Broadcast News and Writing Stylebook

Papper's *Broadcast News and Writing Stylebook* is the go-to handbook in broadcast news, and with the updates in the 6th edition, it is sure to continue this legacy. Through clear and concise chapters, this text provides the fundamental·rules of broadcast news writing. It covers various fields across the board, including crime and government, weather, education, health, and sports. Within each field, readers learn the nuances of reporting, grammar, style, and usage.

Written by a professional who has overseen major industry research for the past 23 years, this edition presents the data on news writing in a relevant and digestible manner. With the business of broadcast news changing rapidly, this text reflects the current news environment and explores where it will head in the future. With an expanded social media chapter and additional insight into the newsrooms of today, *Broadcast News and Writing Stylebook* incorporates all the skills and knowledge reporters and journalists need to prepare for their careers.

Robert A. Papper is Emeritus Distinguished Professor of Journalism at Hofstra University. A graduate of Columbia College and the Columbia Graduate School of Journalism, he has worked as a producer, writer and manager at television stations in Minneapolis, Washington, DC, San Francisco, and Columbus, Ohio and radio stations in Maine and Indiana. He has won both the top award in broadcast journalism (DuPont-Columbia) and the top award in broadcast journalism education (Ed Bliss Award).

Broadcast News and Writing Stylebook

Robert A. Papper

Routledge
Taylor & Francis Group

NEW YORK AND LONDON

First published 2017
by Routledge
711 Third Avenue, New York, NY 10017

and by Routledge
2 Park Square, Milton Park, Abingdon, Oxon, OX14 4RN

Routledge is an imprint of the Taylor & Francis Group, an informa business.

© 2017 Taylor & Francis

The right of Robert A. Papper to be identified as author of this work has been asserted by him in accordance with sections 77 and 78 of the Copyright, Designs and Patents Act 1988.

Library of Congress Cataloging-in-Publication Data
Names: Papper, Robert A., 1947– author.
Title: Broadcast news and writing stylebook / Robert A. Papper.
Other titles: Broadcast news writing stylebook
Description: New York, NY : Routledge, 2017.
Identifiers: LCCN 2016037050 | ISBN 9781138682603 (hardback) |
     ISBN 9781138682610 (pbk.)
Subjects: LCSH: Broadcast journalism—Authorship. |
     Journalism—Style manuals. | Report writing.
Classification: LCC PN4784.B75 P36 2017 | DDC 808.06/607—dc23
LC record available at https://lccn.loc.gov/2016037050

ISBN: 978-1-138-68260-3 (hbk)
ISBN: 978-1-138-68261-0 (pbk)
ISBN: 978-1-315-54502-8 (ebk)

Typeset in Utopia
by Apex CoVantage, LLC

For Sol, Renee, Dana, Cristian, Daisy, Matt, Bria, Zack, Jen, Xavier, Sloane, Kate and especially Carole.

Contents   ●●●●●

Acknowledgments   ● ● ● ● ●

Broadcast News and Writing Stylebook was first published in 1986—more than 30 years ago. The first book of its kind, it was initially designed for professionals, and the Ethics and Excellence in Journalism Foundation in Oklahoma enabled the book to be distributed to every TV station and radio newsroom in the country. I am forever grateful to the Foundation for its support.

I am also indebted to so many friends and colleagues who have read (and reread) this book and offered so many valuable suggestions. My thanks to active and past practitioners, faculty members, former students and friends: Laird Anderson, Dave Arnold, Mary Baer, Ken Barcus, Andy Barth, Alex Batres, Steve Bell, Jackie Benson, Amanda Billings, Ed Bliss, Merv Block, Justin Burton, Tim Calahan, Mark Christian, Dane Claussen, Liz Claman, Aubrey Clerkin, Ron Comings, Bob Conley, Evan Cornog, Carol Costello, Christine Davidson, Sue Drucker, Camilla Gant, John Doolittle, Bob Dotson, Emily Edwards, Irving Fang, Mike Ferring, Kelly Fincham, Brad Fitch, Carol Fletcher, Kymberly Fox, Wayne Freedman, Eric Galvan, Jeff Gillan, Peter Goodman, Tom Grimes, Jessica Harrington, Steve Hartman, Craig Helfant, Dave Hickcox, Chris James, Kelli Johnson, Steve Johnson, Phil Jurey, Laura Kaufmann, Mike Kiernan, Eric Knecht, Bill Knowles, Nick Kotz, John Larson, Bill Louthan, Carol Luper, Jim Mancari, Mark Masse, Christine Caswell McCarron, Jack McWethy, Mel Mencher, Nick Mills, Joe Misiewicz, Beth Montagno, Mackie Morris, Mike Murrie, Chad Myers, Mark Neerman, Jacki Ochoa, Nathan O'Neal, Stacie Osadchaya, Charles Osgood, Jenn Palilonis, Bill Payer (who developed much of the guide to super usage), Ian Pearson, Jeff Porche, Deborah Potter, Lou Prato, Andy Rooney, Crosby Shaterian, Robert Siegel, Marc Silverstein, Gregg Smith, Mary Spillman, Susan Stamberg, Leeza Starks, Alan Thompson, Carl Twentier, Dan Van Benthuysen, Sara Vesser, Lafe Williams, Maria Williams-Hawkins and many others at Hofstra University, WSYX-TV, KPIX-TV, KRNV-TV, KSNV-TV, KERO-TV, WTOV-TV, WWJ and other stations across the country.

My thanks to Ross Wagenhofer and Nicole Salazar at Routledge, and to the following reviewers, who made valuable suggestions for this latest effort: Barbara Nevins Taylor, Emily Corio, Elena Jarvis, and Cassandra Clayton.

Most of all, I want to thank my wife, Carole. Along with putting up with me and this book generally, she read and critiqued so much of this material . . . through so many drafts and so many editions. The English teacher in her did its best not to let me get away with abusing our language too much. She tried.

Bob Papper
Distinguished Professor Emeritus
Hofstra University

1

●●●●●

Ethics, Legality and the RTDNA Code of Ethics and Professional Conduct

●●●●●
Ethics

Proper ethical decision-making shouldn't be tough. After all, it's just doing what's right, isn't it? Yes, but apparently that's harder to do—or perhaps harder to stick to—than it sounds.

Inventing quotes and interviews, stealing (plagiarizing) columns, inadequate fact-checking, running PR-supplied video or stories as if they're news . . . the list of print and broadcast news failures has been widely reported.

The toll on the public's perception of journalism is incalculable. The notion that it might be necessary to tell people not to cheat or invent or plagiarize seems absurd. Surely some things should go without saying. Apparently not.

Broadcast appears to have less of a problem with invented quotes and stories, but it's probably just the nature of the beast. Television must have pictures, and it's hard to fake that, although one network did use its "green screen" to make it look like their reporters were outside on location rather than inside a studio. Broadcast also relies heavily on bites which it either has or it doesn't. Since broadcast journalists seldom ever quote (other than running bites), making them up would most often be a meaningless exercise.

There are still plenty of potential failings available. Getting the bites right doesn't prevent them from being taken out of context. And editing one part of a bite to another could well change the meaning of what someone said.

Where broadcasters can and too often do go wrong:

■ Stations periodically run video that they get from public relations or government sources without identifying the source of the video. A few stations were embarrassingly burned when it turned out that they ran PR-supplied video complete with a PR-supplied "reporter"—again, without identifying the source of the video.

■ At least one station has run what looked like a news interview program without identifying that the people interviewed had paid to be on the program. The station justified the practice by arguing that active news people didn't produce or host the show. But a more relevant question is what the audience thought.

■ Electronic altering of images is now so easy that it's not hard for the unscrupulous or thoughtless to change backgrounds, signs or other visual elements. Of course, this is also a danger in print.

There are probably two bigger threats to journalistic credibility and integrity. Not unique to broadcast, to be sure, but problematic.

1. Advertiser influence. Is a station willing to take on an advertiser if that advertiser has done something wrong? Think about how often you've seen news reports—print or broadcast—critical of a local car dealer. Hardly ever.

2. Sensationalizing and the consequent cheapening of the news. It's probably worse in promos and teases than the news stories themselves, but that's not a distinction the audience is going to make or care about. Every time journalists say a word, every time a picture airs, media credibility is on the line. It's infinitely easier to damage a reputation than regain one.

A useful guideline: If you wouldn't tell the audience everything you did to gather and report the story, then don't do it.

Advocacy journalism (like that practiced by Michael Moore in *Sicko* and *Capitalism: A Love Story*) has its place and a long history in this country. But it's not what we do day in and day out. The news audience shouldn't be able to determine where a reporter stands politically based on what's supposed to be an impartial report. At the same time, allowing a politician to make a blatantly false claim—without challenging that assertion—misleads and disserves the audience. It's all in how you handle the material.

While charges of bias get more attention, journalism is probably more at risk from the sheer volume of mistakes made every day. Talk to anyone who has been touched by journalists, and they'll complain about how a reporter confused dates, misspelled the name of the street or town or people, misstated the number of something. The list goes on and on. Death by a thousand cuts. There will always be issues of interpretation or emphasis. Someone may feel that a journalist didn't emphasize a particular point enough or left a subtle misimpression. That's a different and debatable issue. Not open to interpretation or debate is getting the facts right.

Journalism is neither rocket science nor brain surgery, but everyone needs to remember that people's lives, livelihoods and reputations are at stake in virtually every story.

Consider this a plea for more care and attention to detail to help preserve your reputation, the reputation of the news outlet you work for and, most importantly, the reputation of the people whose lives you touch.

Ethics isn't simply a topic handled in one chapter of a book. You'll find issues involving ethical decision-making and ethical behavior in almost every chapter.

●　●　●　●　●

Ethical Decision-Making Starts at the Top

Ethical decision-making is easier if it's clear that the news organization you work for cares and values that approach. Having a written code of ethics or guiding principles is a good start. You'll find the RTDNA Code of Ethics and Professional Conduct at the end of this chapter. Other organizations, like the Society of Professional Journalists, offer equally meaningful guidance. A good organization should subscribe to one of these codes or have developed their own. Critically, they should reinforce that code through their actions.

Writing for the RTDNA *Daily Communicator*, News Director Treena Wood at CKWX-AM in Vancouver, British Columbia, noted that her station had been successful by adhering to internally developed guiding principles. Number 1:

> *First, we get it right. Nothing goes to air or online before it's independently confirmed. We wait, make phone calls, put out the emails, gather the evidence, and get our facts straight before rushing to get something out there, no matter what everyone else in the media is doing. No one remembers who got it first, but everyone remembers who got it wrong.*

●　●　●　●　●

Issues in Media Law

A few words about media law in a chapter on ethics is not a substitute for a media law course. Still, a few words seem appropriate.

We are still guided and most often sheltered by the First Amendment to the Constitution:

> *Congress shall make no law respecting an establishment of religion, or prohibiting the free exercise thereof; or abridging the freedom of*

speech, or of the press; or the right of the people peaceably to assemble, and to petition the Government for a redress of grievances.

We may consider the First Amendment to be a bedrock of our society—and it certainly is as far as the news media is concerned, but it has always been controversial. If it wasn't controversial, it wouldn't have been required as an amendment to the Constitution; it would have been included in the original. And it remains controversial.

A recent (2015) study by the Pew Research Center found that 40% of Millennials (ages 18–34) said that government should be able to limit statements offensive to minority groups. All other (older) age groups ran from 12% to 27% agreeing that government should be able to limit speech offensive to minority groups. The example tested in this survey may be among the most difficult to judge, but isn't that how you judge whether we have free speech for all—or just for some? Or for just some viewpoints?

Note that we're talking about the *first* amendment—the first individual liberty stipulated by the founding fathers is designed to restrict federal or state limitations on individual liberties.

Without freedom of speech and freedom of the press, there is the real potential of converting journalism into someone's or some group's version of public relations.

As it is, freedom of speech and freedom of the press are not without limitations or consequences. Freedom of speech does not include the right to yell "Fire!" in a crowded theater—one of the classic examples of limitations. You also cannot incite people to riot.

In addition, the U.S. Supreme Court has found that broadcasters (unlike print journalists) may be regulated based on a scarcity of channels (licenses for radio and television stations), and that scarcity allows for content-neutral regulation of radio and TV. As an example, tobacco companies have always been free to advertise cigarettes in newspapers and magazines, but Congress banned cigarette advertising on radio and TV starting in 1971.

Clearly, different technologies are treated differently. While the Supreme Court has upheld regulations and restrictions on broadcasting, the Court has recognized full Constitutional protections for the internet since 1997.

It's also critical to understand that the media possess no rights beyond those afforded to every American. The freedom to speak and publish views is no greater for CBS or your local hometown newspaper than it is for you.

But expressing those thoughts can still have consequences. That's true for both individuals and for the media. The three legal areas where the media are most likely to get into trouble include *libel, entrapment* and *invasion of privacy.*

There appears to be a widespread belief that these are potential problems most often of concern in investigative reporting. That's probably not the case. When the news media spend a lot of time on investigative work, part of that time frequently includes meeting with lawyers to go over scripts and documentation to ensure that the station is on solid ground. That doesn't preclude lawsuits; anyone with money can file a lawsuit regardless of the merits or lack thereof. The point is that the material is typically thoroughly vetted. Stations probably more often get into potential trouble in the day-to-day reporting when oversight might not be as carefully provided.

The distinction between libel and slander is in the delivery. Libel involves written material, (published or broadcast) and slander involves spoken (but not including broadcast). In either case, it generally includes the false or malicious publication of material that damages someone's reputation or relationships with family, friends, coworkers or neighbors. Obviously, including someone's name is a form of identifying an accused individual, but identification can also be done by picture or a description that may single out a particular individual.

Truth is the best and, most often, an absolute defense against libel. In journalism, there's never a good substitute for being right and being able to prove that you're right. That's the gold standard, and that's what you should be prepared to argue based on the journalistic work you do. The one place where truth may not be enough of a defense is if someone can show malice. In other words, a statement may be true, but if the person can show that you, as a reporter, were out to get someone for personal gain, then truth may not be an adequate defense.

Opinion may be used as a defense against libel. That's most often the case in things like critical movie or restaurant reviews. This defense is also known as fair comment. There is a clear line that's drawn. In a restaurant review, for instance, saying that you thought the beef burgundy was bland or overcooked is fine. That's opinion. Saying that the kitchen is dirty, and the place is a breeding ground for mice is only okay if you can prove the truth of that statement.

Privilege is another defense against libel. The issue there is that statements made by people testifying in court or speaking at a government public hearing, for example, would be okay as long as you, the reporter, don't take sides in the case.

Consent may be a defense—where the person who feels injured in fact agreed to the publication of the material.

Public officials have a harder time arguing that they have been libeled. They must argue that not only was the material false, but that the reporter or news organization either knew it was false and broadcast it anyway or exhibited a "reckless disregard" for the truth. Public officials include not just politicians but also actors, sports figures, celebrities, and so on. The issue of publishing or republishing, reposting and linking have also raised new issues associated with developing and evolving notions of defamation liability.

Entrapment is another potential area of legal trouble. In arguing entrapment, the injured party is arguing that the libelous behavior only happened because the reporter or news organization induced the person to do something he or she would not have otherwise done. For instance, if you simply walked up to people and asked them to do something that would be considered libelous—like a crime or performing an embarrassing act—that could well be considered as entrapping the person. Don't do that.

Invasion of privacy can be pretty complicated. Let's say you're on public property—a public sidewalk for instance—and you see an accident on the street. You can take pictures of that scene, and you're not invading anyone's privacy. There is no reasonable expectation of privacy on a public street. What if something happens in someone's front yard? Can you take and use pictures of that from the public sidewalk? Yes. Still no expectation of privacy. What if you're on that sidewalk and see something happening inside a house? No good. Just because the curtains may not have been closed doesn't mean that the people inside still don't have a reasonable expectation of privacy. Generally, if you're on public property, anything you shoot that's outside or also on public property is fair game, and you're not invading someone's privacy.

Related to all this, if you walk up to someone on the street, camera or notebook in hand, and ask a question, you do not need a signed release in order to use that material. You have what is called *implied consent*. They see the notebook or camera and spoke with you. They have, in effect, given their consent.

If you have any concerns about the legality of any action, check with competent and appropriate legal counsel.

● ● ● ● ●

Drones

What about the use of drones? Be careful here. New FAA rules, in effect as of the end of August 2016, clarify and change a number of rules about how stations can use drones.

The new rules prohibit flights directly over people not involved in drone operation. That's actually a loosening of restrictions. Drone operation must be done by someone with a drone-specific pilot's license. Operation still must be done within visual line of sight. Stations can apply for waivers of certain conditions.

There are record-keeping requirements, and plenty of other restrictions still in force. The bottom line is you better know the rules before attempting to shoot video of something with a drone.

The use of ever more powerful technologies has added to privacy concerns. Telephoto lenses, parabolic microphones, camera-equipped drones and "public" online places have all raised increasing questions about public spaces and expectations of privacy.

● ● ● ● ●

The Radio-Television Digital News Association (RTDNA) Code of Ethics and Professional Conduct*

Guiding Principles:

Journalism's obligation is to the public. Journalism places the public's interests ahead of commercial, political and personal interests. Journalism empowers viewers, listeners and readers to make more informed decisions for themselves; it does not tell people what to believe or how to feel.

Ethical decision-making should occur at every step of the journalistic process, including story selection, news-gathering, production, presentation and delivery. Practitioners of ethical journalism seek diverse and even opposing opinions in order to reach better conclusions that can be clearly explained and effectively defended or, when appropriate, revisited and revised.

Ethical decision-making—like writing, photography, design or anchoring—requires skills that improve with study, diligence and practice.

The RTDNA Code of Ethics does not dictate what journalists should do in every ethical predicament; rather it offers resources to help journalists make better ethical decisions—on and off the job—for themselves and for the communities they serve.

Journalism is distinguished from other forms of content by these guiding principles:

■ Truth and accuracy above all

  ■ The facts *should* get in the way of a good story. Journalism requires more than merely reporting remarks, claims or comments. Journalism verifies, provides relevant context, tells the rest of the story and acknowledges the absence of important additional information.

  ■ For every story of significance, there are always more than two sides. While they may not all fit into every account, responsible reporting is clear about what it omits, as well as what it includes.

  ■ Scarce resources, deadline pressure and relentless competition do not excuse cutting corners factually or oversimplifying complex issues.

  ■ "Trending," "going viral" or "exploding on social media" may increase urgency, but these phenomena only heighten the need for strict standards of accuracy.

- Facts change over time. Responsible reporting includes updating stories and amending archival versions to make them more accurate and to avoid misinforming those who, through search, stumble upon outdated material.

- Deception in newsgathering, including surreptitious recording, conflicts with journalism's commitment to truth. Similarly, anonymity of sources deprives the audience of important, relevant information. Staging, dramatization and other alterations—even when labeled as such—can confuse or fool viewers, listeners and readers. These tactics are justified only when stories of great significance cannot be adequately told without distortion, and when any creative liberties taken are clearly explained.

- Journalism challenges assumptions, rejects stereotypes and illuminates—even where it cannot eliminate—ignorance.

- Ethical journalism resists false dichotomies—either/or, always/never, black/white thinking—and considers a range of alternatives between the extremes.

- Independence and transparency

  - Editorial independence may be a more ambitious goal today than ever before. Media companies, even if not-for-profit, have commercial, competitive and other interests—both internal and external—from which the journalists they employ cannot be entirely shielded. Still, independence from influences that conflict with public interest remains an essential ideal of journalism. Transparency provides the public with the means to assess credibility and to determine who deserves trust.

  - Acknowledging sponsor-provided content, commercial concerns or political relationships is essential, but transparency alone is not adequate. It does not entitle journalists to lower their standards of fairness or truth.

  - Disclosure, while critical, does not justify the exclusion of perspectives and information that are important to the audience's understanding of issues.

  - Journalism's proud tradition of holding the powerful accountable provides no exception for powerful journalists or the powerful organizations that employ them. To profit from reporting on the activities of others while operating in secrecy is hypocrisy.

  - Effectively explaining editorial decisions and processes does not mean making excuses. Transparency requires reflection, reconsideration and honest openness to the possibility that an action, however well intended, was wrong.

  - Ethical journalism requires owning errors, correcting them promptly and giving corrections as much prominence as the error itself had.

■ Commercial endorsements are incompatible with journalism because they compromise credibility. In journalism, content is gathered, selected and produced in the best interests of viewers, listeners and readers—not in the interests of somebody who paid to have a product or position promoted and associated with a familiar face, voice or name.

■ Similarly, political activity and active advocacy can undercut the real or perceived independence of those who practice journalism. Journalists do not give up the rights of citizenship, but their public exercise of those rights can call into question their impartiality.

■ The acceptance of gifts or special treatment of any kind not available to the general public creates conflicts of interest and erodes independence. This does not include the access to events or areas traditionally granted to working journalists in order to facilitate their coverage. It does include "professional courtesy" admission, discounts and "freebies" provided to journalists by those who might someday be the subject of coverage. Such goods and services are often offered as enticements to report favorably on the giver or rewards for doing so; even where that is not the intent, it is the reasonable perception of a justifiably suspicious public.

■ Commercial and political activities, as well as the acceptance of gifts or special treatment, cause harm even when the journalists involved are "off duty" or "on their own time."

■ Attribution is essential. It adds important information that helps the audience evaluate content and it acknowledges those who contribute to coverage. Using someone else's work without attribution or permission is plagiarism.

■ Accountability for consequences

　■ Journalism accepts responsibility, articulates its reasons and opens its processes to public scrutiny.

　■ Journalism provides enormous benefits to self-governing societies. In the process, it can create inconvenience, discomfort and even distress. Minimizing harm, particularly to vulnerable individuals, should be a consideration in every editorial and ethical decision.

　■ Responsible reporting means considering the consequences of both the newsgathering—even if the information is never made public—and of the material's potential dissemination. Certain stakeholders deserve special consideration; these include children, victims, vulnerable adults and others inexperienced with American media.

　■ Preserving privacy and protecting the right to a fair trial are not the primary mission of journalism; still, these critical concerns deserve consideration and to be balanced against the importance or urgency of reporting.

■ The right to broadcast, publish or otherwise share information does not mean it is always right to do so. However, journalism's obligation is to pursue truth and report, not withhold it. Shying away from difficult cases is not necessarily more ethical than taking on the challenge of reporting them. Leaving tough or sensitive stories to non-journalists can be a disservice to the public.

A growing collection of coverage guidelines for use on a range of ethical issues is available on the RTDNA website—www.rtdna.org.

Revised Code of Ethics, adopted June 11, 2015
Reprinted with permission.

● ● ● ● ●

Summary

Get the facts right, and behave like a responsible and caring human being.

2

• • • • •

News

Although this book focuses on writing, it takes as a given the reader's acceptance of the basic tenets of broadcast journalism: to be accurate, fair, clear and interesting. Accurate because no manner of clever word-weaving compensates for wrongful injury to the people we cover or the self-inflicted damage of a correction that could have been avoided. Fair if we are to be trusted. Clear because without clarity what we do has no meaning. Interesting because it really doesn't matter what we do if no one's out there listening and watching.

• • • • •

What Is News?

There are common characteristics or values that make up the typical news story:

1. **Importance or significance**. Some stories are news because they involve events that have a meaningful impact on people. War, famine, an outbreak of a dangerous disease are all significant on a global basis. A zoning decision or a school board election could be an important event in a small town. Generally, for an event to be significant or important, it should have a meaningful impact on a meaningful percentage of the audience. A fatal car accident on a lonely stretch of road may be a disastrous event for the people involved and the family, but it's not a news story based on significance or importance. On the other hand, the story may well be considered news based on human interest.

2. **Prominence**. Some people—by virtue of who they are by birth or deed—make news no matter what they do. The president, a major Hollywood or sports star and British royalty all make news by doing almost anything at all. Or nothing. Some people acquire temporary prominence—their 15 minutes of fame—by some extraordinary action, good or bad. The person who rescues a family from a burning home and the newly accused serial killer both achieve a measure of prominence. Every area has its local prominent figures and

characters, but few people rise to the level of prominence such that we recognize who they are by name alone.

3. **Conflict**. War is obvious, but conflict can just as easily be over ideas like abortion, charter schools, separation of church and state, any election and most crimes. If there were no "other side" or "opposing view," then many of the stories we cover could simply be calendar listings rather than news stories.

4. **Human interest**. Some stories are just interesting. Yes, that includes the newscast filler of the waterskiing squirrel, but it also includes the wide range of stories that describe what we do with and to each other—like a daring water rescue in a faraway city or a child's battle with a ravaging disease or that fatal accident noted above. CBS's Steve Hartman provides us with extraordinary stories that report on the human condition.

Some people consider *impact*—as in having a strong or significant effect on a (large) group of people—as a separate characteristic of news; some view it as a part of the above list.

A story only needs to be strong enough in one of those four characteristics in order to be newsworthy, but many stories include more than one. The remaining two characteristics are relevant to every story—either positively or negatively.

5. **Time**. Time factors into all stories. A story is most newsworthy when it happens, but news ages quickly. Absent a new development, news generally has a life cycle of no more than 24 hours. A major event that breaks on the 6 p.m. news is likely to be on the 11 p.m. news and probably again on the next morning's newscasts. The story might get on the noon news but would not likely air on the next day's 5 p.m. newscast, and it certainly wouldn't (or shouldn't) be repeated on the next day's 6 p.m. news. But that's only the case if there are no new developments. New developments restart the news cycle. Along with that overall life cycle, absent new developments, a news story typically becomes less newsworthy with each succeeding newscast. So time figures into every story or potential story as either an ally—if it just happened—or an enemy—as it ages. What about an old story that a journalist just learned about? Those are trickier. If the story isn't too old, and if it has other strong values, the standard 24-hour life of the story will exist. But because the story is old (even if new to the reporter or audience), the story must be stronger in other categories to get on the air at all.

6. **Proximity**. Again, all stories involve proximity since all stories are based somewhere geographically. As with time, proximity is either a help or a hindrance. Geographically, the closer the story is to the audience, the easier it is for the story to be considered newsworthy

by other standards. Conversely, the farther away a story is from the audience, the higher the story must score in other categories to be considered newsworthy. The arrest of a small-town mayor for drunk driving will be a huge story in that small town. It might well be a small story in the nearest large city. A state or two away, the story will likely get no attention at all.

For a story to make it on the air, it must have one or more of the first four values in sufficient quantity to be worth telling, and it must pass separate tests for time and proximity.

● ● ● ● ●

Balancing News Values

There's no absolute scale. There's no way to assign numbers for every case and call something news if it exceeds some total score. Worse, reasonable people will always disagree on _how_ important or interesting a story is. Part of the discrepancy is just human judgment. Part of it involves the background and interests of different people. Older people may find any story on Social Security to be extremely important, while younger people may be largely indifferent. Because the general audience is a diverse group, the people deciding what news is should have a similar diversity, otherwise the news organization may miss stories that a significant segment of the audience really cares about.

We put those definitions of what is news into practice in the day-to-day decisions of exactly what news to cover and how. That takes us to another list: the types of news stories that we broadcast.

● ● ● ● ●

Types of Stories

From a newsroom coverage and story assignment standpoint, stories break down into six categories.

Breaking News

More and more loosely defined, this is hard news that the station and the audience are just learning about that day. Breaking news has become the bread and butter of TV newscasts. Usually handled by live reporting, there's no way to plan for the specific event; it's simply what a station reacts to, preferably with a plan for responding, generally, to breaking news. Real breaking news will inevitably alter newscasts and coverage plans a station made earlier in the day.

Examples:

- A surprise political resignation
- A seven-car pile-up on the interstate
- A triple murder
- A flash flood or tornado or earthquake
- An unexpected major business development

If a station knew about the event ahead of time and could plan for coverage, then it isn't breaking news. Note that with rare exceptions, all competing stations are likely to learn about breaking news at just about the same time. They may react differently, but breaking news is seldom a secret or exclusive, so stations differentiate themselves on breaking news not by whether they have the story on the air. All are likely to have it. The difference comes in how each station handles the breaking news.

Planned Event Reporting

While some stations will label almost everything breaking news, much of what stations cover they knew about in advance. Calling it breaking news may work from a promotion standpoint, but it's certainly not an accurate portrayal. This category includes coverage that comes out of a city council or school board meeting; a court case; a scheduled news conference. Anything that you knew in advance was going to happen.

Advancing an event would also be included in this category. That's when a station does a news story before (in advance of) a school board meeting or any planned event. Ongoing coverage of an event also goes here—even if the original event was breaking news. For instance, hurricane coverage is breaking news, but the inevitable series of follow-up stories are really planned events because you know in advance that you're going to continue coverage.

Examples:

- A story on the top agenda item on the evening school board meeting
- A story on the scheduled report issued by the city council or the state legislature
- A story on the scheduled local appearance of a prominent politician, actor, sports figure

A news organization reacts to breaking news, but planned event reporting—as the name makes clear—is planned. As with breaking news, all competing stations will normally know about the same planned events.

Enterprise Reporting

Breaking news may be a station's bread and butter, but enterprise reporting, day in, day out, is commonly what separates the top stations from the also-rans. Enterprise reporting combines the hard news values you'd find in a breaking news story or a planned event along with station exclusivity. It's a story a news person comes up with by virtue of being observant, creative or maybe just lucky. The key is that other media don't have the story. A hallmark of enterprise stories involves learning or discovering something that people didn't know, realize or expect.

Examples:

- The discovery that a major local business is in serious financial trouble and about to lay off workers
- The discovery that a major public works project is way over budget and well behind schedule
- The discovery that a new principal at a local high school has established some really unorthodox approaches to education that really seem to be turning students around (or failing miserably)

Because these stories are exclusive to the station that came up with them, they're more promotable, and they make a difference in where the audience turns for news. Some will argue that *all* reporting should be enterprise reporting. Sure, in that perfect world that none of us lives in, maybe that's true. In the meantime, if you're looking for a job in this business, your "reel" of stories should be primarily—if not exclusively—breaking news and enterprise stories.

Investigative Reporting

Real investigative reporting is enterprise reporting on steroids. Typically, this is where you learn something that others didn't know—and that at least some people would rather you not know. Most often seen during sweeps or ratings periods, this is the most time-consuming and therefore most expensive reporting there is. Anyone can make accusations. The key to good investigative reporting isn't making accusations or raising questions, it's about "proving" something.

Examples:

- Proving that a local politician has been accepting bribes
- Proving that a local nursing home has been abusing patients
- Proving that a company is knowingly selling an unsafe product

More and more, stations are working to build their *brand* around investigative reporting. RTDNA research, conducted in 2015, shows that no area of TV reporting has grown as much and increased in station emphasis as much as investigative reporting.

Special Segment Reporting

For the most part, these are usually either planned event reports or enterprise stories about a specific topic. They can be either harder news topics or softer features, but their existence is scheduled and built into various newscasts. Health and consumer reporting are probably the two most common. Stations also run what are sometimes called "franchises"—special segment reports that commonly air weekly.

Examples:

■ Daily health report—especially done by a doctor employed by the station or an outside company
■ "Mr. Food" or other cooking segment
■ Pet or child adoption segment
■ "On Your Side" or other consumer reporting segment

Features

Features have largely fallen out of favor these days. They're typically non-timely stories about who we are and what we do to and with each other. Commonly, these stories have strong human interest aspects and frequently involve the secondary aspects of earlier breaking news or planned events.

Examples:

■ A follow-up on how a family is coping now that the primary breadwinner is out of work due to a plant shutdown
■ A profile of someone who has overcome an obstacle
■ A story about search and reuniting
■ The story of someone with a bizarre hobby or collection

"I'm looking for stories that haven't been told before," says CBS' Steve Hartman, the top network feature reporter today. "Stories that aren't clichés. Stories that aren't copying other people's deeds."

Stories can also cross lines to incorporate aspects of more than one category. The recovery and rehabilitation of a veteran who fought in Afghanistan or Iraq is a feature although it obviously has a timely aspect to it. In fact, many if not most stories cross boundaries at least to some degree.

● ● ● ● ●

Where Story Ideas Come From

Stations get story ideas from a variety of places:

- **Wire services** like the Associated Press
- **Social Media** like Facebook, Twitter and others
- **News releases** from government, businesses and organizations
- **Agendas** from governmental or quasi-governmental organizations
- Scheduled **news conferences**
- **Follow-up notes** from previous stories
- **Other media**, including newspapers, books, magazines, radio, cable, blogs, tweets, other television stations and so on
- Story idea **services and consultants**
- **Reporters** and other news people who have seen something, talked to someone or just had an idea
- **People who call** the station with information, tips or stories

The wires supply a steady stream of news and information all day. Most of that news is national or international, but some involves state and local news. Stations are always looking for state, regional, national or international news that has local implications. A U.S. military plane that crashed on the other side of the world could have been made in your community. Or maybe the same kind of plane is flown at a military base in your area. Or the crew flying that plane could have been stationed in your community not too long ago.

More and more, the first stop for reporters and news managers is social media. That includes Facebook, Twitter and others where people post video and comments about events that they've seen or heard about. Some of those ideas are on a station's website or Facebook page as a comment or response to an earlier post; some may be on community websites or Facebook pages, or other media sites.

News releases tell us what some organization or company or government agency would like us to run a story on. Maybe that's a worthwhile story like a new program to help feed poor people or a local business expanding and adding new jobs to the community. Maybe the information ties in with another story a reporter is working on. Maybe within the press release is information on a more interesting story. Maybe the information simply gets you thinking about a story idea. Most news releases contain little real news, but that doesn't mean that they can't inspire terrific news stories.

Agendas tell us what's slated to come up at various government or organization meetings. Some of the topics may clearly be newsworthy.

With others, we may need to make a phone call to gather additional information. Remember that a meeting agenda doesn't tell you what old or new business might come up . . . and that could be the most interesting news of all.

News conferences commonly tell us information that we probably should have found out already by good reporting. But sometimes that's not possible, and the news conference also tells us when we'll have access to people that we may want to question—even if those questions have nothing to do with the topic of the news conference.

Every time we work on a story, we're talking with people who should be giving us information that we can use for other stories. Sometimes those stories relate to the one we're working on, and sometimes they're completely different. Or maybe we just want to remember to follow up the original story that we did. If the story was meaningful enough to put on the air the first time, maybe we should keep track of it to provide progress or follow-up reports.

We constantly monitor other media to see what they have and to compare what and how we did with the competition. A good, timely story that we didn't have might force us to play catch-up. An interesting feature might be worth putting aside to do on our own in a few months or so.

There are a number of private services that supply story ideas—and news consultants do that as well. Also, check out places like Al's Morning Meeting at Poynter.org.

We'd also find a lot more stories if we just opened our eyes and our minds. What's going on behind that new construction fence? Why is a school teacher moonlighting as a waitress at a local restaurant? Why does it take so long to register your car or get a new driver's license? What are the issues your neighbors are concerned about or service people are talking about? We all probably walk through a dozen good story ideas every day. Too often, we're too busy with less important issues to see them. Too often, our outside-of-work personal interactions are limited to other news people. You'll pick up no story ideas there; get to know real people who live and work and play in the community.

For seven years, Steve Hartman told amazing stories in a feature called "Everybody Has a Story." At the end of each story, the person profiled threw a dart at a map of the U.S., and Hartman and his photographer would travel there and randomly pick a name out of a phone book. Hartman did a story on the first person who agreed to see them. "There was always a life lesson," notes Hartman. "Not only does everybody have a story, but everybody has a story worth telling." That's a lot easier said than done, but part of the point is that good, meaningful stories are lurking almost everywhere.

Sometimes people call in great story ideas, but it's rare. More than rare. Mostly, people who call feel abused and want to get even; people misunderstand something or how the system works, but they want the station to fix it; people try to get someone in trouble. Worse, there seems to be a rule requiring every unbalanced person in America to call their favorite television station at least once a day. On the other hand, there was a very strange woman who called a large television station in the Midwest to complain that a U.S. congressman was having sex with her underage daughter. The woman was probably unbalanced, but her underage daughter really *was* having sex with a U.S. congressman. That's why we listen.

● ● ● ● ●

The Assignment Desk

The assignment desk is the nerve center of the newsroom. Commonly overseen by the assignment manager or managing editor, the assignment desk monitors police, fire and emergency frequencies on the scanners; regularly checks the wire services; makes regular calls to police, fire and hospitals (among others) to find out what's going on; maintains the future file or daybook to keep track of scheduled events for the day, the week, the month and the year; frequently handles the logistics of pairing photographer and reporter (assuming they're separate); and makes sure events are covered, people are where they should be, even whether crews are getting off for meals.

The assignment desk works with producers, managers and others to make sure that everyone is on top of events of the day and how the newsroom is going to deal with them. It's a great job for people who require constant stimulation and truly enjoy juggling lots of balls at the same time.

● ● ● ● ●

Morning and Afternoon Meetings

In order to determine how to deploy news people and what stories to run on the day's newscasts, most stations have a morning meeting— usually starting around 8:30 a.m. or 9:00 a.m. or 9:30 a.m., running no more than a half hour or so. The morning meeting sets the agenda for what the station plans to cover that day and determines, in large measure, what will air on the afternoon and early evening newscasts, and even on the multiple stations that many newsrooms program for— assuming that breaking news doesn't alter the landscape.

Who runs the morning meeting varies from station to station. Commonly, it's the news director or assistant news director, managing editor or executive producer. In other words, one of the top managers in the newsroom. Sometimes it's the assignment manager or assignment editor. Some stations rotate the person in charge.

Who attends the meeting varies as well. Some stations require everyone who's working in news at that hour to attend and participate; others require only a small group of managers, assignment editors and producers—with reporters welcome but not required; others are somewhere in between. In some cases, everyone is required to propose an idea; in other places, reporters simply wait to be handed an assignment.

Who isn't there? The morning producer is likely done for the day, and the morning show is already over or nearly over. The noon producer may listen in, but the noon show is already set unless a reporter will cover something in the morning that might offer a live shot possibility for noon. The nightside producer and crew aren't in yet. The point is, the meeting is primarily about the afternoon/early evening newscasts.

As stories are discussed and accepted or rejected, producers of the various afternoon/early evening newscasts are likely to claim stories for their shows. Generally, it's not a battle of equals, with the 6 p.m. producer commonly getting first shot because that's likely to be the newscast with the largest audience. Even that varies, however. And when a newsroom handles the news on multiple stations, it's likely that there's a primary station and a secondary one or ones.

In order to determine what to cover, stations—implicitly or explicitly—ask two fundamental questions:

1. What's important?
2. What are people talking about?

A station commits its resources in response to the answers to those two questions. When a single story is the top answer to both questions, then you have a clear lead story for the day. More often, the answers are different and less definitive.

Commonly, stations have a second assignment meeting in the afternoon, usually around 2:30 p.m. or 3 p.m. This smaller meeting involves the "nightside" crew—afternoon/evening assignment editor, 10 p.m. or 11 p.m. producer, nightside reporters and, perhaps, others. The concept is the same as the morning meeting, but the target is the late evening newscast. At some stations, the afternoon meeting includes a late review of the early evening newscasts and an assignment desk handoff from the dayside assignment editor to the nightside assignment editor.

● ● ● ● ●

Following the News

At least part of how we learn what news really is . . . is by consuming it. If you're interested in going into the news business, you should be reading newspapers and magazines, listening to radio news (especially NPR), watching local and network television news and consuming news online. If you don't follow news on a regular basis, it will be pretty hard for you to determine whether something you hear about or come across is actually news or just life as usual. We're not surprised when we run across someone who is crazy about sports who says that he or she wants to be a sports reporter or sports anchor. Someone who wants to be a news reporter or news anchor needs to have the same passion for news.

●●●●●
Summary

The basic tenets of broadcast journalism—or any kind of journalism—involve a news person being accurate, fair, clear and interesting. What we call news isn't simply random facts, it's material that contains one or more of four basic news values: importance, prominence, conflict and/or human interest—and passes additional hurdles of timeliness and proximity. From a station coverage standpoint, those news stories break down into six categories: breaking news, planned event reporting, enterprise reporting, investigative reporting, special segment reporting and features. Ideas for those stories come from a wide variety of sources and are discussed at the morning and afternoon meetings, where the afternoon and early and late evening newscasts are planned in response to two underlying questions: What's important, and what are people talking about?

●●●●●
Key Words & Phrases

accurate . . . fair . . . clear . . . interesting . . . importance or significance . . . prominence . . . conflict . . . human interest . . . time . . . proximity . . . breaking news . . . planned event reporting . . . enterprise reporting . . . investigative reporting . . . special segment reporting . . . features . . . the assignment desk . . . future file or daybook . . . morning and afternoon meetings

●●●●●
Exercises

A. Watch or listen to a local or network television or radio newscast and evaluate how each story measures up in terms of accurate, fair, clear and interesting. Check facts to see if the stories were correct. If the story involved something controversial, how were the different sides treated? Does treating people fairly mean giving everyone the same amount of time and space? Did you understand all of the stories? Were the stories interesting to you? Even if they weren't, do you think others might find the stories interesting? If so, who?

B. Watch or listen to a local or network television or radio newscast. Do you think all the stories were really newsworthy? Might others think so? List each value or characteristic of news and score or explain whether each story scored high or low in that category. Why was each story on the air?

C. Watch a local or network television newscast and determine what type of story each item was. Do you notice any organizational plan in the sequence of those stories? How does each story answer those two fundamental questions that stations ask to determine what to cover?

D. Which news values do the following scenarios exemplify?

1. A local factory that employs 1,500 people will shut down in 90 days.

2. Two local teens who were drag racing collided, and one of the cars hit and killed a pedestrian.

3. A local business announced that it had received an award from the company's headquarters (in another state), recognizing the local business for its "service excellence."

4. The Labor Department reports that the consumer price index rose 1.5% last month in the local area.

5. Scientists at a local university say that the community is not prepared for the possibility of an earthquake that might hit the local area sometime in the future.

6. A local city council member has just announced her resignation in order to spend more time with her family.

7. The weather service just announced that a major storm with wind gusts as high as 60 miles per hour may hit the local area tonight.

8. The Food and Drug Administration has just announced a recall for packages of fresh chicken manufactured by The Very Best Company. One of your local supermarket chains carries the brand, but other stores do not.

9. The State Environmental Protection Agency released a report that says the local water supply has 65 ppb of Pb.

10. Local police announce that because of a shortage of manpower, they're going to stop responding to non-injury traffic accidents.

11. Charity Navigator notes that a local group that raises money for veterans spends 33% of its income on administrative and fund-raising expenses.

E. If you're putting together a local newscast, on a scale of 1 (lowest) to 5 (highest), which stories in D (above) are the most newsworthy?

F. Rank the stories in D (above) that you'd run in a local newscast from most important to least important.

3

•••••

Collecting Information

We gather much of our information—along with radio actualities and video bites—through interviews, so how well we do in the field and on the phone determines what we have to work with later on. As with many things in life, the more interviews we conduct, the better we tend to get. Bites and actualities are the same thing: the actual sound of someone in the news. It might be a statement from the mayor, the argument of conflicting protestors or an interview with a young kindergartner. It involves sound that we can clearly understand and that tells some part of the story. In radio the term is *actuality*; in TV it's *bite*. Otherwise, they're the same.

An interview is any exchange during which the news reporter or writer collects information. In radio, interviewing is most commonly done on the phone. That's not nearly as good as doing it in person, but it's efficient and inexpensive. Even in television, we conduct many— perhaps most—interviews on the phone. In fact, our calls to set up interviews are in many cases interviews themselves. After all, we need to know that the prospective interviewee really has something to say, will say it to us and can say it well.

In TV, we increasingly conduct interviews via Skype. Mostly that's reserved for people we can't readily get to because of time or distance. We used to do phone interviews with those people that we'd run with a still picture (if we could get one). Now we at least try to get video (usually via Skype) rather than just audio.

We also deal in mass interviews. Those include news conferences at which a speaker or speakers take questions. We also conduct interviews in groups—some newsmakers call them packs—in which we question a city council member, the police chief, a hospital spokesperson and so on.

Along with actualities and bites, we also collect natural sound. Called variously *natural sound, nat sound, background sound, ambient sound* and possibly a few other terms, it's the sound of real life captured by the microphone. It might be the chatter of children in a playground, the sound of traffic on the highway or an explosion.

●●●●●

Conducting Successful Interviews

Understanding What Makes Good Bites

Most bites on radio and television probably aren't worth putting on the air. Most bites involve a simple recitation of facts that the reporter or anchor could usually say better, clearer and in half the time.

Good bites—the best bites—generally fall into one of four categories:

1. Personal account. These are the bites in which people tell us what they saw, heard, felt, smelled or tasted. Note the response of the senses. These are the first-person accounts of what happened, told best by people who have an emotional stake in the outcome. These are the bites from people who survived the earthquake, searched for the missing child, got fleeced by a con man, ran the marathon and so on. Their firsthand account of having been involved cannot be duplicated by the writer or reporter. These people bring their passion and feeling to the story because it's their story.

2. Witness account. Sometimes as strong as personal account, these are the stories of people who saw or felt what happened. They witnessed the fire; they saw the accident happen; they heard the cries for help. Although usually missing the personal involvement, these bites can be just as strong because they can supply us with a sense of what happened that we, as writers or reporters, would have to cite as sources to explain.

3. Personal opinion. Everyone has an opinion, and these bites can be good if they're short and to the point. This is the person reacting to news of a tax hike, the election outcome, the demolition of a city landmark, the construction of a new highway or shopping center. Man-on-the-street (MOS) reaction stories fall into this category. Remember that these may or may not be informed opinions, and they should not be presented as representative of a larger group unless you actually have real survey data to back that up.

4. Expert opinion. There are experts on just about everything, and most places have several on any given topic. That puts the onus on the reporter to locate people who not only know the subject well, but can also speak about it clearly and succinctly. Keep in mind that in many cases, different experts see the same data or circumstances differently. Don't limit yourself to one interpretation or viewpoint because you've located someone who speaks in good sound bites or who may share your own perspective. Aggressively seek out a diverse group of experts from which to draw.

From a *content* standpoint, weak bites fall into two categories:

1. Hard data. A recitation of numbers or facts is almost never a good bite. Rarely can someone we interview express numbers or facts as clearly and succinctly as we can. Invariably, they hem and haw, they stumble and restate, they give us too much data or too detailed data. Talk to people and collect that information, but it's almost always better to include relevant hard data in the reporter track or anchor script, rather than letting weak and tedious bites on the air. The fire chief may tell us it was a three-alarm fire that took firefighters two hours to get under control, but the better bite comes from the sweaty, soot-streaked firefighter telling us that he had to run for his life when he heard the roof start to go.

2. Anything not well said. Even if you talked to the right people, not everyone has something compelling to say or is capable of saying it well. Bites can confuse the audience just as easily as they can enlighten. Just because you recorded someone for a story doesn't mean you should burden the audience with the material. Don't punish the audience with a long, tedious bite because it took someone a long time to explain the situation. Children and teenagers can be especially difficult to get good bites from.

"Kill the babies," says former NBC reporter Don Larson. He's referring to a producer he knew who had trouble getting rid of bites she had worked so hard to gather. They became "like her babies." Be ruthless. If the bite won't really mean something to the audience, don't use it.

Former NBC national correspondent Bob Dotson also argues that the quality of a sound bite has nothing to do with length but whether it's something that will stick with the audience. "Robert Frost used to say that a good story starts with a lump in the throat," says Dotson. The whole point of sound bites, then, is to add texture to a story or pound home a point.

"I'm looking for [bites] that are emotional," says Wayne Freedman, a reporter at KGO-TV in San Francisco. "I don't want facts, I want emotions. I want somebody to tell me how they feel. The story is about the *people* in the story."

Plan

This is the most important part of a successful interview. Going into a major interview on an investigative story will obviously require extensive planning, but you should plan for *every* interview you do. Why are you interviewing this person? What are you after? What would make this a successful interview? How does—or might—this interview fit in with others? If you can't answer those questions, how will you know what to ask? If you can't answer those questions, how will you know when to end the interview?

Inexperienced reporters commonly conduct long interviews. That's frequently because they don't know what they're after, and if you don't know where you're going, it can take a long time to get there. That creates two problems. You use too much time conducting an overlong interview, and then you use too much time going through the whole interview to figure out what you have and what to use. Time is too precious for that.

Even on breaking news, there's planning to be done. Take a house fire, for example. You've got a few minutes in the car on the way. Think about what kind of story it's likely to be. Who do you talk with first? Who's next? Who comes after that? What are the human elements you're after?

The answers matter because people leave and memories and emotions fade. Resist the temptation in the above example to start with the fire chief. If you talk to the chief at all, do so at the end. First are the people who live there. They're most involved in the story, and depending on damage and injuries, they may leave. Remember, the best bites are personal accounts, and this is where you get them. Next come the neighbors. They're potential witnesses, and they're readily available. Soon, they won't be. Talking to them when they're outside watching is usually easy. Once they go into their homes and shut the doors, you'll have a harder time convincing them to talk. Then interview the firefighters. Pick the dirtiest ones first. They're the people with the greatest personal involvement in the fire. Remember what makes for good bites. The hard data that the fire chief may be able to supply you also belongs in the story, but you're almost always better off incorporating it into your script.

Keep in mind how people think and what's important to them. In fires or natural disasters, after people and pets the next greatest loss involves personal items—especially pictures. We have insurance for furniture and clothing and other largely meaningless possessions. The real value lies in the stuff of our lives that can't be readily replaced. But if you didn't plan or think about these things, would you watch for and see them? When you see people picking through the rubble after the fire or earthquake or tornado, think about what it is they're really looking for.

Listen

Along with planning, listening—really listening—is the second most important skill for successful interviewing. It's the most critical skill you *must* develop to be a good interviewer. Don't simply hear; listen to every word.

Generally, the biggest impediment to listening is our inability to cope with silence. Especially starting out, we're frequently so concerned about what we're going to ask next that we're not listening closely enough. We're worried that the person will stop talking, and we won't know what to say, so we focus inward on ourselves and what we'll ask next instead of focusing outward on the people we're talking to.

If it will help you to focus on the people you're interviewing, make a few notes of topic areas and put them in your pocket. Use that short list as your security blanket to enable you to focus on the people you're interviewing. All your attention and energy must go toward these people. If you pay enough attention—to what they have to say, how they say it, what they don't say and body language—they'll tell you where to go next in your interview. In most cases, the best question to ask next comes logically out of the previous answer. Remember that ideally, an interview is just a conversation between two people in which the person being interviewed does most of the talking. The ability to listen and focus on the person or people you're talking to will make all the difference in the success of your information gathering. Planning may be step one, but if you don't listen, you won't know whether that planning worked out for you.

Technical Concerns

In broadcast we generally record our interviews, and you must record high-quality sound and pictures. The audience will notice technical flaws before they notice anything else, and *all* of the audience will notice. You must get it right.

In radio, much of the listening takes place in a car, so you're already competing with road noise, traffic and other people for the listener's attention. People will not strain to hear or understand an actuality; they will not turn up the volume and quiet down the environment. If the technical quality of the actuality isn't good, people will simply miss it. Having tuned out the actuality, they've now tuned out the story and the newscast. If the technical quality of an actuality isn't on a par with that of the newscaster, don't put it on the air.

Television offers a little more flexibility—but not much. It's easier to understand people when we see their lips moving, so that gives us a little more leeway. A really compelling (or self-incriminating) bite that proves a story can always be supered on the screen to make sure the audience understands. But again, technical quality matters, and the typical bite for television should be crystal clear.

Natural sound that runs under a reporter track doesn't have to rise to the same standards, but if you want to bring the natural sound full—and you should, as part of the story—then that, too, needs to be high quality.

In radio, listen to the environment, and make sure there are no distracting noises that will ruin the recording. The same goes for TV, and you also need to think about focus, framing, light and color—among other things.

Always check your equipment in advance. Make sure you have everything; make sure it's working; and make sure you know how to operate it. There are rules in this business that say that everything you don't check is likely to break or fail.

Make the Interviewee Comfortable

In breaking news stories, you interview people where and when you can. In other cases location can make or break an interview. The more comfortable the people you're talking with, the more open and forthcoming they're likely to be.

People are usually most comfortable in their own homes, so that's frequently a good place to conduct interviews. Offices pose more of a challenge. That desk they're sitting behind serves as both a physical and a psychological barrier. Equipment noise can make an interview unintelligible. Try to avoid having to contend with those kinds of obstacles. Look for a couple of comfortable chairs or another site. In radio, a conference room may work. In television, look for an interview site with a background that helps tell the story. Offices make common but boring backgrounds.

Watch out for the phone. Once a phone starts to ring, the interview is over—at least temporarily. The ringing makes that spot in the recording unusable, and the distraction derails everyone's train of thought. Try to get the phone turned off (both desk phone and cell phone), have phone calls held or move someplace where there's less chance of a distraction, such as outdoors.

Remember that many of the people we interview are nervous about the whole process. They're worried about how they'll look, what they might say, how they'll sound and whether they'll do a good job. Nervous people give poor interviews. Make them comfortable, and make them comfortable talking with you. The more they talk before the interview, the more comfortable they're likely to get. But *don't* talk about the interview subject until you're actually recording. Talk about the weather, talk about sports, talk about pictures on the office wall—talk about anything *except* the subject at hand. Generally, you'll get good, animated, responses to your questions one time and only one time. If you're not recording when they first say it, you've lost the moment. The second time around, the life will be sapped out, and the person will say things like, "Well, like I told you before. . . ." But since the audience didn't hear it before, that kind of comment should not be used on the air.

Ask Questions That Deliver What You're After

Questions that start with *Do, Are* and *When* are fine as long as answers like *Yes, No,* and *Yesterday* are what you're looking for. And they may be. If you're after hard data and concrete information as background for your story, questions that start with *Do, Are* and *When* may be the fastest way to get it. But if you're after usable bites to put on the air, it would be dumb luck if those questions generated worthwhile answers.

If you're after bites, ask people to *Explain* something. Ask *Why* or *How come.* Ask people to *Describe* what they saw, heard, felt, smelled or tasted. Those are most likely to produce good bites.

Again, the issue comes back to planning. If you know what you're after, it can help frame your questions so that you get what you need.

Unless you're attending a White House news conference and have one chance to ask the president something, don't ask complicated, multipart questions. Don't make speeches. Generally, don't share your personal experiences. Train yourself to be brief and direct. The more straightforward you are, the better the responses are likely to be.

The fewer words you use in your questions—delivered cleanly and crisply—the greater flexibility you have in putting together the story. A one- or two-word response to a question commonly won't work for a bite. But sometimes it can—if you asked the question in about the same amount of time. It is possible to make a quick series of tight questions and answers into a bite. Given the difficulties in interviewing young children and teenagers, this approach may be your best shot at usable bites with difficult groups or individuals.

Generally, start with the easiest, least controversial questions and end with the hardest. First, the more comfortable someone is talking to you, the more likely that person is to respond—even as the interview may move to touchier subjects. Second, even if the interviewee is so offended by a tough question that the interview is terminated, at least you have something. Third, most controversial decisions made sense to someone at the time they made them. So you're better off starting with questions that take the interviewee back before the critical moment you actually want to ask about.

Use Silence

That same silence that you're uncomfortable with (see the earlier section entitled "Listen") generally works the same way for the person you're interviewing. You can use that as a technique. After an answer that may seem incomplete, don't say anything. Just look at the person expectantly, as if to say, "Where's the rest of the answer?" Frequently, that's when the person, uncomfortable with the silence and/or perhaps sensing your lack of understanding, will blurt out the real story. It's not about tricking someone; it's about searching for the truth. If they just look back at you and smile, they know about the technique. In that case, just move on.

Maintain Strong Eye Contact

Don't stare at interviewees, but do engage them. Strong eye contact demands that someone look back at you. It says you're interested and involved. It says you care. It also helps to take someone's mind off the equipment, and in the case of television it increases the odds that the person you're interviewing will look back at you and not directly at the camera.

It's hard to maintain strong eye contact if you're reading questions from a pad of paper. If you need that kind of preparation because it's a complex story with lots of data you must refer to, then you do it. Otherwise, you're always better off acting like a real person asking questions, rather than reading from a prepared script.

Learn to Respond Inaudibly

Almost everyone in the business learns the importance of this the hard way. You need to respond to the person you're interviewing, or the person will stop talking. But if you respond out loud, you'll ruin the audio. Many interesting interviews never made it on the air because constant *uh huh, uhhh, okay, I see* responses by the interviewer simply made the audio unusable. Maintaining good eye contact helps. Nodding is all right, but mindlessly bobbing your head up and down could make it appear that you're agreeing to some sort of outrageous comment the person is making. Facial expressions can help a lot. Just make sure you respond silently.

Follow up and Clarify

Any time the person you're interviewing uses a name that you (and/or the audience) don't know, a technical term that you don't understand, or a peculiar phrasing that isn't clear, you have an interruption in the flow of information. In all likelihood you can't use that material on the air because the audience won't understand.

If this happens in a live interview, you must interrupt and clarify the point right then. Otherwise, you've lost the audience, who will be puzzled over what they don't understand. In a recorded interview, you can wait until the person finishes the sentence or thought and then go back for an explanation.

This is another critical reason to listen. If you're not paying full attention, you'll miss the problem spots in an interview, and you won't hear the kinds of statements that require follow-up questions to make sure you—and the audience—understand. If you don't understand something, there's no way that you're going to be able to make that clear to the audience.

Maintain Control

Never hand over the microphone to someone else. This is *your* interview, and you have to remain in charge. It's up to you to maintain the technical quality; interviewees who take the mike from you will commonly not use it properly on themselves and will almost never hold the mike in a way to pick up your comments or questions. Without the microphone you have no way to interject to clarify; you're completely at someone else's mercy. If you give up the mike, you're no longer conducting the interview. Whoever has the mike is the person who's in control.

Ask for More . . . Twice

In an important interview, it's frequently a good idea, at the very end, to ask whether there's anything you missed, any ground not covered. In most cases the answer will be no, but sometimes people will come up with pertinent material. Occasionally, it's something useful for the story at hand. More likely, if there's anything at all, it's an interesting, related point. While it may not belong in the story you're working on, it may be a great story idea or nugget for a future story. Make note. You should always be collecting future story ideas.

Finally, after you shut off the equipment, watch for a sigh of relief. The interviewee survived. If you see this happen, ask again whether there's anything you missed. "Well," the person might say, "of course I can't really say much about such and such." Now comes the dilemma. Technically, of course, you're still on the record, you're just not recording. But what is the perception of the person you're talking to? We're back to ethical decision-making. If you're talking to a politician, he or she knows the rules, and, absent a clear understanding, everything is on the record. Not so with others. In any case, your job as a reporter is to convince them to let you turn your equipment back on and talk about this unexplored area. If you work at it—and care about the outcome—most of the time you'll succeed.

Make Notes Afterward

No camera or recorder will register every nuance you may have seen or noticed. Telling details such as the weakness of a handshake, an odor of stale cigars or the chill of a drafty room can make or break a story. Pay attention to these things, and make notes right away. Later, in the rush to air, it's easy to forget, and then they're lost forever.

●●●●●

Beyond the Interview

Being Human

The toughest interview is the "grieving widow"—the person (widow or otherwise) who has just suffered a loss. It might be a fatal car accident, a drowning or a devastating loss from a tornado. How do we talk to the person in grief? Should we talk to that person at all?

In some respects the answers vary depending on the particulars and the particular reporter. Without question, some people in grief will be highly offended at the notion of speaking to a reporter. But others find the experience cathartic or an opportunity to publicly memorialize a victim. Don't prejudge how *you* think someone should behave. It's really not up to you to pre-censure what someone should or should not say.

But be a human being first. *Without* a recorder or camera aimed and running, offer the sympathy any human being would extend to another at a time of loss. Offer to talk if the person would like to. Make yourself available. If people are interested or willing, they'll say so. If not, you wouldn't have gotten a usable bite anyway. In either case you'll be able to sleep better at night.

Never ask victims of tragedy *how they feel.* If you don't know the answer to that question already, find a different career.

A Closing Thought

One advantage that we have in this business is that we do record our interviews. That means the audience gets to hear exactly what someone sounds like, and it means that our quotes are completely accurate.

It also means we get a chance to learn from every interview we conduct. Don't just listen to your interviews for good bites; listen to learn about interviewing and yourself. How were your questions? Did you listen completely? What can you learn to make the next interview better?

● ● ● ● ●

Summary

Bites and actualities involve the actual sounds of people in the news. We call them *bites* in TV and *actualities* in radio, but otherwise there's no difference. Natural sound is the actual sound of life (traffic, kids on a playground, and so on). Beyond making sure the technical quality is high and the sound clear, the best bites involve personal account, witness account, personal opinion and expert opinion. Generally, weak bites involve hard data and anything not said well. The quality of our bites and actualities depends heavily on the quality of our interviews. This chapter contains a dozen points for better interviewing: 1) Plan; 2) Listen; 3) Get the technical side right; 4) Make the interviewee comfortable; 5) Ask questions that deliver what you're after; 6) Use silence; 7) Maintain strong eye contact; 8) Learn to respond inaudibly; 9) Follow up and clarify; 10) Maintain control; 11) Ask for more—twice; 12) Make notes afterward. Be human, and remember that a good interview is generally just two people having a conversation—with the interviewee doing most of the talking. Never ask victims of tragedy how it feels.

●●●●●

Key Words & Phrases

bites . . . actualities . . . nat or natural sound . . . personal account . . . witness account . . . personal opinion . . . expert opinion . . . plan . . . listen . . . the use of silence . . . strong eye contact . . . follow up and clarify . . . maintain control . . . ask for more

●●●●●

Exercises

A. Come up with three solid story ideas (no profiles allowed) based on interviewing people not like you. That means no college or graduate students. Find out what their concerns and interests are . . . and what stories they think the media have ignored. Write two paragraphs on what they had to say, include their name and a way to reach them— either phone or email—and a third paragraph based on your research that determines either that the proposed story idea is valid or that it's not. And why.

B. Watch one of the Sunday morning talk shows like Face the Nation (CBS), Meet the Press (NBC) or This Week (ABC). What did you notice about the interviewing? What worked and what didn't? Make a list of the three best questions the interviewer asked. What made them good?

C. Watch a 60 Minutes or CBS Sunday Morning piece that's primarily an interview. What did you notice about that interview, and how did it compare with the Sunday morning talk show? What were the best questions the interviewer asked? Why?

D. Record at least one of the interviews in Exercise A. Pick out the best bites from the interview you conducted and evaluate the questions you asked that elicited the best answers. What do you notice about those questions? Make a list of your three best and three least effective questions. Explain why each question made the list.

4

● ● ● ● ●

Stories

No one said writing is easy. At least, no one should have said that. "People think, 'You're good at this, it must be fun to you,'" says CBS' Steve Hartman. "It's not . . . it's work." Hartman knows the secret to writing success that all good reporters learn sooner or later: It's not about the writing . . . it's all about the rewriting.

The first time I write something down, it's never any good, says Hartman. "Sometimes it might take you five times, and sometimes it might take you 25 times. Don't ever think you're going to be a great writer on the first pass. That's not how it works."

There has always been a debate about whether good writers are born that way or whether they've learned to be good writers. Is it an art or a craft? "It's not a gift you're born with," says Hartman. "It's a craft, and like any craft you get better at it the more you practice it. If you do it repeatedly, as I have, you're going to find that eventually you get better and better."

● ● ● ● ●

Stories Are Like Music

Composer Stephen Sondheim said that the best, most important advice he ever got came from lyricist Oscar Hammerstein:

> A song should be like a play; it should have a beginning, a middle and an end. It should have an idea, state the idea, and then build the idea and develop it, and finish. And at the end, you should be in a place different than you began.

That's why Charles Osgood, recently retired from CBS News, says we should think of broadcast writing in terms of music. "Good writing has to be musical, with a sense of balance, a sense of beauty, melodic, a sense of phrasing." As with music, sentences should be constructed in a "graceful way." As with music, "the beginning should sound like the beginning and the end should sound like the end."

The point is, we call them stories, and we do best telling them that way. It doesn't apply to every item in the news. There are timely events that simply require a straightforward recitation of significant information—well written and constructed. But they're still stories.

There is no one right way to tell a story. Regrettably, there are considerably more wrong ways than right ones, and most stories that don't work start out badly and never recover. That's why the lead is so important. The keys are thinking and planning. If you figure out both how you're going to start the story and how you're going to end it *before you start writing*, you're most of the way home.

Stories also frequently fail because they're illogical in telling the information. Call the concept *story logic*. The phrase is easier said than explained, but it starts with understanding the story itself.

● ● ● ● ●

Plan and Focus

Why Run the Story?

Why should this story go on the air? If you can't answer that question, the rest is probably hopeless. There are lots of plausible answers.

The story is of sufficient importance to the audience that it needs to be in the news:

■ A chemical spill that endangers people
■ A major plant closing
■ The results of the day's election

The story is useful to the audience for day-to-day living or long-range survival, sometimes called "news you can use":

■ Consumer stories
■ How to make your way through new highway construction
■ Surviving unemployment

The story is particularly interesting or particularly unusual:

■ Senior citizen beauty contestants
■ The wranglings over whether someone can keep his pet alligator at home
■ The dramatic rescue of a young child (not in your area)

The story involves important and/or well-known people:

- Almost anything the president does
- A big-name celebrity visits your town
- The high-profile leaders and leading characters every community has

Other reasons are possible. Other factors such as timeliness or proximity certainly enter into the decision. Think about why the story should be on the air, and think about what's *new* in the story because the lead must address the issue not only of why the audience should care but also why they should care *now*. There's an old saying that "three-quarters of news is new." Stories are not on the air *now* because of something that happened in the past.

Former network correspondent Deborah Potter says there are two steps to follow *before* you actually start writing. The first is to answer the question, "What is this story really about?"

It's not enough to say what happened, she says. It's what happened, and what are we supposed to make of that? What does that mean? Come up with a focus statement that's short and tight. Potter says that if describing that focus takes more than one sentence, you're not yet ready to write the story.

Former NBC correspondent Don Larson says you should be able to determine the focus because, "It will make you smile, it will make you shake your head in disgust, it will make you sense a shared truth. It might make you think of your own neighborhood, your own childhood, your own family."

In a story about a kid in juvenile detention, Potter says the focus statement might be, "Ernie survives jail." Or maybe, "Jail breaks Ernie." Once you figure out the narrow focus, get rid of everything that doesn't fit. That includes bites you collected along the way. Even good bites, if they're not right on point, have to go. Remember Larson's phrase, "Kill the babies."

Do You Understand?

Do you understand all the aspects of the story? Nothing *you* don't understand will ever get clearer on its way to the audience. If you don't fully understand what's happening in the story and the answers to all of those basic *who, what, when, where, why* and *how* questions, then you're not ready to start writing anything. If there's something in the story you don't understand, you have three choices: get the issue(s) cleared up, drop the part you don't fully understand or drop the story. If you don't understand something, it's inconceivable that the audience will.

The following story, word for word, went on the air on a top station in a top 15 market:

> Incinerators in the metro area may get their plugs
> pulled. The Air Control Commission will review a
> letter today that would shut down incinerators that
> pose potential health and environmental hazards at
> hundreds of schools.
>
> According to Department of Natural Resources
> records, there are 733 burners on school and college
> campuses in the area. Some may not be running. If
> the letter is approved, it will be sent to every
> school district. Today's meeting could be the last
> for the commission; it will close down in January as
> part of the governor's reorganization of the
> department.

Even leaving aside some serious writing problems, it's clear that the writer had no idea what this story was really all about. Neither did any of the people who heard it. In most of this book, I provide corrected versions of bad stories and bad phrasing. I can't do it here, however, because I'm really not sure what the story was supposed to be about either.

And this story must have left its Midwestern (but nowhere near Chicago) audience a bit puzzled:

> Fog blanketed Chicago's O'Hare Airport today.
> Ninety-eight percent of the flights out of the windy
> city were canceled before noon.
>
> That pea soup covered all of northern Illinois.
> The F-A-A is blaming the fog for the cancellation of
> all landings at O'Hare today as well.

That story is at least understandable; it just suffers from inadequate thought in the telling. Why split up the takeoffs and landings? And because this story was broadcast outside of Chicago, the far greater *local* effect would be on flights going in to Chicago from the city where this broadcast took place. That's the primary local story, along with the secondary effect of planes from Chicago that don't get to land in your local city. Either start with the local story:

BETTER: Make sure you call ahead before heading out to
the airport today. We're feeling the effects of
a fog-inflicted shut down at Chicago's O'Hare
Airport ...

or at least combine the Chicago information:

BETTER: Dense fog has virtually shut down Chicago's busy
O'Hare Airport ...

The problem in the original O'Hare story is nothing compared to the following story, which went on the air, exactly as written, on a top 50 market TV station:

```
Thinking of investing in the stock market? Well,
now's the time to do it. The consumer price index
is down ... the inflation rate is, too ... and that
makes the market ripe for the picking. And you don't
need a lot of money. Analysts say if you do it
right, you can be successful with as little as six
thousand dollars. The trick is to diversify. Put
a little in a short-term option. And, above all,
be honest with yourself about how much you want
to risk ...
```

Having a news anchor offer advice like this is frightening. Among other things, the market is never *ripe for the picking;* most people think of six thousand dollars as a lot of money; and short-term options are among the riskiest investments someone can make. This story went well beyond both the reporter's area of knowledge and the proper role of a journalist. Don't write what you don't know.

What's the Story About?

Think what the story is about. Remember, we're still talking about all the things you need to do in your head—or on paper if it's complicated—*before* you actually start writing. While you're writing is no time to be thinking about where you're headed; you need to know that beforehand.

That's a lot harder than it sounds. It's easy to get overwhelmed by facts and try to deal with information in the sequence in which you collected it rather than digesting the whole thing and figuring out the story. Unfortunately, there are no shortcuts. Collect all the information, figure out what the story is really all about and then figure out how you're going to tell the story—the whole story.

THE FACTS: A young girl gets out of a defective child restraint, wanders from her yard and falls into a river. She is pulled out by her father, revived by mouth-to-mouth resuscitation by a neighbor and taken to a local hospital by paramedics.

The facts are simple enough, but should this be a story of safety, survival or rescue? Since you can't say everything in a lead, what's most likely to capture the attention of the audience? The issue isn't as simple as choosing the right path versus the wrong one. It's picking a single, simple story to concentrate on.

THE FACTS: A small fire breaks out in a service room, filling apartment building corridors with smoke, upsetting residents of the senior citizens' complex, who must leave their apartments and wait outside in the cold while the fire department deals with what turns out to be a minor fire resulting in little damage.

Is there a story here at all? If so, what part of it would get anyone's interest and attention in a lead?

What's the Lead?

Find the lead. A story that's broadcast because of its importance, newsworthiness or usefulness will most often demand a fairly straightforward lead. If you've selected the story properly, that kind of information should capture the attention of the audience. A story that's broadcast because of whom it's about should obviously include the *who* in the lead. A story that's broadcast because it's unusual or interesting frequently allows more leeway in how you get into it. But don't confuse leeway with sloppiness. This kind of story is harder to write because the facts of the story won't write themselves. You've got to sell them. See Chapter 10 for more on leads and endings.

In What Order Do You Tell the Story?

We tell stories to one another in a manner in which we think the other person will best understand. If we do that face to face, we have the advantage of visual and perhaps oral feedback. We can usually tell whether the person we're speaking to understands and cares, and we can adjust accordingly. We don't have that feedback in this business. We have to think about the story from the standpoint of the audience the whole time we work on it. Generally, after an appropriate lead, telling stories chronologically will be easiest on the audience. That means that we first get the audience's attention with a strong lead. We then tell the story from beginning to end, in the same sequence in which it actually happened.

GOOD

LEAD AND

BEGINNING: Two men teamed up for a dramatic rescue of a young girl today. Six-year-old Sally Jones ... [starting at the beginning and going to the end of that sequence of information from the previous page]

GOOD

LEAD AND

BEGINNING: Clouds of smoke drove elderly residents from their apartments today. It all started ... [again, from the beginning to the end of the information given on the previous page]

Good

LEAD AND

CHRONOLOGICAL

STORY

DEVELOPMENT: Police have arrested an unemployed truck driver for yesterday's robbery at the Jones Trucking Company. Police say John Smith went in to see his former employer armed with a sawed-off shotgun.

An employee at the firm said the robber demanded all the money kept in the company safe — and that he threatened to shoot anyone who moved. Police say Smith made off with two-thousand dollars, which police say they recovered in Smith's south side apartment this afternoon.

Note that after the lead—which is a simple statement of what took place—all the information is relayed in the same sequence as it happened. Note also all the attribution in the story. It feels a little cumbersome, but each one is necessary to avoid *your* accusing Smith of a crime. (See attribution in Chapter 8 and the crime and legal section of Chapter 19.)

The robbery story above is a clean, clear, straightforward development that will be easy for the audience to follow and understand.

Here's another example of a story that takes an unfortunate turn out of sequence:

ILLOGICAL

SEQUENCE: Meantime, Democratic presidential hopeful Hillary Clinton is planning a stop in Nevada on her way to the Democratic National Convention next week.

The convention begins a week from Monday in Philadelphia, and Clinton's schedule calls for her to be in Las Vegas this coming Tuesday.

Campaign officials say she'll talk about the need for investing in our infrastructure at the international convention of the American Federation of State, County and Municipal Employees.

The lead is acceptable, but, after that, the writer lost track of what story she was telling. The story is supposed to be about Clinton's trip to Nevada, but after the lead, the writer tells us about the convention instead. That's better handled in an information ending.

BETTER

SEQUENCE: Meantime, Democratic presidential hopeful Hillary Clinton plans a stop in Nevada on her way to the Democratic Convention next week.

```
    Clinton is scheduled to appear in Las Vegas on
Tuesday ... where she's expected to talk to a
meeting of municipal workers about investing in the
country's ailing infrastructure.
    The Democratic convention begins a week from
Monday in Philadelphia.
```

● ● ● ● ●

Story Logic

Handling the Basics

As reporters, every statement we hear leads us, or should lead us, to the next logical question. We want answers to all of the *who, what, when, where, why* and *how* questions, but we don't ask those questions at random. Each one has its place. The same is true when we're writing the story for the audience. As we go along, logical questions come up in the minds of the audience. If each succeeding line in our story answers the next logical question in the minds of the audience, we have achieved story logic.

```
    Florida officials sprayed an 80-acre marijuana
field with the controversial weed killer, paraquat.
It's the first time the chemical has been used on pot
in the U-S. Opponents fear some of the treated drug
might get on the market where its use might damage
smokers' lungs. But officials say the spraying saves
time and labor getting rid of the stuff — and that
the field will remain under 24-hour guard until all
the plants are destroyed.
```

The story starts with a hard lead: what happened. The second sentence really functions as part of the lead, splitting up material that would overload the sentence if written all together. The lead says the weed killer is controversial. Sentence three must explain why. Having said that officials did this controversial thing and what the potential hazards are, the next logical question is why, then, did officials spray? The last sentence answers that and brings the story to a logical information/future ramification close.

The story above is tight and straightforward, but it's certainly not the only way to deal with the information. Alternative leads include:

```
    Florida officials are trying a new way to get rid
of marijuana.
```

or

> A marijuana field in Florida is under 24-hour guard
> right now.

The first alternative will require that line two explains what the new method is. The second example will require that line two explains why. The point is that every line you use in a story takes the listener or viewer deeper into the information, and each line should lead logically into the next. Where that logical flow doesn't exist, there's a problem.

> Students who skip school may really get hit where
> it hurts.
> The Ohio Senate passed a bill that would take away
> the drivers' licenses of kids under age 18 who drop
> out of school.
> Officials in West Virginia say a similar law there
> has cut the drop-out rate by one-third.
> The Ohio version is expected to be approved by the
> House and signed by the governor some time next
> week.

This clean, clear story starts with a soft main point lead. Line two gives the specifics of what's taking place, followed by what could be an answer to the question, *Can this work?* The story ends logically with a future ramification close. Nice, straightforward story.

Will It Stand on Its Own?

Every story should be able to stand on its own, as if it were the first time the audience ever heard about the subject. Although we should not underestimate the audience's intelligence, we cannot overestimate the audience's knowledge and background on a story. News people talk to themselves too much; most people don't follow the news with the kind of interest and intensity that reporters do. Many people receive only bits and pieces of news for days at a time—or longer. People frequently miss the news completely.

With a few exceptions for major, ongoing stories, think of each story as taking the audience from a clean slate to some measure of understanding. The lead line takes the audience from point A (nothing) to point B (some new information). Point B should include, depending on the kind of story it is, something of the significance of the item—why it's on the air and why it's on the air now. Having written the lead, stop. Think about where you've taken the audience. The choices for line two are limited. You've raised certain questions in the lead; you've given partial explanations in the lead. What's the next logical question? The answer to that is line two. Now that you've taken the audience from A to

B to C, stop again. Where will you go next? Use this process all the way through the story. If your _answers_ to logical questions come when the _questions_ do, you've achieved story logic.

WHAT

HAPPENED: The city council today voted to raise property taxes by 20 percent.

WHAT IT

MEANS: If signed into law, the cost to a homeowner with an average 150-thousand-dollar house — an extra 220 dollars a year.

WHY—

AND ONE

SIDE: Council chairman John Smith proposed the tax hike — saying it was the only way the council could balance the city budget.

WHY NOT—

THE OTHER

SIDE: Council member Jennifer Jones was the lone dissenter in the five-to-one vote. She warned that the tax hike will drive businesses out of the city.

WHAT WILL

HAPPEN

NEXT: The mayor did not attend the meeting — and has not said whether he'll sign the measure.

Answer the Logical Questions

Never leave logical questions unanswered. Some people will always want more detailed information about a given story. That's not the issue. The issue involves logical questions that a good portion of your audience is likely to wonder about. It might be the possible effects of something; what someone thought about the event; why the person did that anyway. Sometimes you don't know the answer to a logical question, as in the example above on the mayor's position. Then say so. But don't ignore it. If it's not in the story, there's no telling what the audience will assume, but there's no guarantee they'll assume you would have told them if you knew. In the story above, leaving out the last line would leave a logical question unanswered. Even though the mayor's position is unknown, the script above means the audience knows that it has all the relevant answers the reporter has. Remember that the audience looks to you for answers. That's your job.

After inaccuracies and confusion, leaving logical questions unanswered is the next greatest sin in news writing. Look at the problem created in the following story, which ran on a large-market television station:

```
    Last night, police found themselves in a tense
situation after busting a crack house.
    Narcotics and SWAT officers charged into the house
on Main Street and came face to face with four kids
armed with semi-automatic weapons.
    Detectives found about six-thousand dollars worth
of crack inside the place, and they also confiscated
a tech-nine and a 45-caliber semi-automatic. The
teenagers ... 16 and 17 years old ... are charged
with drug trafficking.
```

But what happened to the *tense situation?* What happened when the officers found themselves *face to face with four kids armed with semiautomatic weapons?* That's likely to be exactly what the audience was thinking about as the rest of the story slid by unnoticed. The writer needed just one more line to take the audience, logically, from the *tense situation* to the aftermath.

● ● ● ● ●

Story Structure

Make the Writing Structure Interesting

Vary sentence length and structure. There are only so many words that can be read well together, but if sentence after sentence is structured the same way grammatically and close to the same length, the story will sound choppy and boring. Be careful with sentence structure variations, though. You still need to keep sentences short and simple, or they'll be confusing. Go back to the city council story on page 43. It's a short, simple story, but notice the variation in sentence length and structure even in a quick story like that.

```
    There was another chemical leak in Delaware
County. It was the second chemical leak this week.
    A couple of officers with the state highway patrol
noticed some sort of fluid leaking from this tanker
this morning.
    They stopped the driver. The fluid turned out to
be hydrochloric acid. The driver himself fixed the
leak. The officers charged him with carrying an
insecure load.
```

The story is reasonably clear and told in the right sequence, but it's boring and badly in need of some writing variation and connector words to smooth it out:

```
Another chemical leak in Delaware County — the
second one this week.
    Highway patrol officers pulled over this tanker
this morning when they spotted some fluid leaking.
    The fluid turned out to be hydrochloric acid — a
dangerous chemical, although it caused no problem
here. The driver himself fixed the leak, but the
officers charged him with carrying an insecure load.
```

What made the second version better? The second version took the first two identically-structured, passive sentences and combined them into two short sentence fragments without the weak *to be* verbs. The resulting lead is one-third shorter than the original two sentences—and a lot punchier. The next sentence of the new version again combines two sentences of the original version while tightening up the writing. In fact, the new version trims the wording of the middle of the story by almost half. The new version and the original start the next sentence exactly the same, but the new version adds new information—that hydrochloric acid is a dangerous chemical—and answers a logical question that was unanswered in the original: Did the chemical cause a problem? The revised version then combined the last two sentences of the original using a conjunction (*but*) to smooth out the copy. The second version of the story actually contains more information, reads better and is still a little shorter than the original. In this business, shorter is almost always better.

● ● ● ● ●

Transitions

Use transitions to smooth out the writing.

Transitions within Stories

Within stories, transitions help the audience understand the story better by drawing connections and improving the flow. Transitions ex.

- **cause and effect:** *because, so, that's why*
- **comparison and contrast:** *but, on the other hand, however*
- **groupings:** *and, with, along with, also, in addition*
- **size or quality:** *more* or *most important, even (bigger* or *older* or whatever)*

spatial relationships: *nearby, just down the street, on the other side of town*

time relationships: *in the meantime, at the same time, just as, meanwhile, now, then, so far, when, while, yet, soon*

Look at how the use of transitions helps to smooth out this copy and draw connections and contrasts:

```
Three years' worth of city reports have called
for programs aimed at going beyond homeless
shelters ... and helping people restart their lives.
But three years later, almost none of it exists.
According to city officials, there hasn't been a new
low-cost or subsidized housing project built here in
more than five years. And none is planned.
```

The story uses three conjunctions. The first one serves more to provide a breathing point than anything else. The next two—one *but* and one *and*—serve to smooth out the copy by drawing a contrast between two facts in one case and adding additional information in the other.

Make sure you use conjunctions correctly. The following examples, which were actually used on the air, were more likely to puzzle the audience.

PROBLEM: The project will be built over the next
   10 years, and won't start for several months.

Given that the above two bits of information are really *contrasting*, the conjunction should be *but*, not *and*.

BETTER: The project will be built over the next
   10 years ... but won't start for several months.

The correct conjunction helps the audience understand what's taking place.

PROBLEM: They arrested one man, but another man in the
   house tried to run out the back door but was met by
   SWAT officers.

The second *but* does its job well—contrasting situations. But because the second man was arrested, too, the first *but* really doesn't make any sense. In fact, the audience is likely to be confused because the word sets up the idea that the guy got away. Better to drop that first *but* completely:

BETTER: They arrested one man. Another man in the house
  tried to run out the back door but was met by SWAT
  officers.

This version will be far easier for the audience to follow.

PROBLEM: No charges have been filed against the 16, but
  officials say most were in their late teens and early
  twenties.

Don't force transitions and connections where they don't exist. Since
there's really no known relationship between the filing of charges and
the ages of those arrested, the *but* connecting the otherwise unrelated
parts of the story simply confuses the audience. Drop it:

BETTER: No charges have been filed against the 16.
  Officials say most are in their late teens and early
  twenties.

In this case, the copy is clearer with no transition.

PROBLEM: Applications from foreign students for the
  upcoming semester are down 30 percent over last year.

The idea that something can be "down . . . over" just doesn't sound
right. Better to tighten the copy and change the preposition.

BETTER: Applications from foreign students are down 30
  percent from last year.

Conjunctions help the flow of the story, but only if they're used
correctly. Make sure you've used the right transition word to describe
what's happening in the story.

Transitions Between Stories

We don't run stories individually in a vacuum; we run them within
newscasts. Because of that, we also use transitions *between stories* in an
attempt to have one story flow into the next.

Too often, we forget that a newscast is really only organized chaos.
The stories we call news really are related only by the decision that a
given collection of material should go on the air, rather than the many
other choices available. Taken from that standpoint, anything we can
do to make the journey through the newscast a little easier can only
help the listener and viewer.

Transition lines can help light the path of the newscast and make it easier to follow. Only two things legitimately connect news stories. One is *geography*; the other is *subject*. Stories that are connected by either of these common bonds should flow one from the other more logically than stories that have nothing in common. But don't force the transition as this large-market writer did in the last line of a story on a single-engine plane crash:

PROBLEM: Tonight, the F-A-A is trying to figure out why
    the plane crashed and killed the two men.
      Thousands of people on the East Coast are <u>not</u>
    worried about air safety in lieu of the Smith
    Airlines strike ...

In other words, there is no connection between the content of the two stories. A forced and inappropriate transition just sounds stupid—like this bizarre "transition" in the last line of a story on wrong information from IRS personnel:

PROBLEM: Anyway, they say they won't hold you to blame for
    wrong answers if you can document the name of the
    person you talked to, the question you asked, and
    the date of the call.
      You won't find much wrong with Ohio's wineries.
    It's becoming very big business ...

Charitably, these are forced transitions. The first example is really irresponsible. The Smith Airlines story (I'm protecting the name of the innocent airline) that night had absolutely nothing to do with safety. The writer raised the issue in the lead line, in the negative, only for the purpose of contriving a transition. But given that both stories related to aviation, the writer really didn't need a transition at all. The second example is just plain dumb.

Related stories should be easy to handle, like the opening line of a story about people who work on Labor Day, after a story about the holiday itself:

    But Labor Day was just that for many people....

A line like that means a virtually seamless transition from one story to the next.

Even a single word and short phrase can help the flow:

    Also in federal court today, a Newark doctor
    pleaded guilty ...

Individual reporters and anchors may handle each story beautifully, but if someone isn't looking at how they fit together, the newscast just won't flow. That's the job of the producer.

Transitions can smooth the flow from one story to the next, but those transitions have to be logical. If they're not, just move on to the next item in the newscast. See more on this and newscasts in general in Chapter 13, "Producing News on TV."

● ● ● ● ●

Before You're Done

Does the Story Support the Lead?

The lead of a story is like a headline: It catches our interest and attention. If the rest of the story doesn't support it, you've butchered either the lead or the rest of the story.

Will the Audience Understand?

Remember that as reporter, writer or producer, you're close to the story. Even if you do understand the information, there's no guarantee the audience will. Too often, what we know about a story never fully makes it onto the written page. Especially in complicated stories, as we read over what we've written, we may internally supplement what we actually write with information that only we know. Unfortunately, the audience can't do that. Always go back and make sure you've answered all the logical questions and that what you know and mean to say really got down on paper in the manner you intended.

```
     Republican officials say the very survival of
the party in Ohio may hinge on the outcome of the
elections. They say if Democrats are allowed to
dominate the state appointment board for the third
straight time, the G-O-P could be pushed out of
business in Ohio.
```

Other than party officials or students of government, it's inconceivable that members of the audience could have understood what this story was about—although it did go on the air, word for word, as printed above. This is a much-too-shortened story on the complicated controversy of reapportionment. The writer may well have understood the issue, filling in the many gaps in written information with the background and knowledge *within* the reporter. The audience would have had no idea what this story meant.

Another common, related problem is providing accurate information that has no discernible meaning. Take this real story as an example:

> The river is at its highest level since 1982.
> The Louvre is relocating priceless pieces of
> art ... in rooms ... that could be flooded out.
> The Seine burst its banks yesterday and is
> expected to crest at 21 feet. The flooding in Europe
> has claimed 12 lives.
> It could take two weeks before the river returns
> to normal levels.

This is a pretty typical example of your basic flood story, but—as with many if not most flood stories—it doesn't provide useful information. A river cresting at 21 feet means that that's the highest level of water (or wave in the case of an ocean), but that measure doesn't tell you anything about flooding unless you add that information. Without knowing the flood stage—where the water runs over what is normally dry land—the crest number has no meaning. What would be more useful in this story is to know either how much higher the water is than the flood stage or how much area has been (or will be) flooded.

By the way, officials are certainly *not* "relocating priceless pieces of art . . . in rooms . . . that could be flooded out." They're undoubtedly relocating the art *from* rooms that could be flooded.

Contrast that with this nicely handled version of a fairly complex story:

> There is a glimmer of hope tonight that Smith
> Airlines and its disgruntled mechanics may be able
> to avert a strike, set for midnight tomorrow.
> The airline says there's a new proposal on the
> table ... the two sides are talking ... but they
> have a long way to go.
> Smith is demanding 150 million dollars in wage
> concessions from the mechanics. The mechanics say
> the best they can do is accept a wage freeze for
> one year.
> Smith claims it's losing a million dollars a day
> and can't afford that.
> Pilots and attendants today said they will honor
> any picket lines ... and won't fly in planes which
> haven't been serviced.
> Other airlines, though, say they're not sure
> they'll honor Smith tickets if there is a strike.
> We'll keep you posted.

Note the use of short, clear sentences and the back-and-forth approach to the issues: one side and then the other side. Nice, clear summary of a complicated story without any sense of whether the writer is more sympathetic toward one side or the other.

Use Humor Sparingly

If you're really good at humor, you should probably be a comedian. Few news people are nearly as funny as they seem to think they are. Use humor sparingly and only when it's clearly appropriate.

PROBLEM: Those of you who work at Smith Instrumentation
and its neighbor, Jones Company, might want to call
the boss before work tomorrow. Both places are
pretty well gutted tonight ...

PROBLEM: A knock-down, drag-out fight between two women
ended in gunfire tonight on the west side. Witnesses
tell us a woman named "Vicki" lost the fight in the
first round at the Green Apartment complex. And then
won the second round ... not with her fists ... but
with a gun.

Other than changing the names, both of the above stories went on the air as written. They shouldn't have. People who have been thrown out of work and those who have lost everything they've worked for in the first story will find little that is cute or amusing about the situation. And getting shot is seldom funny. Misplaced humor is offensive.

Read the Story Aloud

Always read your story aloud before it goes on the air. That's the only way to tell:

- Real length. Numbers, especially, can easily make a computer's automatic timing highly inaccurate. To most computers, it takes the same amount of time to read *the* as it does to read *999*.
- Whether the lines can really be read comfortably and with proper emphasis.
- Whether you have words that are difficult to pronounce without sounding awkward (try *desks* out loud for example).
- Whether in writing a bit too quickly you have omitted words that you meant to write.
- Whether you've misspelled any words—assuming your errors were oversights rather than ignorance. Misspellings commonly turn into mispronunciations and muddled reading.

• • • • •

Summary

Most stories that don't work either start out with bad leads and never recover or try to convey information in an illogical sequence. To figure out how to tell a story, think about why you're running the story, what's new that the audience didn't know about, what's the lead, and what's a logical sequence. The three biggest problems in storytelling are inaccuracy, confusion and not answering logical questions. Make the writing more interesting by at least some variation in sentence length and structure and use transitions to smooth out the writing.

• • • • •

Key Words & Phrases

Why run the story? . . . What's new to the audience? . . . Do you understand all the facts? . . . What's the story really about? . . . What's the lead? . . . What's the best sequence to tell the story? . . . story logic . . . answer the logical questions . . . story structure . . . transition—within story and between stories

• • • • •

Exercises

A. Convert the following random bits of information into coherent 30–40 second broadcast stories. For this assignment, imagine that you're a reporter in Springfield.

Story 1

a) Yesterday, the Fourth National Bank of Springfield was robbed.

b) Police arrested James Smith and Harry Jones in connection with the robbery.

c) Police are looking for a third suspect in connection with the bank robbery. No name has been released.

d) The robbers made off with an undisclosed amount of money.

e) A bank customer was shot and seriously injured during the robbery. His name has still not been released.

f) Springfield General Hospital says the injured man is in serious but stable condition.

g) Sally Hannon, a bank customer, said the robbers made everyone lie down on the floor and hand over valuables and money.

h) The robbery took place at 4:45 p.m., just before closing time yesterday.

i) The bank branch that was robbed is located at Main St. and 14th Ave. It's the bank's biggest branch outside of the main office downtown.

j) Chief Detective Samuel Greene said that police apprehended the two male suspects at 11 a.m. this morning . . . and that police are confident that they will make a third arrest today.

k) Police said they have not recovered any of the missing money yet.

Story 2

a) General Engine and Aeronautics employed 2,500 workers at its plant in Springfield.

b) That's one of 3 plants in the U.S. The other two are in Bakersfield, CA, and Mobile, AL.

c) GEA also has a plant in Brazil and another in Mexico.

d) The company makes airplane and heavy truck engines.

e) GEA just announced that it will lay off 2,000 workers in Springfield in 60 days.

f) The company will stop making engines in Springfield, and the smaller workforce will just make engine parts.

g) The layoffs are part of a general restructuring of the company.

h) The Bakersfield plant will shut down completely, and the Mobile plant will remain the same. There are 1,500 and 1,800 workers, respectively, in Bakersfield and Mobile.

i) Production—and hiring—in Mexico will increase.

j) No workers will be offered relocation, according to George Hansen, the local company spokesperson.

k) The company said that it had to lower labor costs in order to compete on a global basis, according to Hansen.

l) Theodore Ripson, the head of the local Teamsters union, which represents most of the soon-to-be-laid-off workers, says he is shocked by the announcement, and that the Teamsters will fight the layoffs.

m) Ripson said GEA did comply with state labor laws in giving the workers 60 days' notice.

n) GEA is one of Springfield's largest employers and the largest manufacturing plant in town.

Story 3

a) The state's general fund revenue comes mostly from sales, income and corporate taxes.

b) Newly elected Governor Mary Smith is seeking an 8 to 10 percent cut in pay for state workers who aren't covered by union-negotiated contracts. Smith says that would save the state about $300 million.

c) Smith said that voters must approve a continuation of the state sales tax and vehicle license fees. Those fees will then go to local governments to help pay for the shifting of some expenses from the state to local governments.

d) Smith said her recommendations would close a 12-month budget gap estimated at $18.5 billion, and that everyone in the state must sacrifice at least some in order to bring the state back from the brink of insolvency.

e) Smith's office said the only area of state spending that would not be cut would be K–12 education. That's because that area had already been cut last year. Even so, spending in that area would be frozen for at least 2 years.

f) Smith called for $10 billion in spending reductions, including cuts in social services, welfare, health care and the statewide university education systems.

g) Smith also acknowledged that the restructuring of state government to shift many responsibilities from the state to counties and cities will be complicated and controversial.

h) Smith is proposing a $70.5 billion general fund budget, slightly less than last year's $73.2 billion budget.

i) Smith's new proposed budget would cut funding to most areas of state government and maintain a group of tax increases for five years to close the state's enormous budget deficit.

j) Smith's proposal to extend taxes will require support from both parties in the state legislature, many of whom have vowed to oppose all taxes.

Story 4

a) An out-of-state development group from Montana completed the purchase of approximately three acres of land along East Main Street in Springfield on Wednesday.

b) The soon-to-be-formed Springfield Hotel Group, Incorporated, plans to build a new hotel on East Main Street between the Marriott Hotel and the Hampton Inn.

c) Developer Henry Jones said several people that he has met in Springfield have questioned how there can be enough business for so many new hotels.

d) Jones said he is optimistic about the hotel's long-term success because of the steady growth in the area.

e) Jones said he has already purchased the land, and he expects construction to begin within the next three months. He said it will take 18 months to complete the construction.

f) Construction of a new hotel near downtown is expected to begin within 90 days, according to an announcement by the developer earlier today.

g) The land purchased is a portion of a larger tract of land owned by former Springfield Mayor Marvin Summers.

h) The developers say the total investment for the 160-room hotel will be approximately $19 million. When complete, it will be the third new hotel constructed in Springfield since 2014.

i) The construction phase is expected to mean about 200 new jobs. When the hotel opens, it will mean about 85 full time and part time jobs.

Story 5

a) Land-based pollution is handled by the state, but pollution in the water is handled by the U.S. Environmental Protection Agency. The EPA started Springfield River PCB dredging last spring.

b) New studies will estimate how much PCB and other pollution is present in East Springfield . . . along with how much it could cost to clean it up.

c) A lawsuit by the residents in the area and the town against General Wire and Metalworks for damages is pending.

d) New state grants will pay for studies to spell out cleanup and revitalization plans for two polluted sections of East Springfield. Those areas make up over 300 acres and include 6 "brownfield sites."

e) Money for the studies will come from a $400,000 grant from the state, announced this morning, under a program meant to clean up so-called industrial brownfields. Those areas sit nearby the old GWM plant that released PCBs and other chemicals into both the river and the land decades ago.

f) Residents nearby have complained for years that the contamination makes their homes almost impossible to sell or even refinance.

g) In that area of East Springfield, GWM has installed basement ventilation systems in some homes to exhaust tainted air left from underground industrial pollution.

h) East Springfield Mayor Janet Burroughs said the state will cover 90 percent of the study costs, but the town will have to cover 10 percent, which is likely to come in services rather than actual cash.

i) Burroughs said East Springfield has been struggling for decades to recover from its history of pollution . . . and has trouble attracting new development because of the perception of widespread contamination.

j) A state-mandated cleanup of a nearby storage area by GWM began in 2013 where as much as 100,000 pounds of PCBs were believed to be buried.

B. Now convert those random bits of information (above) into coherent 20 second broadcast stories.

5

Working with Bites, Actualities and Natural Sound

The most important concept to understand when writing into or out of bites, actualities and natural sound is that those elements are as much a part of the story as the script itself. Since you can't rewrite what someone says, you must frame your writing to blend in the bites and sound so that everything flows smoothly and logically and becomes one cohesive story.

The Feel of Natural Sound

In both radio and TV, we collect natural sound to help give the audience a feel for "being there." We run the natural sound *under* the voice track of the reporter. In radio a report from a city council meeting will commonly have the natural sound of the meeting under the voice of the reporter. In television the reporter track is recorded and blended with the natural sound under whatever we're seeing in the video. The natural sound under the voice track gives the audience a sense of being there and puts an audio presence under the reporter's voice.

We also use natural sound full. In both radio and TV, that's when we bring up that natural sound—the meeting, the kids playing, the crowd cheering and so forth—so that it's full volume in the story. It's a short pause in the story, usually no more than a few seconds, when we let the story breathe and give the audience a real feel for what the location, meeting or event was like.

What exactly is the difference between natural sound full and an actuality or bite? Frankly, there's no universal standard, but it's easiest to distinguish between the two on the basis of function. Natural sound full is used simply as a pacing device or sound bridge in the story, and the *content* of the sound does not really contribute to the information. When the sound contains real substance and needs to be understood to contribute to the content, then we usually consider it a bite or actuality.

Natural Sound as Pacing and Punctuation

"Sometimes you can use actuality and sound as punctuation," says former KCBS reporter Mike Sugarman, like a period between thoughts.

In radio, Sugarman says that once he's found that "center"—the focus of the story—he needs to find the sound that best represents it. If it's something about homelessness, it might be a car door slamming when they're living in a car or the sound of the soup line. "It's whatever strikes your ear as trying to get that point across," says Sugarman.

"You want just enough natural sound to keep you in a sense of environment or moment," KGO-TV reporter Wayne Freedman says. Not so much, he says, that it breaks the flow of the story but enough to maintain the rhythm that you set.

Steve Hartman says CBS is concerned about the potential to misuse natural sound and make the story harder to follow and understand. "Scott Pelley sent out a directive [to the reporters] when he started at the Evening News," says Hartman, "not to break up sentences with sound because he saw the evil of that." It's all in how you use it.

Former NBC correspondent Bob Dotson says he used natural sound to help people go beyond seeing or hearing about the story so that they're actually experiencing it. That's exactly the point.

●●●●●

Working with Bites, Actualities and Natural Sound

When you write stories, you always have to keep the information flowing. The two most common errors in working with bites and actualities are 1) stopping the story flow dead in its tracks and 2) repeating in the lead-in what the bite or actuality is about to say.

Don't Stop the Story

Here are some examples of the most common ways to kill the flow of a story:

TERRIBLE: The mayor had this to say on the proposal.
    (bite)
TERRIBLE: The mayor explains what she thought of the proposal.
    (bite)
TERRIBLE: I asked the mayor how he felt about the proposal.
    (bite)

None of the above lead-ins has any redeeming qualities. In all of those cases the lead-in brings the story to a dead stop because the audience learns no information from the sentence. Those are just empty words whose only function is to tell the audience that a bite is coming. We would never put a line into a story saying that, "the next sentence will contain information on what the mayor thinks," so never go into a bite using anything like the above examples.

Don't Repeat

The other common error is to repeat in the lead-in what the bite is going to say:

ALSO
TERRIBLE: The mayor says he's against the proposal.
        Mayor bite: "I'm against the proposal."

Doing this makes it sound as if you have no idea what's going on in the story. It's not that the lead-in is bad per se. The problem is the repetition of the material. Even having the lead-in repeat just a key word or phrase from the bite makes the whole thing sound repetitious.

PROBLEM
LEAD-IN: The mayor says the proposal is counter-productive.
        Mayor bite: "I just think that the plan is
        counter-productive."

Even though the bite only duplicates one word from the lead-in, it's going to sound repetitious because it repeats a key word from the lead-in.

Watch Out for Partial Lead-Ins

Generally, don't go into a bite that's being played live with a partial sentence lead-in:

RISKY
LEAD-IN: But the mayor says:
        Mayor bite: (bite)

If the bite doesn't come up—usually because of technical problems that seem to be reserved specifically for when you've violated this rule—you're left hanging there with you and the audience waiting, knowing something went wrong. Even in packages, in which all the material is prerecorded, you should be cautious about partial sentence lead-ins where a bite completes a sentence started by the reporter. The audience adjusts their listening each time there's a change in who's speaking. It doesn't take long, and a pause built into the end of one sentence and the beginning of the next will usually handle the adjustment. But when you switch speakers mid-sentence, the edit is tighter, the adjustment period is shorter, and it will be harder for the audience to follow what's being said. It's even riskier when the voice quality of the reporter or anchor is similar to the voice quality in the bite itself.

Making the Story Flow

All the words in your lead-in must contribute information to the story and keep the story moving. The story flow should not be interrupted just because you're using sound.

GOOD

LEAD-IN: The mayor says he's against the proposal.
Mayor bite: It's too expensive; it won't work; and I think there are better ways to approach the problem.

The transition from the lead-in to the mayor's bite flows as seamlessly as if the writer had scripted everything—including the bite. That's exactly the way it should sound. No wasted words. Easy to follow and understand.

Finding the Lead-In

The best place to look for material for a good lead-in is the first line of a good bite:

GOVERNOR: The issue is jobs. We've got thousands of people who want work here but not enough industry to support them all.

In this case, use as a lead-in the governor's opening line about jobs, and pick up the bite with line two:

LEAD-IN: The governor says the issue is jobs.

GOVERNOR'S
BITE: We've got thousands of people ...

This type of lead-in also won't make you look foolish in the event of technical problems. If you're running this story live and the bite doesn't come up, you simply have a slight pause. Depending on how well you or the anchors know the story, it's possible to ad lib a line summarizing the governor's view—or you can just keep going. Either way, the story will sound reasonably complete.

Occasionally, there isn't good information for the lead-in. In that case, minimize damage:

LEAD-IN: Mayor John Smith.
    (bite)

This type of lead-in isn't nearly as good as the other because it doesn't really keep the information flowing smoothly and seamlessly. But it's a decent second choice, since it's short and to the point. All it does is give the next speaker's name.

Television Lead-Ins

There's less of an issue leading into bites in television than radio because we seldom need to introduce anyone. Mostly, we just cut directly to a bite and super the name and position in the lower third of the screen. That helps to keep the flow of the television story going, and it prevents the painfully weak five or six seconds of video of someone *not* talking (but usually sitting at a desk) while that person is introduced. Introducing people on TV can work if you need to do so and have some interesting video of that person actually doing something. But if that isn't the case, skip the introduction, just go to the person and tell us who it is with a super.

Writing out of Bites

Usually, we don't need to do anything special coming out of a bite or actuality. Normally, the bite is so short that we don't need to remind people who was speaking; we can just move on. In any case, writing out of a bite or actuality involves the same concept as writing in: Keep the information flowing. Never come out of a bite with something like this:

WEAK WRITE
OUT: That was Mayor John Smith.

If you need to repeat the name because the bite was long, include new material:

BETTER
WRITE OUT: Mayor Smith also said....

An Alternative to Traditional Bites

The use of sound can help tell a story, break up the monotony of a single speaker and prove to the audience that we were there covering the event. Even one-word responses or short phrases can work as bites if you write into them and out of them properly. Because they're so short, using them can be risky in a live newscast, but they'll work fine in a pre-recorded radio or television package.

Look at how KGO-TV reporter Wayne Freedman wove one and two word responses through a portion of his script on the clean-up following the last San Francisco earthquake:

FREEDMAN: For people in the quake zone, this has been a
    day for finding and taking care of essentials.
MAN OUTSIDE HARDWARE STORE: Spackle.
ANOTHER MAN OUTSIDE: Metal straps to go around hot water
    heaters.
CLERK IN HARDWARE YELLS: Roofing nails.
Freedman: They're the building blocks of recovery. By
    beginning with little things, the big ones will fall
    into place as well.
FREEDMAN TO WOMAN: So how's the house?
WOMAN: It's standing.
FREEDMAN: And how's the car?
WOMAN: It's dirty.

That entire sequence, including reporter track and bites from four different people, took a total of 18 seconds.

● ● ● ● ●

Packages

Writing into Packages

A TV package (or pack) is a prerecorded report, normally with reporter narration over video, a standup, and bites. Radio's equivalent is the wrap or wraparound, which includes the reporter narration, preferably over natural sound, and one or more actualities. In both cases these go on the air only after being introduced by the news anchor. As with writing into bites or actualities, always try to keep the information flowing. This common form of package lead-in is *not* how you should do it:

WEAK
LEAD-IN: Mayor John Smith has come out against a new
    highway plan for the city. Jane Jones has the
    details from city hall.
        (package)

It's not a terrible lead-in, but it's weak because the last line serves only to introduce the reporter. Otherwise, it says nothing at all. We should be able to do better:

BETTER

LEAD-IN: Mayor John Smith has come out against a new highway plan for the city. Jane Jones at city hall says the mayor is ready to fight the issue in court.
   (package)

That's better because, in this example, the same last sentence that introduces the reporter also says something about the story (that the mayor is ready to fight the issue in court). Make every word count.

PROBLEM

LEAD-IN: XXX's John Smith was in Clark Lake this morning when Virginia Jones got the word of her husband's release and he has more in this report.
   (package)

Strengthen this network lead-in (that went on the air) by eliminating the extra words (underlined) that slow down the story:

BETTER

LEAD-IN: XXX's John Smith was in Clark Lake this morning when Virginia Jones got word of her husband's release.
   (package)

This version is better because it's tighter and more to the point. Those seven extra words that were in the original story just slow it down and weaken the writing.

Introducing a Package That Starts with a Bite

How a package begins determines how the lead-in should be written. Most package lead-ins are designed for a package that starts with the reporter track or, preferably, natural sound full followed by the reporter track. In the above example the dual introduction of the reporter and Virginia Jones would actually allow the package to start either way. If you're going to start a package with a bite, make sure the package lead-in is written in such a way that you don't confuse the audience.

PROBLEM: Reporter John Smith is at City Hall and has the story about what's happening with the city budget.
   (package that starts with a bite from a city council member)

This doesn't work because the lead-in clearly has the audience expecting to hear from reporter John Smith. If you're going to start with a bite, this would be poor form in TV and impossibly confusing in radio. In television, a super can reorient the viewer, but the confused radio listener may never catch up with the story.

BETTER: Reporter John Smith is at City Hall and spoke with
   Council Member Jane Doe about what's happening with
   the city budget.
      (package that starts with a bite from a city council member)

In this example the audience clearly knows that John Smith will report, but they're also expecting to hear from Jane Doe. No one will have any trouble following the beginning of the story.

Understand Where the Story Begins

Nothing improves lead-ins (and tags) to reporter packages as much as the reporter understanding that the story actually begins when the anchor lead-in starts and ends when the next story is about to begin. The reporter may think that the story begins and ends with the package itself, but the audience doesn't see (or hear) it that way, and why should they? The story begins with the anchor introduction.

Too often, reporters write the prerecorded portion of the package first. After that's all done, they go back and try to tack on an intro and sometimes a tag. The problem is they've said just about everything in the package, leaving nothing of consequence to say in a lead-in or tag. That results in weak, sometimes redundant lead-ins and meaningless tags. Reporters should start writing with the lead-in and end with the tag, before recording anything. Even when time is tight, the reporter must at least figure out what the lead-in and tag will say—before writing the package itself.

Package Tags

Generally, a reporter package is self-contained and requires no additional information coming out of it, but that's not always the case. Sometimes there's additional information that is most logically added to the end. Sometimes there's another aspect to the story that is better handled in a short tag. Sometimes TV stations insist on an anchor tag after reporter packages to improve the flow of the newscast and reestablish the anchors for the audience. The concept is good; the execution frequently is not. If the tag doesn't contain meaningful information, the effect is to grind the newscast to a virtual standstill at the end of every package.

TERRIBLE

ANCHOR

TAG: That was John Smith reporting.

NOT MUCH

BETTER: John Smith will be following the story as the petition drive progresses.

MUCH

BETTER: John Smith says the group hopes to deliver a thousand petitions to the mayor late next week.

A good tag can be a tough balancing act. It needs to contain meaningful information but must not sound as though the reporter forgot to tell us something.

● ● ● ● ●

Summary

The key in using sound is maintaining the story flow while giving the audience the sense of "being there." The two most common errors writing into bites are stopping the flow of the story and repeating the same information that's in the bite. Generally, in TV, don't introduce people before bites; that's what supers are for.

● ● ● ● ●

Key Words & Phrases

don't stop the story flow . . . don't repeat the information . . . partial lead-ins

● ● ● ● ●

Exercises

A. For each of the following bites, write a lead-in and all of the words of the bite that you would use on the air at your Springfield television station. You may use all of the bite or just part of it.

1. Lab worker John Smith on the past experience of accused serial killer James Jones:

   "He did not seem to understand why all of this could be important and how deadly the chemicals could be for animals. He never really acknowledged our concerns. We were concerned about him not following the rules that the supervisor had clearly explained to him, and we told him not to return until he was willing to abide by the rules. That was the last we saw of him."

2. Springfield Mayor Marvin Summers on complaints about poor snow removal during the last storm:

"We recognize that we did not do the job that Springfield residents rightly expect of us in the last storm. We were admittedly a little late getting started, and I think we really didn't follow through in all cases as aggressively as we needed to. We intend to make sure that does not happen again."

3. Jonathan Smythe, an analyst for Research Ltd. in London, on the financial difficulties facing Portugal:

"Eighty percent of Portugal's debt stock is held by foreigners. But the flow, now, is being financed domestically. A year ago, the I.M.F. published that the outlook for Portugal's economy is bleak. The staff's baseline scenario envisages modest adjustment, weak growth and continuing unsustainable imbalances."

4. Jonathan Smythe, an analyst for Research Ltd. in London, on the financial difficulties facing Greece:

"A large part of the Greek debt is hidden on the balance sheets of the Greek banks. You cannot just say 'Let's restructure.' It is not so easy. In fact, it will be extremely complex even to untangle the intricacies of the entire financial system."

5. New Jersey Gov. Chris Christie on education:

"I propose that we reward the best teachers, based on merit, at the individual teacher level. I demand that layoffs, when they occur, be based on a merit system and not merely on seniority. And perhaps the most important step is to give schools more power to remove underperforming teachers."

6. Mary Smith, head of Gun Control Advocates, on the shooter of a U-S Representative:

"The reason he was able to be tackled was he had to pause to reload. The problem is, he didn't have to pause to reload until he'd already expended 30 rounds. We need to go back to the slightly saner laws that we used to have where these high capacity clips were illegal. That's the way it used to be. If that were still the case, then maybe at least some of these innocent souls would still be alive today."

7. Deborah Parsons, head of Guns for Protection, on the shooter of a U.S. Representative:

   "The criminals are going to have guns, so why should we as law-abiding citizens be punished for what a criminal does? Maybe if more people attending the event had been armed, they could have done something before so many people were hurt. The judge who was killed knew how to shoot, but he'd just been to church, and he probably didn't have his gun."

8. East Springfield Chief of Police Evan Coulter:

   "A man was fatally stabbed in Springfield County on Monday evening in the 10th violent attack there in 10 days. We have stepped up efforts to curb the outbreak of deadly violence that has provoked concern and alarm in the suburban jurisdiction. In the most recent incident, the victim was stabbed during a fight in a supermarket parking lot in East Springfield."

9. Springfield Mayor Marvin Summers on the new convention construction in downtown:

   "Now we have a convention center and hotel set-up, airport and downtown that few cities in this nation can match. This will allow us to compete for some of the biggest and most important conventions in the country. And don't kid yourself, it's serious competition. Sure there's pressure. But all the pieces are in place here."

10. National weather service forecaster Carmen Hyde on the upcoming snowstorm:

   "At this point, right now in the Springfield area, there will be 4–6 inches of snow when it's all said and done. Wind will enter into the weather picture tonight, so blowing could become a problem by morning. Temps during the day will be in the 20s. The accumulation by rush hour this morning means commuters — as well as buses and parents taking their kids to school — will need to slow down. As we've seen, you don't need a lot of snow to create a lot of problems. Conditions are going to be deteriorating throughout the day. Take necessary precautions."

11. Gerald Jones on the fire that destroyed his home today:

   "I left with my two dogs to run an errand, and when I returned home, my house was on fire. I think it started between 9 a.m. and

9:30 a.m., maybe near my wood stove. I left the house to go to the post office, and when I got back it was fully engulfed. My neighbors are helping all they can. I'm sure it hasn't hit me yet. If I'd have been home 20 minutes sooner, I maybe could have gotten enough water to it to put it out. But I couldn't even get into that room. There was too much smoke."

12. Springfield Mayor Marvin Summers on an ongoing dispute with a private water company on whether the company's assets are taxable:

"Hopefully we can work out a solution. We have a good relationship with the company, and there are going to be issues of discussion moving forward. We're not trying to pull a fast one here, we just have different interpretations of the law and we need to resolve that. A legal opinion provided by the state Municipal Association stated that the activity is taxable, and the town attorney concurred."

13. Springfield City Council Chair Helen MacDonald on a new proposal to clean up the town:

"I'm concerned that the plan would be making too many demands on businesses that are already having a hard time. I also think that some recommendations in the draft plan, that seem to be very personal, such as that specific driveways or yards be improved, might alarm people. A few business owners were alarmed. I explained that we wouldn't force anything on them and that the implementation committee, if so charged, would contact the owners and discuss possibilities of volunteer work or other options to help them spruce up their properties. We're not trying to be draconian; we just want to spruce up our image."

14. Jayne Darrow, head of the Business Development Office for Springfield:

"While downtown business comparisons turned negative for the first time since January 2013, we believe today's results simply reflect a minor bump along the road to a broader Springfield recovery. I know business conditions are difficult and painful, but recoveries take time. Our conversations with local retailers lead us to believe the next quarter of this year will see results largely exceeding expectations."

15. Sarah Devine, Springfield Police Chief:

"We found Springfield dancer Mary Flores's body in concrete 2 miles from her home. The coroner said she died from asphyxiation due to neck compression. Her death has been ruled a homicide. We have arrested Jason James, her ex-boyfriend, and have charged him with murder. It appears that this was a crime of passion that occurred in the heat of the moment after an argument."

16. Daniel Clemente, State Corrections Chief:

"State correctional officers can be given one unpaid furlough day per month without jeopardizing public safety. The last time we did this, we saw no increase in incidents in our prisons. Since those are the facts, and all other state workers are being forced into furloughs in order to save the state money, I simply cannot justify exempting correctional officers from the same pain that every other state worker is experiencing. Those furloughs will save the state $312,700 a month."

17. Alexander Mullins, professor of economics at Springfield State University:

"That's a big reason why much-ballyhooed loan modification and foreclosure mediation programs aren't saving people from losing their homes. There are issues because we have banks that not only hold their own mortgages, but they sold off mortgages. It's difficult for the homeowner to work with servicers and investors. Much of the time, it's hard to tell who even owns the mortgage — much less getting that company or those companies to give the owner any kind of break."

18. Jermaine Hathaway, Assistant Chief of Police in Springfield:

"A 3-year-old boy was taken to Springfield General Hospital this afternoon after he was found at the bottom of a swimming pool on North 17th Street. The boy was unconscious. We do not know exactly how long he had been in the water, but we do not think it had been long. A neighbor spotted the child and pulled him out. At this point, the boy is in critical condition. We have no information that indicates this is anything other than a horrible accident."

B. Which one or ones would you change if you were running the bite on your Springfield commercial radio station? On your Springfield public radio station?

C. List the bites in A in order from strongest/best to weakest . . . and explain why.

6

• • • • •

Readability

Broadcast news writing involves not only the basic elements of all good writing but a number of special conventions and peculiarities of its own.

News, generally, must be understood immediately, and in broadcast, it must be understood via the ear.

[Broadcast copy must be easily readable. Because breaking news and the nature of the business may result in last-minute changes in reading assignments, there are basic rules to give any announcer a fighting chance to convert words into meaningful and readable copy.

• • • • •

Broadcast News Writing

Broadcast writing is like writing a screenplay or a song. Composer Stephen Sondheim was asked whether the song lyrics he writes are like poetry. No, he said. "Lyric writing has to exist in time," Sondheim explained. "The listener cannot do what the reader of poetry [or a newspaper] does. He cannot go at his own speed; he cannot go back over the sentence. Therefore, it must be crystal clear as it goes on. That means you have to underwrite. You have to lay the sentences out so there's enough air for the ear to take them in."

Exactly like writing for broadcast. Writing for the ear is special—not better or worse than its print or web counterparts—but different. Think of how many times you've found yourself rereading material only moments after your first journey through it. Perhaps your mind wandered. More likely, the material simply wasn't well-written, well-organized, or logically presented. The written word can perhaps tolerate those lapses; the spoken word cannot. As with music or plays or films, the broadcast audience gets one chance and one chance only to understand what's being said. The wrong word, the right word in the wrong place, too much information too quickly, words mismatched with pictures—all can result in an audience lost in information. In broadcast, you cannot afford even a momentary loss because the newscast continues, and the words and stories keep coming. Every time viewers or listeners must stop to sort things out, they miss even more.

Beyond writing for the ear, the broadcast writer must think about how words sound together. Are they easily readable? Can the announcer read the words with proper emphasis without gasping for breath? How much meaning can be inserted with inflection rather than text? Does the sound of the words match the story those words tell? How do the words blend with accompanying video?

● ● ● ● ●

Writing for the Ear vs. Writing for the Eye

Broadcast copy differs from print and web in two critical conceptual points. First, it's designed to be read aloud; second, it's written to be understood by people who only get to hear it. Those two points, flip sides of the same coin, lead to virtually all of the rules about writing broadcast copy. Broadcast writing isn't different from print or web for its own sake, it's different because it's produced and consumed differently. This chapter focuses on the first of those differences: reading out loud.

Today, essentially all newsrooms use some sort of computer system, and that system dictates some of the stylistic rules. The latest numbers (RTDNA 2015) show the Associated Press' ENPS system in a majority of TV newsrooms (55%). Then came Avid's iNews (33%) with Comprompter and others splitting up what little is left.

Every system is just a little bit different, and all are customizable, so there are even some differences within the same software. The first challenge on the job is to learn how to use the station's software. It's basically just a word processor and archive library within a newscast environment. More and more stations are integrating that newsroom writing and producing system with character generators for automatic supers and desktop audio and video editing.

TV video editing software, incidentally, is all over the map. A plurality (36%) use Grass Valley Edius. Fewer than one in five use Avid (18%) with Final Cut Pro (15%) and Adobe Premier (13%) not far behind. Harris Velocity, Sony Vegas and a bunch of others make up the rest.

● ● ● ● ●

Rules of Readability

Although every station does things a little differently, and newsroom computer systems tend to dictate technical form, these are the general guidelines accepted in the industry. The whole point of these rules is that anyone should be able to pick up any piece of copy and read it well.

Newsroom Computer System

The computer ensures that everything is typed. Most stations double-space, although many computer systems display single-spacing on the terminal but double-space or 1.5 spacing on printed scripts and prompter copy.

See more on today's newsroom computer systems in Chapter 13, "Producing News on TV," and Chapter 16, "Social Media and News."

The Slug

Each story must have a slug, a heading that separates that story from all others that day. Usually written in either the upper left or across the top of a page, it includes a one- or two-word name for the story, the writer's last name or initials, the date and the time of the newscast the story is being written for. In most TV newsrooms (and large radio operations), newscast producers or assignment editors determine the slug for each story. Again, newsroom software dictates exactly how all of these things are recorded.

```
FBI arrest
Smith
1/12/16
6 pm
```

The Printed Word

Use paragraphs, indenting the first word of each. Radio copy normally goes across a full page and runs three and a half to four seconds a line, depending on type style and margins. TV copy goes on the right side of a split page and runs one to two seconds a line, depending on type size.

Radio	TV	
	Video	Audio
The FBI today arrested one of its 10 most-wanted criminals.		The FBI today arrested one of its 10 most-wanted criminals.

Most newsroom computer systems time copy automatically, adjusting the projected time for different readers based on reading speeds entered into the system. Even so, view that time as approximate; there's no substitute for having the person who's going to read the copy on the air time it exactly.

Hyphenation

Don't hyphenate or split words from one line to the next. Doing so increases the chances for unnatural hesitation or mispronunciation.

INCORRECT: He went in search of the corporate headquarters.
CORRECT: He went in search of the corporate headquarters.

Fortunately, most newsroom software won't allow this mistake in copy.

Do hyphenate some words within a line for the sake of readability. Words like *pre-disposition* and *anti-missile,* although not grammatically correct, are much easier to read correctly with hyphens. Be especially careful with prefixes that create double vowels, such as *pre-eminent.* But don't overdo it. Words like *cooperate* and *coordinate* we recognize easily and don't need to hyphenate.

Abbreviation

Don't abbreviate. Not everyone understands what a given abbreviation stands for, and some, such as *St.,* can stand for different things (Street and Saint). Exceptions are *Mr., Mrs., Ms.* (pronounced "miz") and *Dr.* We see them so often, day in, day out, that we have no trouble reading them. Incidentally, *Dr.* in broadcast usually refers to medical doctors, including physicians, dentists and chiropractors. *Ph.D.s* should not be called doctor without making clear their area of expertise.

Symbols

Don't use symbols. Symbols such as %, & and $ are too easily missed, require translation and, in the case of $, come out of sequence in how it's read.

INCORRECT: ... 40% ...
CORRECT: ... 40 percent ...

Some experienced anchors will use the dollar sign in copy (*$4-thousand*). That's what they're used to, and it works for them. But it's safer to use the word instead (*4-thousand-dollars*).

Initials and Acronyms

Almost everything uses initials or an acronym these days, but don't assume that the audience will remember and understand them without some help. In almost all cases, use the full name in the first reference with initials or acronym thereafter. A few will work for first reference, like FBI and CIA. Don't make up your own initials or acronyms for a group in an effort to shorten the name. For many organizations there are no shortcuts.

When initials are to be used, place dashes between the letters:

```
N-C-A-A    I-R-S
```

When the letters are to be read as an acronym, use all caps without dashes:

```
OPEC    MADD
```

OPEC is unusual because it's one of the few acronyms that's preferable to the full name. More people are familiar with OPEC than the full, formal Organization of the Petroleum Exporting Countries.

Names

Generally, write names the way people are known. If the governor is known as *Joe* Smith rather than *Joseph,* use *Joe.* But don't use names that only family and close friends use; if you're unsure, stick with the formal name. Nicknames present more of a problem. Ultimately, the issue is less one of right and wrong than of consistency. Stations should establish a set form—and make sure everyone knows what it is—for any problem name.

Generally, don't use middle initials or names. That's because few people are popularly called by their middle name or initial. Two exceptions: when someone *is* popularly known by his or her middle initial or name:

```
Michael J. Fox
Mary J. Blige
Ruth Bader Ginsburg
```

or when someone with a fairly common name has been charged with a crime or is involved in something controversial. In that case the middle initial or name (and perhaps even an address) helps to isolate the individual from others with similar names:

```
Police charged John S. Smith of State Street with
yesterday's robbery at the First National Bank.
```

Numbers

Minimize the use of numbers in broadcast copy. Numbers are hard to take in and understand when we only get to hear them, so always try to use a word description (e.g., *almost all*) instead of the number. When you must use them:

■ **Write out all numbers one through nine.** A single digit is too easily lost on a page, and 1, 2 and 5 can look a lot like I, Z and S.

■ Use numerals for numbers 10 through 999.

■ Use names for thousand, million and so on. You can't expect an announcer to count the digits of a number to figure out what to say.

■ Newsrooms are split on numeral and word combinations. Some stay with the same form listed above—mixing numerals and words as appropriate (e.g., one-thousand, 22-thousand). Others use only numerals when they're connected to a word by a hyphen (e.g., 5-thousand).

■ Write out *a hundred* or *one hundred* to prevent an announcer pausing or stumbling over the decision of which way to pronounce it.

■ Ordinals may be written as numerals or words (*2nd* or *second*).

■ Write out fractions in words (*one-half, two-thirds*).

■ Numbers below 1.0 such as .4 (in economic reports, for instance) should be written as *four-tenths of a (or one) percent.* Above 1.0, the use of *point* is fine (e.g., *one-point-two percent*), but round off when possible.

■ Write numbers coming next to each other in contrasting style (e.g., *the score was 162 to 140, fourteen points shy of the record*).

■ Write years as numerals (e.g., *1999* or *19–99, 2017 or 20–17*).

For TV, always think about ways to visualize numbers through graphics, but don't use TV graphics as a crutch for countless and usually meaningless numbers. The audience is not interested in wading through a sea of charts and graphs. Graphics involve a better way of demonstrating numbers that are still best rounded off and held to a minimum.

Look at all the numbers in this copy—which went on the air on a large market TV station:

PROBLEM: So far this year, calls to the I-R-S telephone assistors are producing wrong answers 30-point-8 percent of the time. That's worse than last year, when the error rate was 28 percent. The I-R-S says it's trying, but of its five-thousand assistors, 15-hundred are new to the job, and tax questions can be tough to answer.

And broadcast copy can be tough to follow, especially a short story with four complex numbers, most of them not essential to the story.

BETTER: So far this year, calls to the I-R-S are producing wrong answers more than 30-percent of the time. That's slightly worse than last year. The

```
I-R-S says it's trying, but that nearly a third of
its telephone assistors are new this year.
```

Note that part of the solution above involves the substitution of words that express relationships (*a third*) instead of actual numbers.

Ages

Generally, we report ages only when they're an important or interesting part of the story. Newspapers and the web can give ages quickly and easily (e.g., *Mary Smith, 41, was injured* . . .). In broadcast, we have to tell the audience that *Mary Smith is 41 years old*. Since it's so much more cumbersome in broadcast, think about whether the age really adds something to the story.

Unnecessary: ```The accident injured 41-year-old Mary Smith.```
Necessary

and

interesting: ```The driver of the car was nine years old.```

An exception: If the story includes information about someone's death (e.g., in a traffic accident), then we usually do include the age. That's because the story serves as something of an obituary, and we always give the age in an obituary.

Emphasis

Broadcast copy is to be read aloud with meaning transmitted through both words and inflection. Indicate emphasis through underlining or capitalization or whatever a given newsroom computer system provides:

```
The mayor says he will not run for re-election.
The mayor says he will NOT run for re-election.
```

Indicate pauses with dashes (—) and ellipses (. . .), with spaces before and after the dashes or ellipses. But don't use either where a period should go. And double-spacing after all periods makes for cleaner-looking and easier-to-read copy.

Correct: ```The mayor shouted — then grabbed his chest.```
Correct: ```The mayor shouted ... then grabbed his chest.```

Pronouncers

Every word that might be mispronounced, especially a name, should have a pronunciation guide immediately after it in parentheses.

Watch out for easily mispronounced names such as Lima (LEE ma), Peru and Lima (LI ma), Ohio. Indicate emphasis by capitalizing the emphasized syllable or, if you're writing in all caps, by putting an apostrophe after the emphasized syllable:

```
LIMA (LEE' MA), PERU AND LIMA (LI' MA), OHIO
```

Note: A pronouncer is not a substitute for the correct spelling. Names and places on scripts frequently wind up being supered (the words superimposed on the lower third of the TV screen) and used as keywords for computer searches somewhere down the line. All too often, phonetic spellings have been supered on the air because the writer never used the correct spelling or didn't make clear which spelling was correct and which was phonetic. Be careful.

Wherever possible, avoid words with the same spelling but different pronunciations and meanings. *Suspect, read, wind* and the like can all be dangerous to an announcer who hasn't been able to pre-read copy.

Spelling

Spell correctly. Any word that's misspelled is likely to be mispronounced on the air. And remember that between computers and closed captioning (for the hearing impaired), some of the audience gets to see all of our spelling.

● ● ● ● ●

Summary

Broadcast writing is different than traditional print or web because there's an announcer reading it out loud, and the audience only gets one chance to hear the material. Although newsroom computer systems frequently determine style, there are generally accepted universals in writing broadcast copy. Use paragraphs, be careful with hyphenation, generally don't use abbreviations, symbols, middle initials or ages. Use numbers sparingly, and learn how to write them properly. Indicate emphasis to determine how copy is to be read, and use pronouncers for unfamiliar names. Spelling counts.

● ● ● ● ●

Key Words & Phrases

newsroom computer systems . . . slug . . . paragraphs . . . hyphenation . . . abbreviation . . . symbols . . . initials and acronyms . . . names . . . middle initials . . . numbers . . . ages . . . emphasis . . . pronouncers . . . spelling

●●●●●

Exercises

A. Write each of the following words or phrases correctly based on standard broadcast writing:

NCAA	2-thousand	422	Dr. Jones
17th	10,000	alot	point-7
8-percent	persons	says	fortitude
male	will not	deceased	tuna
2	one hundred	34	19-95
one-half	point-five	$55	FCC
Houston St.	Mrs. Smith	ACLU	998
halibut	John A. Church	1600	3RD
can't	seperate	female	goldfish
sattelite	2-hundred	english	1/3
IU	N-C-double-A	kids	U-S
989 point-3			

B. The following sentences have errors and/or words, phrases or means of expression not acceptable for broadcast writing. Make them acceptable.

1. Their are alot of rules for writing broadcast copy that you must understand.

2. Fore instance they're about 8 rules for writing numbers including things like how to deal with numbers and phrases like 6.4% and 3/4 and 200,000.

3. Many of these rules are about readibility — so that the announcer won't have to struggle thru your copy in order to figure out what you meant when you talk about a $2.46 pay rise per hour for workers in Nassau Co., NY or a new record low temperature of-27 in Albany.

4. Goverments, goverment agencies, and political organisations like O-P-E-C and the IRS may work to muddy our language and the meaning of words, but your job is to simplify and clarify with in the rules of writing for broadcast writing.

5. It really doesn't matter whether your reporting the news from Lima, Peru or Lima, OH — you've got to seperate the facts and make things clear.

C. Re-write the following story using a proper slug, and correct any errors you find:

According to sources inside the Teamsters union, 4 labor leaders are being investigated for misappropriation of funds. The amount of money involved hasn't been disclosed, although its believed to be almost $1,000,000. The names of the 4 have been witheld as the FBI investigation continues.

7

●●●●●

Words

Good writing has nothing to do with word length or complexity. Good writing—including broadcast news—involves choosing words that convey a meaning that's accurate, a tone or feel that's appropriate and, wherever possible, a sound that matches the meaning.

First, get it right. You have no better friend than the dictionary. You can't have too many of them, and they should be handy whenever and wherever writing is possible. Beware the thesaurus. This potentially useful tool can mislead writers into substituting longer and more complicated words of only approximate similarity to the original. Meanings must be precise, not approximate. A *ship* is not a *boat; burglary* is not the same as *robbery*.

Second, use words whose primary meaning and feel match what you're trying to say. When the audience gets only one chance to understand what's being said, we can't defend our word choice because the fourth or fifth definition matches our intended meaning. The audience simply doesn't have the luxury of thinking over what we're trying to say. Use words the same way people most commonly do.

Third, think about sound. It's called *onomatopoeia* when the sound of the word matches its meaning. Words like *buzz* and *cuckoo* are the most obvious, perhaps, but even the use of soft or hard sounds to describe soft or hard issues or events can strengthen your writing. *Weed killer* is almost always better than *herbicide*. Same length, same meaning, but *weed killer* is universally understood, easier to pronounce and has a far more graphic and harsh feel.

●●●●●

Keep It Simple

Use simple words expressed in simple ways. Not simplistic, but simple. Broadcast news is *not* written for 12-year-olds; by and large, children neither watch nor listen to news. It *is* written for a large, diverse audience. There's nothing wrong with using a big and, perhaps, not universally known word if it's the most appropriate. But use such a word only in a context in which its meaning is clear. Don't make the audience's ability to understand a line dependent on knowing the definition of an obscure word.

Obscure: The suspect will be arraigned later today.
Clearer: The suspect faces court arraignment later today.
Better: The suspect faces formal charges in court later today.

● ● ● ● ●

Keep It Conversational

Informal Words

Use informal words—not slang or colloquialisms but informal. Broadcast news is a blend of written and spoken language. The way we tend to write is commonly too formal, but the way we commonly speak is a bit too casual. Broadcast writing is written the way we *would* speak if we could plan it out well. It's what we *wished* we had said—after we were less eloquent extemporaneously.

A word you're unlikely to hear in spoken English is rarely appropriate for broadcast. Only newspapers refer to legislators as *solons* or talk of people being *feted*—no normal person would do that. And only journalists call a *fire* a *blaze* or use the word *some* to mean *about*. Normal people don't do that; you shouldn't either.

Contractions

Use contractions; that's how we speak. But be careful about contracting the word *not*. If the meaning of the sentence hinges on the audience hearing the *n't*, you probably should not contract it.

Risky: The senator says he isn't running again.
Better: The senator says he is not running again.

The riskiest contraction is *can't* because the difference between the positive *can* and the negative *can't* rests solely on the ability of the announcer to pronounce the *t* sound clearly. Generally, don't take the chance.

Formal Terminology

Avoid formal terminology like *male, female* or *juvenile*. Other than police and the military, most people don't talk that way. With rare exception, use *man/men, woman/women, child/children* or *kid/kids*.

Avoid pretentious or oblique terms. Generally, in broadcast, people do not *pass away*, nor are they *late—they just die.*

People . . . Not Persons

Although grammatically correct, the use of *persons* is, at best, stilted. One *person* is right, but more than one should be *people*.

● ● ● ● ●

Keep It Clear

Common Usage

Use words in the same context in which they're normally used. Almost every word conjures up an image in the minds of the listeners and viewers—an image based on the *common* usage of the word they're hearing. You can play with words for effect, and it's wonderful if you can pull it off. But if you're not careful, you'll just confuse—as did the following examples used on the air by some large-market TV stations:

PROBLEM: Governor Smith's popularity isn't looking very nice. In fact, it's on a downhill slide.

PROBLEM: Ministers in town are crying for a citizen review board to keep an eye on police.

PROBLEM: A house subcommittee has fattened the governor's tax package to support the next two-year state budget.

In all three cases the writers used words in ways that just don't compute. We don't refer to popularity as *nice*. Popularity may be *up* or *down* or perhaps a few other things—but not *nice*. Ministers in town may be *asking for, arguing for, demanding*, perhaps even *pleading for*, but not *crying*. It's also not likely that *all* ministers are involved, as the wording of this sentence suggests. And the word *fattened* just doesn't make sense. People get *fat*; animals may be fattened up; there can be fat in a budget. But we're just not used to hearing about a tax package that's *fattened.*

BETTER: A new survey says Governor Smith's popularity is heading down.

BETTER: Some local ministers say we need a citizen review board to keep an eye on police.

BETTER: A house subcommittee has tacked on more taxes to the governor's tax package. It's all part of figuring out how the state will cover the next two-year budget.

All the above examples use common words and terms the way we expect to hear them used.

PROBLEM: Today people are spending a lot of money on
    new-fangled gadgets for their home. The latest is an
    electronic brain which does all the housework. All
    you have to do is push a button.
        The oven can be started from telephone beeps. The
    furnace can be turned on from a button on the TV
    screen.
        About two thousand homes have this stuff in them
    nationwide.

The problem in this copy, which also went on the air, is that turning on the oven and furnace may be this unmarried, male reporter's idea of housework, but it doesn't match the way most of the audience thinks of it. That electronic brain doesn't sweep, vacuum, dust or do dishes—all of which are part of what most people think of when you say housework.

BETTER: This could be the gadget-lover's heaven on
    earth ... an electronic brain for the ultimate in
    remote control. Telephone beeps can start your
    oven ... a button on the TV screen can turn on the
    furnace.
        About two thousand homes have this Star Wars stuff
    in them nationwide.

The pictures in TV are more likely to amplify the problems of a poorly selected word than compensate for it. Not only does the word have to be accurate and logical, it also has to blend with the picture the audience is seeing, which may further limit the writer's choices. Words that fight with what viewers see can wind up canceling out both, leaving a bewildered audience.

Technical Terms

Technical terms are fine for technical publications; they don't work in broadcast. It's true that some technical terms do creep into everyday lexicon; however, unless the term has not only crept in but firmly implanted itself, it must have an explanation. Problems in scientific terminology tend to be obvious. Watch out for legal terms. *Certiorari* means various things depending on who's asking for or granting it. It means nothing to most people in the audience.

And don't invent your own terminology.

Problem: Researchers have discovered a body chemical that lures the cold virus away from its targets inside a nose — where a cold starts.

By the time the audience figures out what a *body chemical* is in this copy (which went on the air), they've missed the rest of the line. Sometimes the shortest way to say something isn't the best. Here, what the reporter means is a chemical found naturally in the body.

Better: It isn't a cure, but researchers have discovered a chemical that can help fight the common cold. The chemical — which is found naturally in the body — can lure the virus away from its targets inside a nose — where a cold starts.

Definite and Indefinite Articles

Watch out for the definite article *the*. This innocuous-sounding word can get you in a lot of trouble if misused. Frequently, *the* acts to single out a specific thing or person.

Problem: Police arrested a man for the robbery last night.

Problem: Police arrested the man for a robbery last night.

Both examples have problems created by the word *the*. In the first example, if the audience isn't familiar with last night's robbery, the line raises as many questions as it answers: What robbery? Use *a* instead of *the* when the described person or thing is not specific or when referring to something you have not yet mentioned in a story. The same applies in the second example. What man? *The* may also indicate *the one and only*—as it does in the examples above. There's a good chance more than one robbery took place last night, and more than one man may have been arrested.

Better: Police have arrested a man for robbery.

Notice that *the* can frequently be omitted when it precedes a plural—as in the above example, in which we say *police* rather than *the police.*

By the way, with rare exception, pronounce *a* as "*ah*" and pronounce *the* as "*thuh.*" Those are the more informal ways to say the words, and they're how we usually say them when we're not paying attention to our pronunciation.

●●●●●

Keep It Tight

Don't write phrases when words will do:

Wordy and Weak Phrases	Tighter and More Direct Words
subsequent to	after
prior to	before
in an effort to	to
for the purpose of	to
in order to	to
is of the opinion that	believes
due to the fact that	because
with the exception that	except
in the near future	soon
at this point in time	now
being that	since

●●●●●

Make It Powerful

Use Strong Nouns and Verbs

Use nouns and verbs that say something, not just take up space. If the meaning or feeling of a phrase depends mostly on adverbs and adjectives, your writing is lazy. Rewrite.

Weak: The noisy crowd did not like the speaker.
Better: The crowd jeered [or booed] the speaker.
Weak: Dozens of motorists were left stranded by a blizzard.
Better: A blizzard stranded dozens of motorists.

See Chapter 8 for an explanation of writing in the punchier, preferred, active voice rather than the weaker, passive voice.

Avoid Weak Qualifiers

Avoid meaningless qualifiers that weaken the copy. Words like *somewhat, fairly* and *very* rarely add anything to copy.

Problem: Smith's corporate wallet was somewhat emptied
tonight. A federal court fined the defense contractor
five million dollars ...

In this example, used on the air, the use of *somewhat* makes a bad sentence even worse. What does a *somewhat emptied* corporate wallet look like? Stay with stronger terms that people know.

Better: A federal court says Smith double-billed the
government ... and will have to pay five million
dollars in fines ...

● ● ● ● ●
Get It Right

Grammar

There's simply no excuse for writing that's ungrammatical.

Not acceptable: If you want to lose weight ... clean out
your kitchen! A group of women were left in untidy
and clean kitchens ... along with a batch of
cookies. The group ate less cookies in a clean
kitchen! Experts say ... one possible reason is
that a chaotic environment makes people feel out of
control.

The experiment may be valid, but the grammar in this story that went on the air is not. It's *fewer* cookies ... not *less*. We're in the language business, and if we can't get that right, why would we think the audience would trust us to get the facts right?

Says

We use *says* all the time in journalism to convey someone's thoughts to the audience:

Common
usage: The mayor says he's against the plan.

The word has the advantages of being short, to the point, universally understood and neutral in meaning. The biggest disadvantage in broadcast is the constant repetition of the word. Look for places where a substitute will work. Some possibilities are:

acknowledge	contend	recite
admit	declare	recount
agree	demand	relate
allege	disclose	remark
announce	divulge	repeat
argue	explain	reply
challenge	grant	report
charge	indicate	respond
cite	insist	reveal
claim	maintain	speak
clarify	mention	specify
concede	narrate	swear
confess	pronounce	tell
confirm	react	testify

Substitute words say more—and might be better—if they're right. But keep in mind that substitute words that express more meaning than *says* also run the risk of being inappropriate. Some of the words in the preceding list have clear legal implications (e.g., *allege, claim, confess* and *testify*). If the possible substitute isn't completely accurate and appropriate, stay with *says*. Because we use the word all the time, we may get tired of it in broadcast copy; there's no evidence the audience shares that concern. Note that it's most often *says* and not *said*. More on that in Chapter 8.

Saying Too Much

Avoid words that convey editorial meanings. Words or phrases like *only, tiny,* and *so-called* are frequently pejorative and have no place in good broadcast writing except in direct quotes. Words like *finally* commonly imply that something took too long. Be careful. The audience rightly resents being told how to feel or what to think; stay with the facts.

One of the points that many of the great reporters make is that we work way too hard trying to manipulate the audience into feeling a certain way, instead of letting the audience feel the story—and come to their own conclusions.

"Why are you shouting at me?" Deborah Potter, former network correspondent and current Executive Director of NewsLab, says the audience is complaining. "Just tell me what happened."

"Our writing is overstuffed and needs to go on a diet," she says. "You end up with stories full of emotion-laden adjectives like 'tragic' and 'terrifying' and 'horrible' and 'unthinkable' and 'unbelievable' and those kinds of words, all of which are designed to tell our viewers and listeners how they're supposed to feel about a story, but that eat up the time we could be spending on providing the detail that would allow our viewers and listeners to feel something."

Think

Write as if you had to defend every word you use. Is it the best choice possible? Is it the most accurate? Is it the most telling? Does it work with the video? From time to time we do have to defend every word to an irate listener or viewer—or in court. We'd be better off all the time if we thought that way before we started.

● ● ● ● ●

Common Problems

These are some of the many words and terms commonly misused, misunderstood or mispronounced.

accident: BE CAREFUL. Accidents happen all the time, but so do intentional acts. Don't predetermine cause by a haphazard word choice.

ad hoc: Means for a specific purpose only. It's redundant and wordy to say: *The governor has just created an ad hoc committee to study the issue.* In this case, leave off *ad hoc.*

admit: BE CAREFUL. Other than meaning to grant entrance (a usage that should be avoided in broadcast because of its awkwardness), the word means to concede or confess and implies an acknowledgment of wrongdoing. Generally, limit use of *admit* to legal and quasi-legal issues where it's clearly appropriate.

alleged: BE CAREFUL, and in general, don't use this word. See Chapter 8, "Phrases and Phrasing," and the crime and legal section of Chapter 19, "Reporting: Specialized Coverage."

alumna, alumnae, alumni, alumnus: *Alumna* refers to one woman graduate or former student of a specific institution; *alumnae* is the plural for women. Use *alumnus* for one male graduate or former student; *alumni* is plural for men and should be used as the plural for a group of men and women.

among, between: Generally, use *among* when something is in the midst of more than two people or things; use *between* when something is in the midst of two people or things.

and/or: Don't use this stilted expression in broadcast copy.

as: See *because.*

average, mean, median: Take the numbers 2, 6 and 7; the *average* is the total (15) divided by the number of items being totaled (3). The *average* here is 5. The *mean* is the same as the *average*, but use *average* because it's more widely understood. The *median* is the middle figure in an ascending or descending series—in this case, 6. Generally, stick with *average* and write around the others.

because, since, as: *Because* shows a cause-and-effect relationship; *since* or *as* usually reflects a time relationship (one took place after the other), but the relationship is more indirect than cause and effect.

between: See *among*.

bi-, semi-: Unfortunately, depending on the source, *bi-* means either *once every two* or *twice a*. Those opposing meanings suggest that not using the prefix may be best in the interests of clarity. *Semi-* means *half* or *twice a*, but use the term only in a familiar context.

boat, ship: These terms are not synonymous. A *boat* is generally considered a small vessel, although ferryboats, PT boats and submarines are exceptions. *Ships* are larger, frequently oceangoing vessels.

bring, take: *Bring* involves transporting something to the speaker (here); *take* involves transporting it away from the speaker (there).

casualties: Includes dead and injured or sick.

cement, concrete: *Cement* and *concrete* are not the same. Cement powder is one of the ingredients in concrete.

centers around: Makes no sense; use centers *on* or revolves *around*.

claim: BE CAREFUL. *Claim* means to demand or assert a right (generally in a legal sense). Keep usage of this word in that context; it's not synonymous with *says*.

concrete: See *cement*.

consensus: General majority agreement, but not unanimous. The phrase *consensus of opinion* is redundant.

continual, continuous: *Continual* means ongoing at intervals; *continuous* means ongoing without stop.

convince, persuade: *Convince* generally means inducing someone to believe something; *persuade* involves inducing someone to some action.

cop: Slang for police, police officer. Better to say police.

crisis: Not every problem—or even every dangerous situation—is a crisis. Don't overuse. Plural is crises (KRI seez).

currently: *Currently* means now. *Presently* means soon.

daylight saving time: Note that daylight saving time is singular. See pages 240 and 243 for more.

dialogue: An overused word that all too frequently replaces the simpler and more accurate *talk*.

die, kill: All people eventually die; some people are killed. Use *die* when death results from natural causes.

drugs: This word has taken on the meaning of narcotics (illegal, controlled substances) and should generally not be used as a synonym for medicine.

elderly: BE CAREFUL. This may be viewed as negative or simply inappropriate. As health care improves, the age at which people are "elderly" gets older. If you use the term at all, limit its use to over 70 or even 75.

emigrate, immigrate: *Emigrate* means to leave a country to settle elsewhere; *immigrate* means to enter a country from outside.

ensure, insure: Unless you're speaking about insurance, the proper word is *ensure*—to guarantee, to make sure of.

equal time, fairness: In broadcasting, equal time (passed by Congress) relates to political candidates only. Better called *equal opportunity*, it means that all candidates for the same office must be treated equally (outside of news), whether in opportunities to buy commercials or free appearances. The *Fairness Doctrine*, repealed in 1987, related to issues only. It said that stations must treat all sides of controversial issues in a reasonable manner—not equally, but reasonably.

execute: In the sense of dead, only governments, by virtue of law, can execute. Terrorists or individuals kill, assassinate or murder; they do not execute.

Fairness Doctrine: See *equal time, fairness*.

February: Although difficult to pronounce properly, there are two *r*'s in February. See also *library, hundred* and *nuclear*.

fewer, less: Both mean the same, but *fewer* relates to numbers and *less* relates to amount, more abstract ideas, bulk numbers and singular nouns and pronouns. Someone has fewer dollars, but less money.

figuratively, literally: *Figuratively* means like (as in a metaphor); *literally* means exactly, precisely.

firefighter, fireman: Although common in usage, use the gender neutral term *firefighter*. If you wouldn't say *firewoman* (and you wouldn't), don't say *fireman*.

flammable, inflammable: Both mean exactly the same thing—easily ignited—but use *flammable* because too many people think *inflammable* means the opposite of its correct definition.

gay: This word's only current usage relates to homosexuality, and it should be used as first reference.

ghetto: BE CAREFUL. This means a section of a city overwhelmingly inhabited by members of a minority group. The term also implies that a minority group has been forced to live in that section, so don't use this term lightly.

good, well: *Good* is almost always an adjective meaning well-done, worthy, kind and the like. *Well* is almost always an adverb meaning properly (except as an adjective meaning healthy).

gun: Acceptable term for any firearm.

half-mast, half-staff: What takes place in honoring the dead. *Half-mast* is for ships and naval stations; *half-staff* is on land.

Halley's Comet: Currently accepted pronunciation is HAL (as in pal) eez, not HAIL eez.

hang, hanged, hung: Everything hangs. People are or have been *hanged*; everything else has been *hung*.

hundred: Pronounced HUHN dred, not HUHN derd.

illegal: BE CAREFUL. Use this word only in reference to a violation of law—and with proper attribution. See the crime and legal section of Chapter 19, "Reporting: Specialized Coverage."

immigrate: See *emigrate*.

impact: Don't use this word as a verb.

indict: Use this word only in its legal context of bringing charges. See the crime and legal section of Chapter 19, "Reporting: Specialized Coverage."

inflammable: See *flammable*.

insure: See *ensure*.

irregardless: Not a word. Use *regardless* instead.

issue: Saying that something is a *controversial issue* is redundant; it wouldn't be an *issue* if it weren't controversial.

key: Another overworked word that only works, if at all, in the spirit of its original meaning of opening a lock.

kid, kids: Perfectly acceptable in broadcast for child, children.

kill: See *die*.

knot: See *mile*.

lady, woman: Use *lady* only in quotes and in formal titles (as in *Lady Marian*); otherwise, use woman, women.

less: See *fewer*.

library: As with February, there are two r's in *library*, and both must be pronounced.

literally: See *figuratively*.

major: Another overworked word.

majority, plurality: *Majority* means more than half; *plurality* means more than any other (as in the winner of a three-way race, perhaps).

massive: Another word worth resting.

mean, median: See *average*.

media: Includes all *media* and requires a plural verb (singular is *medium*). Use *media* rather than *press* unless you're specifically referring to print media only.

mile, knot: *Mile* is a measure of distance (5,280 feet), as distinguished from *knot*, which is a speed of one nautical mile (6,076.1 feet) per hour. See the weather section of Chapter 13, "Producing News on TV."

none: Usually means no one or not one and almost always takes a singular verb.

NOW: National Organization *for* Women—not *of*.

nuclear: Pronounced NU klee ur, *not* NU kyu lur.

persuade: See *convince*.

plurality: See *majority*.

presently, currently: See *currently*.

press conference: Most broadcasters prefer *news conference* because *press* refers to print media only, although some argue that the term *news conference* elevates most of these gatherings beyond their substance.

rebut, refute: *Rebut* means to argue against with evidence; *refute* means to prove wrong. Don't confuse the two.

semi-: See *bi-*.

ship: See *boat*.

since: See *because*.

some: Means an unspecified number. Its use to mean *about* (e.g., *some one hundred years ago*) is classic journalese. Normal people don't talk like that. If you mean *about*, say *about*.

sources: An overworked, meaningless term that should be used more carefully. Don't use the word alone; it doesn't say enough to give any credence to a report or bit of information. Don't use with *unnamed*. The source does have a name, making the correct term *unidentified*. Even so, use some accompanying word or substitute phrase that provides more substance to the source (e.g., a *senior White House official* says . . .).

survey: BE CAREFUL. Don't use this word when there really hasn't been a formal survey.

take: See *bring*.

that, which, who: As pronouns, use *who* to reference people; use the appropriate choice of *that* or *which* to reference things.

toward: *Not* towards.

unique: Means the one and only. No adjective modifying *unique* makes much sense. Things cannot be *more, less* or *very unique.*

viable: Means able to live. Much overworked term.

warn: Means to inform of possible trouble. Don't use the word when what's involved is really a statement and not a warning.

well: See *good.*

whether or not: Should almost always be just *whether.*

which, who: See *that.*

wide-ranging: Overworked phrase.

woman: See *lady.*

●●●●●

Summary

Choose your words carefully, making sure that they're accurate, are used the way most people use the word, and, if possible, have a sound that matches the meaning. Keep your word choice simple and conversational. Use contractions, but watch out for technical terms and words that may convey editorial meaning.

●●●●●

Key Words & Phrases

accuracy ... tone ... sound ... simple ... conversational ... contractions ... common usage ... definite and indefinite articles ... loaded words

●●●●●

Exercises

A. The following sentences have errors and/or words, phrases or means of expression not acceptable for broadcast writing. Make them acceptable.

   1. An unidentified man was hurt this morning when he was shot by robbers during a hold-up at Smith's Supermarket.

   2. Certiorari was granted today in the case of Smith v. Jones by the State Supreme Court.

3. The superintendent of schools has stated that the air quality tests conducted in all of the districts 70 schools might be invalidated for 45 of the aforementioned schools.

4. Extensive rebuilding, reconstruction and renovation is what the building inspector said would be required for the dilapidated and run down housing project.

5. Last month the consumer price index took a 0.4% increase.

6. Although the 2 females and 1 male were searched for by members of the police department, but the men in blue weren't able to locate them.

7. The ruling by the state's highest supreme court has many local attorney's in the legal community here very displeased.

8. The govenor has decided to dulcify his critics by reluming the capitol dome.

9. The leader of Belize will travel to America to meet with members of Pres. Obama's administration over the new 6% import duty, according to the leader.

10. Being that there were 3 robberies last night, the police decided to elevate the number of units that would be driving around the apparently endangered area.

B. Record the first block of a radio or television newscast, and rewrite at least one story using fewer words and tighter phrasing — without sacrificing any important information.

8

Phrases and Phrasing

How well you piece all those appropriate, descriptive words together determines both the quality of the writing and how well the audience understands it. Remember, the audience gets only one shot at what you're saying. Phrases that are too cute or simply don't work with the pictures may wind up merely puzzling the audience.

After inaccuracy, the second greatest writing sin is creating confusion. And there are lots of ways to confuse the audience: a word or phrase that's out of place or that doesn't mean exactly what it should, a phrase that's awkward, even wordiness itself. If the audience has to stop and think about what you mean, you lose them. Do it often enough, and you lose them permanently.

How to Say It

Voice

Write in the active voice. If the subject of the sentence does something, that's active. If something happens to the subject, that's passive.

Passive: The First National Bank was robbed of two thousand dollars this afternoon.
Active (and better): Robbers stole two thousand dollars from the First National Bank this afternoon.
Passive: The area was hit by a devastating winter storm.
Active (and better): A winter storm devastated [or battered] the area.
Passive: The car was driven by an escaped convict.
Active (and better): An escaped convict drove the car.
Passive: The bond issue was approved by the city council.
Active (and better): The city council approved [or passed] the bond issue.

The active voice is shorter, punchier, more interesting, more direct, and it's part of what broadcasting is all about. Of all the writing skills you can master to improve and strengthen how you use the language, none compares to writing in the active voice.

There are occasional times when passive makes more sense:

■ When what has been acted on is much more important than what's doing the acting:

```
The president was surrounded by the crowd.
```

■ When the cause is unknown or you want to avoid assigning blame:

```
Union leader John Smith was shot this afternoon.
```

■ When active voice would be too awkward:

```
The man was pinned between his own car and the
guardrail.
```

Consider those the exceptions that prove the rule. Write actively.

Tense

Broadcasting's ability to be current in the news demands that we be current in our phrasing. First choice is present tense. Second choice is future tense. Third choice is present perfect tense. After that, it really doesn't matter.

```
PRESENT: The city council votes on the sales tax bill
    today.
FUTURE: The city council will vote on the sales tax bill
    later today.
PRESENT PERFECT: The city council has voted on the sales tax
    bill.
PAST: The city council voted on the sales tax bill
    today.
```

Note that present perfect's use of *has* and *have* makes the action sound as if it happened recently. Make sure you use it that way.

Remember, updating a story or looking to future implications of a past (tense) action will frequently allow you to use present or future tense:

```
UPDATED: The sales tax stays [or will stay] right where
    it is. The city council today rejected a bill that
    would have increased ...
```

Note that even though the action already took place (the vote came earlier), by focusing on the *outcome* instead of the vote itself, we can make the phrasing present or future tense.

Don't strain so hard to use present tense that the phrasing sounds awkward and strained.

Former network correspondent Deborah Potter says much of the news writing today is phony and doesn't sound like real people talking. "There's been a terrible crime committed against verbs in broadcast newsrooms across America," she says.

Potter offers her favorite example of this strange, new way of bullet-pointing the language:

```
Less resilient ... local business ... Dwight's
concession stand ... in the family ... three
generations ... sales this summer ... over 75
percent.
```

Potter notes that there's no verb, just phrases. What happens, she says, is that an effort to sound more urgent simply winds up sounding awkward and largely unintelligible. Take this example that recently went on the air at a top 50 TV station:

```
A terrifying attack caught on camera.
Surveillance video showing a parking garage
attendant fighting off a man with a knife ... as he
tried to get some quick cash.
The car drove in with the license plate covered
early yesterday morning. The driver forced his way
into the booth, wrapping a shirt over his face. He
pulls a knife and demanded money the attendant
fought back. You can see him drop the knife and then
pick it up ... before he tried to get into the cash
register. He gave up and took [off] and now Miami
police need help finding him.
The worker is fine but she quit her job.
```

No normal person talks like that, and the constant, seemingly random changes in verb tense makes the information not only not conversational but also difficult to follow.

Clarity

As with words, use phrases the way people are used to hearing them. Twisting a phrase here and there can work, but if you're not careful, you'll only confuse.

PROBLEM: The General Assembly is putting a quick stop on
    legislation passed last year on strict handling of
    teenage drunken drivers.

Quick stops may apply to cars, but the audience that heard this copy read on the air probably never figured out what the reporter was trying to say.

Better: The General Assembly is back-pedaling on tough legislation passed just last year to deal with teenage drunk drivers.

Make sure you use phrases correctly. Things center *on*—not *around;* they revolve *around*—not *on.*
And watch out for mixed metaphors:

Problem: And the race is on ... the battle over who gets your long-distance nickels and dimes is at the front line.

Even giving the benefit of the doubt that the *front line* in this copy used on the air refers to a *battle,* neither refers to a *race.*

Better: Battle lines are forming in the war over who gets our long distance nickels and dimes.

Here, at least all of the references (*battle lines* and *war*) share a common theme.

Conciseness

Don't waste words or phrases; don't be redundant. There isn't time, and the more words you use to say something, the greater the chances for audience confusion.

Redundant: The councilman argued for extensive rebuilding and renovation in the downtown area.
Better: The councilman argued for extensive rebuilding downtown.
Wordy: The car couldn't finish the race due to the fact that the engine in the car gave out.
Better: The car couldn't finish the race because the engine gave out.
or
The car couldn't finish the race ... the engine gave out.

Clauses and Phrases

Short introductory clauses and phrases work fine; parenthetical ones do not. With rare exceptions, a parenthetical phrase makes a sentence difficult if not impossible to follow because it requires the audience to remember what the writer was talking about before the phrase started.

INCORRECT: The U-S Forest Service, responding to criticism from environmental groups, has agreed to review its policies.

For the audience to understand this line, they must remember that the line started with the *U-S Forest Service*—which will review its policies. This is better handled:

INTRODUCTORY
PHRASE: Responding to criticism from environmental groups, the U-S Forest Service has agreed to review its policies.

Or split

UP: The U-S Forest Service has agreed to review its policies. The decision comes in response to criticism from environmental groups.

An audience that only gets to hear the information will find both of the above examples easier to follow and understand. These rewritten examples also put the verbs closer to the subjects; that, too, helps the audience follow what you're saying. News stories are not quizzes for the audience. Each sentence should take the listener or viewer from point X in knowledge, information, and understanding to point Y. That journey must be straight, clean and clear. Parenthetical phrases are side trips the audience can't follow when the journey is conducted by ear.

Positive Phrasing

Keep your phrasing in the positive. The issue isn't good news or bad news; it's whether you tell the audience what *is* going to happen or what's *not* going to happen. Negative phrasing is wordier and harder to understand.

NEGATIVE: The sheriff says they will not be charged until tomorrow.
POSITIVE (AND BETTER): The sheriff says they will be charged tomorrow.
NEGATIVE: There's no lack of demand for new single-family homes in Indianapolis.
POSITIVE (AND BETTER): There's new (or strong) demand for new single-family homes in Indianapolis.

Negative: But as reporter John Doe tells us, White House aides maintain any new proposal will not be announced before late January.

Positive (and better): But as reporter John Doe tells us, White House aides say it will be at least late January before a new proposal is announced.

Pronouns

Watch out for pronouns. Pronouns are reference words and make sense only if the audience can instantly figure out what the pronoun refers to.

It's not clear who *he* is in the following:

> An administration official complained that a network reporter asked unfair questions. He characterized the interview as nonsense.

Keep pronouns close to their antecedents, and look for ways to eliminate pronouns wherever you can. In the above example, using a name in line two should take care of the problem.

Problem: He allegedly began molesting a seven-year-old girl three years ago. She's the daughter of some of his close family friends.

Better: Police say he began molesting a seven-year-old girl three years ago ... the daughter of close family friends.

In some cases a pronoun almost next to the antecedent may not be clear enough. The governing rule is that if you give the audience the slightest chance to misunderstand, that's what will happen. Also remember that singular institutions, businesses, and governments are *it* and not *they*.

No: The company has been boxed in wherever they've turned.

Yes: The company has been boxed in wherever it's turned.

That

Watch out for the word *that*.

■ Don't use the word where it's not needed.

Wordy: She says that she'll attend.

Better: She says she'll attend.

■ Do use the word when its absence sounds awkward.

Awkward: He feels the elephant will ...
Better: He feels that the elephant will ...

■ Do use the word to clarify paraphrasing, attribution and meaning.

Unclear: The mayor reports firefighters who called in
sick will be let go.

That last sentence probably isn't what you mean unless the mayor is actually reporting those firefighters who called in sick.

Better: The mayor reports that firefighters who called in
sick will be let go.

The previous example helps keep the meaning clear. The next example points out a potential problem in attribution:

Problem: The governor says his opponent is lying to the
voters and this is the dirtiest campaign ever.

This phrasing could easily be construed as you, the reporter, calling the campaign the dirtiest ever, when attribution is needed to make it clear that that's what the governor says. In this case, *that* indicates continued paraphrasing:

Better: The governor says his opponent is lying and that
this is the dirtiest campaign ever.

Time and Space Problems

Don't use words that require the audience to recall earlier material to figure out what you're saying. Words like *former* and *latter* (e.g., *in the latter case*) require the audience to remember not only what you said, but also the sequence in which you said it. The audience does not memorize copy and cannot follow these kinds of references.

Watch out for *here* and *there*. Think about both where you are and where your audience is before using those terms. Generally, do not use *here* or *there* unless it means the same thing for both the announcer and the audience:

No: Reporter Jane Smith says everyone here is up in arms
over the mayor's proposal.
Yes: The new state measure will mean that people here
will pay twice as much for garbage pickup.

The reason the first example above won't work is that the issue clearly applies to a city or town—where the mayor is. But the audience crosses political jurisdictions, and it's unlikely that people in distant suburbs or outlying towns care much about the proposal one way or the other. In the second example a statewide measure will clearly affect everyone "here"—assuming that you're not in a market that crosses state lines.

Reporters who are live in the field *should* use *here* to emphasize the fact that they're live and on location:

```
Police have surrounded the building here on the
lower west side.
```

● ● ● ● ●

What to Say

Titles and Identifiers

Titles or identifiers go before names:

No: John Smith, State Attorney General, says his office
    will launch a new attack on illegal drugs.
Yes: State Attorney General John Smith says his office
    will launch a new attack on illegal drugs.

In almost all cases the title or description is really more important than the name itself, and what's important should come first. Putting the title or identifier first also avoids the same potential problem we have with parenthetical clauses and phrases.

Frequently, we paraphrase a long title to keep a sentence shorter and more to the point. An *associate commissioner of the state department of energy resources* should most often become *a state energy commissioner* or *a state energy official.*

● ● ● ● ●

Attribution

Attribution is the term we use to describe the concept that we generally cite (or attribute) the source of information that we put on the air, noting either the person or the organization that supplied that information. We don't just tell people, for instance, "There has been a new outbreak" of some disease. We tell them, "The Centers for Disease Control reports a new outbreak . . ." We don't just tell people, "John Doe has committed a crime." We tell them, "Police say John Doe committed a crime." Attribution qualifies statements and puts them into proper context. It makes clear the source of our information; it protects us in controversies and legal disputes.

In broadcast, put attribution before the statement. Although there are occasional exceptions to this, most of the exceptions you hear on the air are examples of a writer opting for effect over responsibility.

UNACCEPTABLE: Busing doesn't work, according to Senate candidate Jane Smith.

ACCEPTABLE: Senate candidate Jane Smith says busing doesn't work.

Attribution after the fact forces us to think back and, perhaps, reevaluate the material. After-the-statement attribution confuses the audience, causes listeners to miss the next few words during the reevaluation process or just angers them because you made a ridiculous statement without making clear at the beginning that the statement should have been taken with a grain of salt.

Attribution is always needed when someone is accused of a crime, but avoid using the word *alleged*. It's a weak crutch that no one uses in normal speech, it won't necessarily keep you out of legal trouble, and you can almost always work around it by attributing information to police, a prosecutor or an indictment.

WORKS: Smith allegedly entered the bank armed with a shotgun.

BETTER: Police say Smith entered the bank armed with a shotgun.

or

Police charge that Smith entered the bank armed with a shotgun.

Part of why the last two sentences are better is that they also make clear who's making the accusation. That's better reporting.

Make sure you use the attribution at the appropriate spot:

NO: Federal and local authorities are looking for two men who allegedly held up a Chicago bank today.

This is wrong because federal and local authorities are looking for the two guys who actually did it. No need for *allegedly* or any other qualifier here.

YES: Federal and local authorities are looking for two men who held up a Chicago bank today.

Don't use attribution for the wrong thing:

WRONG: Police arrested Jane Doe for the alleged murder.

Wrong again. In this example the issue isn't whether a murder took place, it's whether Jane Doe did it. You don't need attribution for an arrest. That's a fact, and someone was either arrested or not. It's not the *crime* that requires attribution, it's the link between a crime and a suspect. If there is a question about whether a crime actually took place, then you'll have to attribute that, too:

Yes: Police say it was a brutal murder.

Otherwise, use attribution in reference to suspects, not crimes. And use it often. Every statement that links an identifiable individual—no matter where in the story that person is identified, no matter whether the identification is by word or picture—requires some form of attribution. One qualifier at the beginning won't protect you. For more detail on this, see the crime and legal section of Chapter 19, "Reporting: Specialized Coverage."

Attribution is also needed when you're dealing with anything that might be considered controversial, especially if it's changeable.

Risky: The company will not relocate any of the laid-off
    workers.
Better: A company spokesman says there are no plans to
    relocate any of the laid-off workers.
Risky: The store will no longer accept credit cards.
Better: The store says it will no longer accept credit
    cards.

In both of the previous cases it's possible that the business involved will change its mind. Without attribution you're the one making the statement, instead of the company, and you don't know what the company might do.

Don't overdo attribution. If the governor's news secretary says that the governor will hold a news conference later today, it's usually fine to say:

    The governor will hold a news conference later
    today.

If the governor has a tendency to cancel these things or the news secretary is unreliable, then it might be safer to say:

    The governor has scheduled a news conference for
    later today.

Avoid making statements about someone's state of mind.

No: The governor believes we need to build a new prison.
Yes: The governor says we need to build a new prison.
No: The governor wants to build a new prison.
Yes: The governor says he wants to build a new prison.

The fact is, you really can't know what the governor believes or wants—only what he or she says. Limit your reporting to what you know. And use attribution where there's any reasonable possibility that the statement might be wrong or questioned in the future.

Quotations

Generally, don't quote. Few statements are so strong that we need to quote them, and we'd obviously much rather have the actual bite of the person making the statement. In most news stories, based on your phrasing, the audience will know you're either quoting or paraphrasing, and the distinction isn't significant as long as the point is accurate and fair. When a *short* quote (the only kind you normally ever use) is necessary, you do have to make clear that you're quoting.

```
The governor said [pause] ...
In the governor's words [pause] ...
The governor said, and I quote ... (Reserve this
more cumbersome phrase for particularly
controversial quotes.)
```

In TV, if a direct quote of more than a few words is worth using, it's frequently worth supering the quote on the screen. In that case, make sure the script and the super go together precisely. You cannot ask the audience to read words on the screen while the announcer says something else.

Numbers

Generally, avoid numbers when substitutes are possible. Think about the story. If it's about a 3 percent hike in real estate taxes, then the figure obviously must be used. That's what the story is about. But if the story is that 98 percent of the city high school students failed a reading test, then the first reference should say *almost all.* Think about the point of the story.

When numbers must be used, try to round off if appropriate: *986* should usually be *nearly or almost a thousand, 103* should usually be *just over a hundred* or *a little more than a hundred, 8.4* should usually be *almost eight and a half, 52 of 74* should usually be *more than two-thirds.*

Never force the audience to perform mathematics to understand what you're talking about. And notice that none of the above examples uses *about or approximately.* Rather than those vague words, use more descriptive ones: *nearly, almost, just over* and *more than* all say more.

If you don't know the exact number, then *about* is clearly preferable to *approximately.* The words mean exactly the same thing, but *about* is much shorter.

Race

Use identification of race only when it's clearly part of a story, and never use racial epithets except in quotes. Race is clearly relevant to the story:

■ when it's part of a specific description of a person being sought by law enforcement

■ when it's a central or significant issue of the story, such as some stories on politics and voting patterns

■ when its absence would make the story less clear or meaningful

A physical description of someone wanted by police should *always* include race in radio writing. Use race in television writing unless you have a picture, in which case there's no reason to include race at all. Also make sure that a physical description is sufficiently detailed that it has meaning. Saying that police are looking for two white men, or black women, or Hispanic men won't allow anyone to make an identification. That lack of description becomes nothing more than a race story. If you're talking about a hate crime, that may make sense; if not, leave it out.

There are lots of "minority" groups, and there are few if any communities where minority equals only one group, so don't use *minority* as synonymous with black or Hispanic or any other single group. Be aware of the impression you leave with the audience—by both the words that you choose and the pictures that you run.

There are leaders who are black and Hispanic and so on. But no one person speaks for any community, and unless you characterize people in your community as "white leaders," don't characterize minorities that way.

Make a conscious effort to ensure that the only time the audience sees or hears from minority groups isn't when it's a story about minorities. Minorities pay taxes; they're lawyers, doctors and experts in any number of areas that we cover. Make sure the audience sees and hears those voices in stories that have nothing to do with race.

And diversity isn't just racial. It's religious, political, economic and so on. Again, make sure the diversity of your audience is reflected in the diversity of voices—and sources—in the news.

● ● ● ● ●

What You Didn't Mean to Say

Dates

Where you place words in a sentence can alter the meaning significantly. Misplacement of the date presents one of the easiest traps to fall into. Notice the difference:

OPTION 1: The State Supreme Court today agreed to review....

OPTION 2: The State Supreme Court agreed to review today....

In Option 1 the State Supreme Court decided today that it will review a case sometime in the future. In Option 2 the State Supreme Court agreed to review the case *today*. Make sure that what you say corresponds with what happened.

Unintended Meanings

Make sure you say what you mean, and watch out for meanings you didn't intend.

PROBLEM: Luckily, only two of the 27 people who came down with the disease have died so far.

Medically, this may be correct. But both *luckily* and *only* are highly judgmental and have no place here. The families of those two people who died will find little luck in this. And don't make the audience do the math.

BETTER: Two people are dead so far ... another 25 are still fighting the devastating disease.

Then there was this interesting gem, which went on the air:

PROBLEM: A Cleveland elementary school is teaching its kids how not to be the target of a crazed gunman. They're teaching the kids terrorist training.

In addition to the awkwardness of the negative lead in this story, the words conjure up an image of hundreds of little Rambos stalking the halls of some Cleveland elementary school, learning how to be terrorists.

BETTER: How's this for a sign of the times? A Cleveland elementary school is giving its kids anti-terrorist training.

Consider this next sentence. It came at the end of a real story about a kid going to the White House based on a letter of suggestions he wrote for the president.

PROBLEM: Other kids had some pretty good suggestions, too ... like build more baseball fields and make parents go to school, not kids.

Most parents who heard this copy read on the air may not have shared the writer's view of how good an idea that last one really is.

Editorials

Avoid editorial statements.

PROBLEM: On a more positive note about firefighters, expect
to see more women than ever dousing fires here in
Columbus.

PROBLEM: When will those big-time musicians stop selling
out? That latest rock band to sing ditties for
Pepsi ...

The writer in the first example got into trouble by trying to force a transition from one firefighter story to another. Unfortunately, what went on the air was a position statement. The second example is just silly commentary. Even if you think most people agree with you or that your view is right and just, skip the editorial.

Clichés

Don't use clichés—ever. Listen to the collective audience groan after the umpteenth *and only time will tell* or *that remains to be seen.* Clichés have absolutely no redeeming qualities.

KGO-TV reporter Wayne Freedman also hates reporters who make themselves the story and tell people how to feel and what to think and use hackneyed phrases like, "something went terribly wrong."

Freedman has his own list of pet peeves: "Reporters saying, 'meet so and so.' Makes me crazy," says Freedman.

Other clichés we can do without:

A parent's [or other group's] worst nightmare ...

The edge of anyone's seat ...

Never seen before (until now) ...

Whole new ball game ...

All and sundry ...

Both feet on the ground ...

Foregone conclusion ...

Been there, done that ...

Rests on his/her laurels ...

Turn over a new leaf ...

Roll with the punches ...

Writing's on the wall ...

See the light ...

Picture of health ...

[Anything] as big as all outdoors . . .

Marriage made in heaven . . .

Time is ripe . . .

At long last . . .

Consider that just a partial list of phrases that should never come out of your computer.

Of all those tired and overused clichés, the worst these days is probably "a _____ 's worst nightmare." The phrase has become so overused that it no longer has any meaning at all. Worse, perhaps, is that it's now being used in clearly non-nightmare contexts. A traffic tie-up, for instance, is not a "commuter's worst nightmare." Getting in a fatal car accident, for instance, is considerably worse. And being stuck on a school bus or getting head lice are also not a parent's worst nightmare. Not even close.

I'm changing the name of the city in this next example to protect the guilty:

THOUGHTLESS: For a lot of people, getting a parking ticket
in downtown Cityville is an absolute nightmare — but
now the city is looking at an alternative way for you
to take care of this ticket through charity.

No, it's not an "absolute nightmare." It's an annoyance—and a self-induced one at that. Stop the writing nightmare.

Sexism

Avoid sexism. Don't use *he* when the reference is really to men *or* women. But also work to avoid *he or she* because it's so cumbersome. It's almost always possible to write around the problem, frequently by using the plural.

SEXIST: If your child goes to Big Walnut, Logan Elm or
Teays Valley ... keep him home tomorrow. School has
been canceled.
BETTER: If your children go to Big Walnut, Logan Elm or
Teays Valley ... keep them home tomorrow.

And avoid male gender job descriptions when neutral ones are available:

■ Use councilors or council members, not councilmen
■ Use senators and representatives or members of Congress not congressmen or congresswomen
■ Use police officers and firefighters, not policemen and firemen (you don't usually say policewomen, and you would never say firewomen).

Don't take the sexist liberties one reporter did with this story:

```
A former school teacher took a shotgun this
afternoon, killed his wife and then killed himself.
     Jeanne Smith was found in the front yard of her
Clinton home. She apparently was running from her
husband Lafe Smith ... a retired math teacher.
     Smith had been depressed about his declining
health. Jeanne must have known this kind of thing
could happen.
```

Dealing with a story involving husband and wife with the same last name may be a bit more difficult than most. But you can't call him *Smith* and her by the too-familiar-sounding first name any more than you can do it the other way around. Either use first and last names for both or use *Mr. and Mrs. Smith.* In addition, the last line of the story is completely inappropriate and irresponsible. How in the world would the reporter know what Mrs. Smith "must have known"?

Personalization

Personalizing news copy is common in our business. Properly used, there's nothing wrong with it. If you (as announcer or reporter) and the audience will be paying a new, higher sales tax, there's nothing wrong with saying:

Yᴇꜱ: We'll be paying more money ...

But don't separate yourself from the audience as one major market all-news station did:

Nᴏ: You'll be paying higher prices for gas than other parts of the country.

The implication here is that somehow the announcer is above all that.

Certain highly charged issues should always be handled with great care and never lend themselves well to personalization:

Pʀᴏʙʟᴇᴍ: If you believe in polls, then most of us do not want things like Uzi machine guns sold over the counter.
     A Newsweek poll released today showed 72 percent of us favor a ban on the sale of semi-automatic weapons. An L-A Times poll showed 80 percent of us favor such a ban.

This story, which aired on a large market television station, is nothing but trouble. The line *if you believe in polls* is, at best, gratuitous.

People will believe it or not as they wish; never say it. Uzi machine guns are not sold over the counter; that's just plain wrong. The issue here involves semiautomatic weapons. Machine guns are automatic, and different laws apply to their sale. In addition, a story like this begs to be misheard. Drop the personalization (*of us*) on stories about gun control, abortion and other highly charged issues.

BETTER: A new poll says most Americans want to ban the sale of semi-automatic weapons ...

●●●●●

Last Note

As with words, phrases must be precise and telling. Write as if you had to defend every phrase you use. Sometimes, you will.

●●●●●

Summary

Inaccuracy and creating confusion are the two worst writing sins you must avoid. Use active voice, and try to stay with present or future tense in stories, especially leads. Be clear and concise, and use positive phrasing. Watch out for pronouns and time and space problems created by words. In broadcast, titles and identifiers go before the name. Avoid state-of-mind statements, generally don't quote and minimize the use of numbers. Be careful with race identification, and avoid sexism and clichés.

●●●●●

Key Words & Phrases

active voice . . . passive voice . . . present, future and present perfect tense . . . problems with pronouns . . . time and space problems . . . titles and identifiers . . . attribution . . . state of mind statements . . . race and diversity . . . editorial meanings . . . sexism . . . clichés

●●●●●

Exercises

A. Put an "A" next to the sentences that are active and a "P" next to passive ones:

1____ The airplane was landed during the storm.

2____ The lawyer wrote an angry letter to the judge.

3____ The man will be arrested by a deputy.

4____ The bell is rung at noon.

5____ A stranger helped police chase a man down the alley.

6____ The spotlight had been focused on downtown.

7____ The man was going to town.

8____ The car was driven by an escaped convict.

9____ The doctor sent an enormous bill to the patient.

10____ The woman will be rescued by a firefighter.

11____ The alarm has been sounded.

12____ An investor wrote a nasty letter to the company.

13____ The athlete is upset with himself.

14____ The lawyer drove the car straight into a ditch by the side of the road.

15____ The jet was brought down on the wrong runway.

16____ The student is two credits shy of graduation.

17____ The reporter has been shut out of the meeting.

18____ The boy was told to get ready fast.

19____ The delivery service spent two days trying to find the address.

20____ The train was stopped at the station.

21____ Police have been unable to find the robber.

22____ Forty protestors were arrested at the barricade.

23____ The man was pinned between the guardrail and the car.

24____ Passengers fled the scene as quickly as possible.

25____ Soldiers lined up for their shots.

B. Convert the passive sentences above into active voice.

C. The following sentences have errors and/or words, phrases, or means of expression not acceptable in writing for broadcast. Make them acceptable.

1. Police announced that only a few people bothered to demonstrate this morning at the Iranian Embassy located in downtown.

2. The number of fire code violations supposedly more than doubled it's number last year, according to the head of the fire department.

3. The unemployment rate plummeted 0.1% last month, according to the Labor Department.

4. The governor spoke with the author of the school bill, but the former said later that his impression of the latter was that he would not do anything to change it.

5. Luckily, only 2 of the 27 men and women taken hostage have become deceased so far.

6. The cops finally caught the man suspected of burglarizing 3 persons over the weekend.

7. Red light cameras located in Springfield intersections have identified twelve drivers who wrongly drove through the intersections after the lights turned red, but officials say that tickets will not go out to the offending drivers until tomorrow.

8. American auto makers, in response to attacks by Democratic senatorial candidate Mike Smith, have asserted today that they are not lagging behind in quality control to foreign car companies.

9. The presidents of IBEW, the Teamsters, the Amalgamated Clothing and Textile Workers of America and the United Mine Workers Union have all agreed to sit down with the Secretary of Labor to discuss what can be done to maintain the beneficially low level of inflation that the country is now enjoying.

10. The tortile remains of the 2008 Ford Explorer were used by police in front of Central High School as a reminder to the students at Central who were to be celebrating their prom tonight.

D. This assignment is about attribution (and good writing). Reread pages 103–105 on attribution and the crime and legal section of Chapter 19, "Reporting: Specialized Coverage," before you start.

The following information comes from the Springfield police. Re-write it, using correct broadcast style, good writing, logical story development, proper attribution, and a reasonable slug.

A former truck driver named John A. Jones has been charged with the robbery yesterday at the Smith Trucking Company. $5,000 was taken in the robbery. Most of the money was found in his home. John Jones, the former driver, was fired by the president of the Smith Trucking Company 2 weeks ago. Jones went into the trucking company office with two handguns yesterday and left with a paper bag stuffed with $20 bills. The office manager called police, saying she recognized Jones. Jones was arrested at his home, which is located at 1324 Highland Avenue in South Springfield early this afternoon.

Sentences

Ultimately, words and phrases are fashioned into sentences, which, of course, are fashioned into stories. Keep broadcast sentences short, simple and straightforward. The most common grammatical sentence structure in English is subject-verb-object. That's what we're used to; that's the way we generally speak; and that's going to be the easiest sentence structure for the audience to understand. Use it often.

Keep It Short

Broadcast writers are frequently told to keep sentences short. There are two overriding principles.

First, there's only so much information that the audience can absorb into the brain through the ear at one time. That's not a reflection of the intelligence of the audience but a reflection of our ability to assimilate information that we only get to hear. There is nothing so lengthy or complicated that it cannot be understood orally. What's involved is breaking down the material into small, absorbable bits. Use more, shorter sentences rather than fewer, longer ones.

Second, an announcer can read only so many words without gasping for air. And no one reads well, using proper life and emphasis, with lungs starved for oxygen. Generally, announcers can read well no more than about two dozen syllables at a stretch.

One Important Idea

As a general rule, a sentence should contain no more than one important thought or idea. All sentences contain many bits of information, but they still should contain no more than one important thought or idea.

TYPICAL

BROADCAST

SENTENCE: Robbers shot a man this morning during a holdup at the First National Bank.

IMPORTANT
>   IDEA: man shot
>
> SMALLER
>   IDEAS: robbers did the shooting
>   this morning
>   during a holdup
>   at the First National Bank

This type of lead also logically takes us to video of the bank, which will, most often, start with the next line.

Put People First

Had a man not been shot, the sentence would be restructured to make the holdup the important idea. Remember that, ultimately, people are more important than things.

TYPICAL
BROADCAST
SENTENCE: Two people are dead and three hospitalized after a house fire on the west side today.

IMPORTANT
IDEA: two dead and three hospitalized

Note the use of *are dead* rather than *died*. It happened recently, it's technically accurate, and we frequently use this phrasing in broadcast because it's more current sounding. However, some prefer the present perfect *have died*, finding that construction more conversational. Note also that it's not *and three others hospitalized*. That would be wordy and unnecessary.

> SMALLER
>   IDEAS: house fire
>   on the west side
>   today

Generally, put people ahead of things, dead before injured or sick. Information on the fire itself will come in line two, having been set up in line one. Again, that's also most likely to match available video. Even if no one had been killed or injured in the fire, the lead would not be *There was a house fire on the west side today*. So what? Lead with people and/or what the story means to people. If appropriate:

POSSIBLE
BROADCAST
>   LEAD
SENTENCES: Firefighters spent most of the afternoon ...

or

```
Fire investigators are sifting through ...
```

Keep it Simple: Subject-Verb-Object

Keep the flow of ideas simple in construction—not simplistic but simple, as in understandable.

COMPLEX: The family of a two-year-old local girl killed
   by a pit bull last year will have to wait to hear
   from the State Supreme Court before the case can be
   resolved.

The contorted sentence construction of this already complicated story makes it impossible to follow. The most common grammatical sentence in English goes subject-verb-object. Not all your sentences have to be constructed that way, but if you deviate too much or too often from that basic form, your copy will be harder to follow. Keep the construction simple, short and straightforward.

SIMPLER: Contradictory rulings in the case of a pit bull
   that killed a two-year-old local girl. Last
   year ...

Note that the lead includes new information, resisting the mistaken temptation to start the complicated story with old news. Always think about what's *new* in a story. History and background may be interesting and important, but they're not why the story is going to air today. Never lead a story with history or background. Never.

Use Some Variety for Interest

The risk in writing short and simple is that the story sounds choppy and tedious. You avoid that by varying sentence length and structure just enough to ride that line between easy to understand and interesting to hear. Note the sentence variety in the following:

```
   About 24-thousand people here will find themselves
homeless — for at least a while — this year. That's
two thousand more than last year ... which was
two thousand more than the year before. Next year,
it'll be worse, still.
   (nat sound bridge)
   The wind chill is 15 degrees, but it feels even
colder when it comes off the river. It's a tough
place to call home.
   This is not the economic fringe of society. This
is beyond it.
```

The basic form is simple, and most sentences are short, but the variety of phrasing and sentence length helps keep the story moving and gives the audience a feel for the subject.

See Chapter 4, "Stories," on the use of conjunctions to smooth out writing and improve story flow.

Split Up Complex Sentences

Simplify complex sentences and information by dividing the material into more short sentences.

COMPLEX: Two local men, John Doe and David Glass, charged in a series of crimes ranging from armed robbery and drug dealing to extortion, today were sentenced to 20 years to life by Judge Jane Smith of the City Municipal Court.

SIMPLER: Two local men will spend 20 years to life in the state prison. John Doe and David Glass were sentenced today after their convictions in a series of crimes including armed robbery and drug dealing.

● ● ● ● ●

Make It Clean, Clear and Concise

Make all your statements clean, clear and concise.

WEAK/WORDY: Adverse weather conditions have caused quite a bit of school closings ...

That's what thousands of people heard a top station in a top 10 market say not so long ago. Make it tighter and more direct:

BETTER: Bad weather has closed lots of area schools ...
UNCLEAR: People who woke up this morning ... saw the ice ... heard all the school closings ... and wished you were back in school with the day off.

That sentence, which actually went on the air on a large-market TV station, must have left the audience wondering—wondering about the people who didn't wake up this morning ... and wondering exactly who wished to be back in school (which wasn't being held) with the day off.

What the reporter wanted to say was something like this:

BETTER: The crystal landscape left from last night's storm ... reminded me of carefree days as a kid when we were lucky enough to have school canceled.

But you're still better off resisting the temptation to romanticize a bad weather day. Parents who suddenly have to cope with kids at home probably don't see much positive in either the weather or what they have to do to cope with its consequences.

Make Every Sentence Count

A sentence that doesn't contain critical information about the story is a waste of words and the listener's or viewer's time. Change it or drop it.

```
    Robbers shot a man this morning during a holdup at
the First National Bank. The First National Bank is
located at the intersection of Main and Green
Streets.
```

The lead is okay, but the second sentence has no meat to it. Even if the specific location of the bank is needed, that's not the way to do it. Not only does it interrupt the logical flow of the story, but it contains no critical information. Work the general location (e.g., the part of town) or cross streets (if that much detail is needed) into a sentence that contains other, more important material.

BETTER: Robbers shot a man this morning during a holdup
at the First National Bank. It's the third robbery
this month at First National's branch at Main and
Green.

Avoid Repetition

Construct sentences so you don't have to immediately repeat the same names or information.

REPETITIVE: Both Hudson's and the United Auto Workers Union
are declaring victory ... after a weekend of U-A-W
pickets at Hudson's Department Stores.

TIGHTER: Both sides are declaring victory after a weekend
of picketing at Hudson's Department Stores by the
United Auto Workers Union.

Stay Positive

Don't introduce material in a negative way. The issue isn't good news versus bad news. Positive statements are always simpler, shorter and easier to understand.

NEGATIVE: The governor today denied charges that he has
no effective drug program. The criticism came from

a special legislative panel that released its
findings this morning.

The problem in this kind of story is that you want to lead with the newest information (the governor's denial), but it just won't work unless the audience is aware of what is being denied. That's seldom the case, and in broadcast, denials cannot precede audience awareness of what the denial is about. It's simply too hard to follow and digest the information that way.

Better: The governor is defending his drug program
today ...

That makes the statement positive, and the writer can then go on to explain why the governor is defending the program.

Make Sense

Make sure you make sense. The audience can judge only what it hears, not what you know or meant to say.

Puzzling: Accidents all over the city as the storm slams
into Columbus. If you haven't been outside yet,
don't bother looking. The weather has turned
Columbus into one big mess.

Don't bother looking? A line like that not only sounds foolish—it's absolutely guaranteed to send people away from their television sets and straight to the window.

Puzzling: Well, we've got a warning here for you that you
may not like. Breathing Ohio air may be hazardous to
your health.

Why would the writer suppose that the audience *might* not like that? Who do we suppose *would* like it? And how many *good news* warnings do we give?

Provide the audience with information they can understand and use, unlike this:

Unclear: Right now, Steubenville residents are paying
two dollars more per one thousand gallons [of water].

But how much is that? Sometimes being correct isn't enough. No one knows how often they use a thousand gallons of water, so they won't have any idea how much extra this is—in terms of dollars and cents. As with tax stories, you have to convert this number into something that people can understand—like the average extra amount a typical family might have to pay per month.

Puzzling: Meanwhile, Democrat Bernie Sanders is gaining
ground on Clinton in California. A Los Angeles
Times/U-S-C poll out tonight shows Sanders in the
lead right now ... by one point. Sanders is
gaining ground thanks to young voters. Still, Clinton
is leading by 10 points among "likely" voters.

So, is Sanders ahead by one or behind by 10? Is the distinction based on overall adults versus likely voters? The audience will never know (nor do I, so I can't help sort it out—although Clinton did win the primary by 12.5).

This next example went on the air as the last line of a story about a defendant who pleaded not guilty by reason of insanity:

Puzzling: Smith claimed he was on a mission from God.
Apparently the jury agreed.

The jury may well have agreed that the defendant was insane, but it's unlikely they agreed that the defendant was on a mission from God.

End Strong

End sentences strongly. There's a natural break at the end of every sentence, and that means the audience gets just a moment to digest what has been said. Use the end of the sentence to bring home an important point. Wherever possible, avoid ending sentences with weak words or phrases. Watch out, especially, for weak prepositional phrases at the end of sentences.

Weak: Several homes and businesses had to be evacuated
this afternoon when a natural gas line was ruptured
by a construction worker.
Stronger: Several homes and businesses had to be
evacuated this afternoon when a construction worker
ruptured a natural gas line.

In this example, restructuring to end on *gas line* creates a stronger ending as well as making that part of the sentence active rather than passive.

● ● ● ● ●

Last Note

Make your point directly in every sentence. Don't dance around ideas, spilling words around a page. Just as you should be able to defend every word you use, you should be able to defend every sentence those words form. If you can't defend it, rework it or drop it.

●●●●●

Summary

Keep sentences short. The audience can only take in so much information at a time, and an announcer can only read so much material between breaths. No more than one important idea per sentence, but make every sentence count. Remember the audience is people, so structure sentences to put people (or what interests them) first. Most sentences should be subject-verb-object, but use some variety (and conjunctions) for interest. Avoid repetition, stay positive, and end strongly.

●●●●●

Key Words & Phrases

keep sentences short . . . one important idea . . . put people first . . . subject-verb-object . . . make every sentence count . . . end strong

●●●●●

Exercises

A. The following stories and paragraphs have errors and/or words, phrases, sentences or means of expression not acceptable in writing for broadcast. Make them acceptable. Do not assume that the sentences are in a logical sequence. Note that for the purposes of this assignment, you are in Springfield.

1. People living in neighborhoods that are tired of living right near to homes in foreclosure or which are abandoned or unsafe and are overrun by animals and insects will have something to celebrate on Wednesday when the city opens bids for the demolition of more than 30 of those properties, many of which have been featured on the website of the local organization, CleanUpOurNeigh borhood.org.

   A variety of animals will be displaced in the clean-up. Sam Smith said that there's a groundhog den beneath the decaying, rundown house at 2000 East Grant St. A black cat wandered around the dilapidated front porch of 1000 West Carnival Ave. Jane Jones said the dilapidated house at 1500 West Hill St. was a den for opossums.

2. It has been more than 20 years that have gone by since a string of home break-ins and sexual assaults had people who lived here in Springfield on edge in the summer and early autumn of 1995. Back then, the arrest of John Paul Smith, then 21 years old, after he made the mistake of trying to break in and rob a city police officer's home not long before Thanksgiving, seemed to bring the crime spree to an end.

   After a jury in May 1996 found Smith guilty — but mentally ill — of criminal deviate conduct, Judge Hank Jones imposed a maximum 50-year prison term. That 50-year prison term passed considerably faster than some might have expected because even though Smith, due to violating parole in an earlier case, didn't officially begin serving the 50-year sentence until 1997, state Department of Correction officials last week confirmed he had recently been released from prison and is currently residing at a relative's house here in Springfield.

3. Springfield Metal Works President John Smith informed metal workers this morning the company will lay off 130 designers and engineers because work on the next generation of R-2000 engines will be moving from the design and engineering phase to the full production phase.

   In a letter that was distributed to all the metal workers today, Smith wrote that while there was going to be a drop in the size of the design staff at the plant, that there was also a corresponding ramping up in the work force that has taken place on the production side of the business where more than 200 jobs have been added over the past year as work to construct the new, state-of-the-art engines has been intensified, Smith wrote. Smith wrote that the 130 announced layoffs will become effective in 3 weeks.

4. People who live in northwest Springfield will have to wait three weeks before finding out more information about a possible settlement proposal that has been offered to the city to stop various litigation over a City Planning Board decision not to grant a variety of permits for a cell phone tower to be built in the Springfield Valley neighborhood. Following the Planning Board's September 28, decision not to grant a conditional use permit for the company's proposed 85-foot bi-pole cell phone tower that the company wanted to construct at 100 Gearly St., the applicant, Capitol Cell Phone Tower III, LLC, filed a lawsuit on October 22, in U-S. District Court for the Southern District, and which has set a court date in February.

   Thursday, the proposed settlement offer, including camouflaging the tower as a pine tree, was one of four items the members of the City Council would be considering to discuss at the next public hearing at the next City Council meeting scheduled to take place in three weeks, before city council members would decide on placing them on the agenda in order to vote on the matter at the special town meeting scheduled to be held three weeks after that.

5. After extensive discussion of several proposed changes to a proposed property maintenance ordinance Wednesday, the Springfield City Council decided to schedule another workshop on the subject for next week, when members of the city council will again continue examining and combing through the document.

Some members of the city council expressed their frustration that the draft ordinance of the property maintenance ordinance did not more clearly reflect their intent for the whole plan, which was to force properties along the Main Street corridor to become more welcoming to travelers to the region. The proposed ordinance called for the city to be able to fine property owners whose tourist zone properties fall into disrepair, including a list of standards including prohibition of broken glass, peeling or missing paint, unkempt yards or weeds, garbage left outside, and unsightly porches or foundations.

10

• • • • •

Leads and Endings

The broadcast lead must capture the interest and attention of the audience. It may announce important developments; it may summarize complicated data; it may scream in joy, cry in pain or wonder in astonishment. But whatever it does and—within reason—however it does it, the lead must grab hold of the audience. That's the only real function of the lead.

Newspaper's traditional inverted pyramid lead attempts to answer, in abbreviated form, most of the basic journalistic questions of a story: the who, what, where and when (and sometimes even why and how).

The inverted pyramid style has no place in broadcast journalism, and the broadcast lead has no real relationship to the print lead. The broadcast lead most closely parallels the newspaper *headline*, boldly demanding the audience's attention. Think of the broadcast lead as the headline for the story.

If geometry helps in understanding structure, then while a newspaper story may be an inverted pyramid, the broadcast story is a circle. The lead is the most important part of the story, and the last sentence of a broadcast story is the second most important. That doesn't mean the last sentence contains the second most important bit of information in the story. It does mean that, structurally, the ending closes and completes the story, bringing it full circle.

Because newspapers' inverted pyramid story form puts the most important information at the beginning and less important material at the end, it works well for both editors and readers. Editors can cut for length simply by chopping off the bottom of stories, and readers can stop reading a story at any point, knowing or sensing that what they haven't read is less important than what they have. Most of the newspaper audience never reaches the end of a story. However, the newspaper model doesn't work in broadcast. If our audience tires of a story, they can't simply move on to the next one, as they can in the newspaper or online. We can't afford to fade out; either our audience is with us for the whole story or they tune us out.

• • • • •

Types of Leads

There isn't a single best kind of lead. What the story is about, how it fits into the newscast, who's going to read it and what precedes it—all help determine each particular story's best lead in a given newscast. And there are plenty of different kinds of leads to choose from. In most cases the reason the audience should care about the story is the story's innate importance. In that case—in the majority of cases—start with a main point lead.

Hard Main Point Lead

Main point leads include four variations. *Hard main point* leads tell what the story is about in an absolutely straightforward manner:

HARD

LEAD: The state legislature voted overwhelmingly today to
    cut back school funding by 20 percent.

This lead tells exactly what the story is. There's no subtlety here, but it's not designed for that. No lead gets you into the meat of the story as directly and quickly. A fairly simple story that's on the air because of its importance to the audience will usually work best with this kind of lead.

HARD

LEAD: A chemical spill on the west side drove hundreds
    of people from their homes this afternoon.

Soft Main Point Lead

Contrast that directness with the *soft main point* lead, which starts with what the story is *generally* about or the general impact of the story. Converted from a hard to a soft lead, the first lead above might look like this:

SOFT

LEAD: School systems throughout the state may have a
    tough time getting by. The state legislature today
    voted ...

This kind of lead delays the real meat of the story by one line, substituting, at the top, a bottom-line sense of what it means. Notice that line two will almost always be a variation of the hard main point lead. So why slow down the details of the story? First, depending on available video, it might make more sense to start with the anchor on camera giving a sense of the story for a line before going to voiceover video with details in line two. Visually, that's how most stories on TV start.

Video	Audio
Anchor CU	((Anchor))
	Two of the crack houses city police raided last night are owned by city police officers.
VO ENG	This one, on Main Street ...

Second, the soft main point lead is an excellent way to start a complicated story. By stating the sense of the story, you make it easier for the audience to follow the twists and turns that may be involved in getting there.

SOFT
LEAD: Another setback today in efforts to end the
    sanitation workers' walkout.

Throwaway Lead

Throwaway leads just introduce a subject using a short sentence or, more commonly, a sentence fragment. The throwaway lead version of that first lead might look like this:

THROWAWAY
LEAD: Trouble for state school systems. The state
    legislature today voted ...

A throwaway lead can give a general sense of the story, as the above example does, or it can create a general feeling or mood or just grab the audience's attention:

THROWAWAY
LEAD: An ominous warning tonight from police.

Throwaway leads can be especially good for varying the pacing of a newscast—especially to speed it up—and provide a short bridge between related stories:

THROWAWAY
LEAD: And another drive-by shooting tonight.

Umbrella Lead

Umbrella leads are among the most underutilized techniques to help add coherence to a newscast. Where some group, government body, business, or individual has taken several significant actions, the umbrella lead can set up the audience for different aspects of a single story:

UMBRELLA
LEAD: The state legislature today passed bills that will
    raise taxes, lower some salaries and change school
    funding.

This approach tells the audience that you're about to give them, in this example, three related stories. Note that when you write the rest of the story, tell each part start to finish; don't try to weave in and out of the different parts.

When an event will be covered from several angles, the umbrella lead can set up the audience for a series of reports:

UMBRELLA
LEAD: The vice president made a whirlwind tour of
    the city today ... looking for support for the
    administration's new tax plan ... stumping for a
    local politician ... and raising money for the
    Democratic Party. We have a series of reports,
    starting with Jane Smith at the airport.

Or the umbrella lead can connect different stories that have a common thread:

UMBRELLA
LEAD: Three unrelated strikes have 50-thousand workers in
    the state walking picket lines. In Smithville ...

Delayed or Suspense Lead

The *delayed* or *suspense* lead works completely differently from any of the others. Typically, the entire story, including the lead, is told chronologically. For most stories, we relate information chronologically (if there is a chronology) after the lead. Here, the whole story is told chronologically, with the punch line or point of the story coming at the end:

DELAYED
LEAD: John Smith drove to his job at Jones Trucking
    today — just as he has every other day. He stopped at
    the nearby Brown Donut Shop — as he has every
    morning. But today, just as he went in, he noticed
    another customer choking. Smith rushed over,

```
administered the Heimlich maneuver — pushing in on
the man's ribcage — and saved the man's life. Smith
said he learned the technique during a short
training session at lunch — yesterday.
```

Normally, we never use a name that is not widely known in a lead. The delayed or suspense lead is the exception. The audience should feel that there's a reason they're hearing this story, even if the exact reason isn't made clear until the end. If the writing is tight, the story short, and the punch line worthwhile, the technique works. It won't work for most stories, and it should be used sparingly for greatest effect.

Question Lead

The *question* lead is just what it says:

Question
lead: Why would you look for an elephant in a church?

For a question lead to work, it either has to be sufficiently intriguing that the audience really wants the answer or a question that the audience will want to answer in the affirmative:

Question
lead: Do you want to make a lot more money?

A question lead like the last one may get people's attention, but if the story doesn't support and answer the question logically, the audience will simply become annoyed.

Use question leads once every blue moon—perhaps less often. Most question leads exist because writers were too lazy to come up with anything else. Questions contain no information; you're supposed to be answering questions, not asking them; and question leads sound more like commercials than news. Save the questions for teases and promos (see Chapter 13).

● ● ● ● ●

Figuring out the Lead

The kind of lead that works best depends on the story. Hard leads tend to work best with hard, breaking stories. Others are more variable. The best newscasts mix different leads. Too many hard leads can make a newscast sound choppy and staccato. Too many soft leads will slow the pacing down and diminish some urgency in stories that should have it. Vary your leads.

What's the Story About?

The most important parts of the writing process are the thinking and planning that take place before your fingers start dancing on the keyboard. Start by thinking, "What is the story about? Why is this story going on the air?" Ask yourself, "Who cares?" and "So what?" The answers to those questions should not only tell you how to write the story, but also answer the critical question of how to start it. The lead should usually be that brief headline you'd use if you were telling a friend about the information—although not quite as informally stated. When we tell a story to a friend, we frequently start with something like, "Did you hear about X?" Maybe that's Dan's accident or Lindsay's storm damage. Figuring out the lead is a similar concept.

GOOD

LEAD: Sunscreen ... the stuff that's supposed to protect you from cancer ... may actually cause the disease.

The lead tells us what the story is about, in a way that gets our attention.

GOOD

LEAD: The mayor went to jail today ... not as a prisoner but as an observer ... to see for himself how serious a problem jail overcrowding has become.

This last example looks like a long, complex sentence, but broken up the way it is—and read properly—it's really a series of short fragments following a short, catchy sentence.

Say Something Meaningful

The lead must contribute to the telling of the story, including why the audience should care. With rare exceptions, meetings aren't news. Don't start the lead with them.

AWFUL: At its monthly meeting tonight, the city council ...

It might be news if the council *didn't* meet, but sheer existence is rarely news. The lead should say something the council (or school board, organization, etc.) did that made the meeting sufficiently significant to justify air time.

BETTER: Good news for city workers. The city council tonight approved a five percent pay raise ...

In this case a soft main point lead tells us the essence of the story. The city council isn't even mentioned in the lead; it's in line two.

Weak: If you think you are paying a lot for
    utilities — News X has learned that some Ohio
    Valley residents may have to pay even more.

The first phrase of this lead (which did, indeed, go on the air) is completely meaningless and just delays telling people what the news is. First, everyone thinks they're paying a lot for utilities. Second, the story isn't about utilities in general, it's about water rates, so the copy is too vague. Third, even if you don't think you're paying a lot for utilities, your water rates may go up. Keep it tighter and more direct.

Better: News X has learned that some Ohio Valley
    residents may have to pay more money for water.

Keep It Simple

Although all broadcast stories must answer the basic questions of *who, what, where, when, why* and *how*, don't try to answer them all in the lead. You can't have more than one important thought or idea per sentence, and the lead should be one of the shortest and simplest sentences in the story. Remove noncritical information that can wait until later; otherwise, you have the all-too-common overloaded lead. Break up the information.

Overloaded: Five people are being treated for smoke
    inhalation today after a two-alarm fire blamed on faulty
    wiring at a small office building on the south side.
Better: Five people are being treated for smoke
    inhalation today after a two-alarm fire on the south
    side. Officials say faulty wiring at a small office
    building ...

Notice that we've used a hard main point lead to get right into the story. We've told the audience *what* happened, and, critically, we've made clear in the lead that it happened *here*. Other aspects are dealt with only in skeletal form.

Overloaded: Thousands of Detroit students and school
    teachers are waiting in limbo on the outcome of
    negotiations between building engineers and school
    officials.

Remember: Keep leads short, and save the detail for later. Not only does the sentence above (which went on the air) try to give way too much information in the lead, it also understates numbers and improperly shifts the focus of the story from the larger group of students and teachers to the much smaller group of school officials and engineers.

Better: Tens of thousands of Detroit students and teachers are waiting to see whether there's school tomorrow.

Again, we've used a hard main point lead. The story is on the air because it's significant to a large number of people in the audience, so a straightforward—but tight—statement of fact is all you need.

Start with New News

The saying goes, "Three-quarters of news is new." Keep that in mind as you work on the lead. No story is on the air because of background and history. It's on the air *now* because of something that just happened. That's what you need to tell the audience in the lead. Background and history—if used at all—come later. There is a natural tendency to want to start with background and history. Resist that. That's not why the story is on the air *now*.

Old news: A district court judge found a local man guilty of murder two weeks ago. Today, John Smith was sentenced to ...

New news: A local man was sentenced to ... [then you can talk about the trial and the crime]

Old news: The Coast Guard rescued two men from the freezing waters off Point Falcon last night.

New news: Two men are hospitalized in good condition today — after the Coast Guard pulled the pair from the freezing waters off Point Falcon last night.

Don't reminisce. Don't start a story with a phrase like *You may remember,* followed inevitably by a recap of the earlier story. Some of the audience will remember, but most probably will not—either because it didn't make that much of an impression or because they didn't see it at all. Regardless, you still have to recap, so why start the story with a weak lead that simply asks the audience to try to remember old news? Instead, work harder to come up with a strong lead for today's story and then note that it's a follow-up with a phrase like *We first told you about.* If all else fails and you can't come up with a strong, fresh lead, then fall back on

So-so lead: A follow-up tonight to a story we first told you about ...

At least this lead says at the top that the audience is going to learn something new, and the audience likes follow-up stories.

Focus on People

Our audience is made up of people, and, generally, what they care most about are themselves and other people.

WEAK: Business is booming for the people who market cell phones, but they're running into some problems.

Smith's cellular business has doubled in the last year, and the company is looking for places to build new transmission towers.

This is an example of what they need. This one is 285-feet tall.

Smith is trying to put up a 200-foot version on this land on the north side. Today they bulldozed the area to get ready to build. But there's a hitch. The people who live around here don't want a big tower in the backyard and are fighting it.

Notice that this story's lead (a real story that went on the air) focuses on people who sell cell phones and ends with homeowners concerned about property values. You can choose to focus on cell phones and the narrow issue of the few people who market them—as the writer of this copy did—or the wider issue of property values that could affect much of the audience.

BETTER: Some north side residents say a local business [or high technology or a cell phone company] is threatening to destroy the value of their property.

In addition to getting to the point of the bigger and more important story faster, the second version also properly shifts the focus of the story from technology to people—and allows us to start video of the story in line two with either people (first choice) or a new tower (second choice).

Focus on Local

Your audience cares most about news that's closest to them. Unless you're writing for a network, that means local—local people, local issues, local events. If you're writing a story with both local and national implications, generally, focus on local first.

NO—NATIONAL
LEAD: Unemployment rose sharply, nationwide, last month.

Yes—local

lead: Unemployment rose sharply here last month.

Both stories would likely contain the same information; the issue is what goes first. Understandably, the local audience cares a lot more about what's going on in their own community and with their friends and neighbors than about a faceless mass elsewhere. Start a mixed local/national story with the local part first.

Put Location in the Lead

Always make clear in the lead where a story is from.

No: Three people have died in a nightclub fire earlier
     this evening.
No: A gunman entered an elementary school and started
     firing today.

Where did those things happen? The audience is likely to assume that they're local stories. If that's the case, make that clear in the lead so there's no confusion.

Yes: Three people have died in a downtown nightclub fire
     this evening.
     or
     Three people have died in a nightclub fire here this
     evening.
Yes: Officials at Smith Elementary School in Cityville say
     it was a miracle no one was hurt. A gunman ...

In all those examples the audience knows right away that they're hearing about a local story. If the stories are not local and you didn't make that clear in the lead, you're likely to have an audience that rightly feels angry and betrayed. If the story is not local, tell people that.

Yes: Three people have died in a nightclub fire in
     Rochester tonight.
Yes: A gunman entered an elementary school in San Diego
     and started firing today.

In both of those cases you have no one in the audience panicking, thinking that it might be a local story (assuming, of course, that the audience isn't in Rochester in the first example and San Diego in the second).

Keep in mind that there are lots of ways to include that mandatory locator in the lead. For stories in your area, the choices include not only the name of the city, community or neighborhood, but also words like *downtown, here, locally, nearby* and so on.

Be Direct and to the Point

Don't back into a story. Give the audience a reason to care right from the beginning.

BACKING IN: An interesting thing happened at the city
    council meeting last night.

The only thing being said in the line above is that the audience will learn something meaningful in the future. We can't afford to waste that much time or be that boring.

BETTER: The city council last night voted to close all
    city recreation areas.
       or
       All city recreation areas will be closing down.
    The city council last night voted ...
       or
       The city plans to close all its recreation areas.

Envision a busy audience taking time out of their day to find out what happened. Just tell them.

BACKING IN: A homemade single engine plane crashed nose-first
    into some Delaware farmland today. It exploded into
    flames, and the pilot, James Smith of Columbus, and
    his passenger, Tom Jones of Powell, were killed.

Although there are advantages to telling a story in chronological order, this story (real except for the names) takes the idea too far. Buried at the end of the long, second sentence is the real news: Two people died. The plane crash is *how* that news happened, but the real news involves the two local men who died, not the crash itself.

BETTER: Two local men are dead after the homemade plane
    they were flying crashed into a Delaware farm and
    exploded.

Notice, again, the use of a hard main point lead to get across the main point of the story. It tells the audience what happened and how. Again, the lead makes clear that the story is local. It also doesn't use the names of the men in the lead but sets up the use of the names in line two. If one or both of the men were well known in the area, the lead might include that information.

Save the Name for Later

Unless the person the story is about is extremely well known (such as the president, the local mayor, or a popular celebrity) or you're using a delayed lead, don't include the name in the lead. The answer to the question *who?* must be in the lead, but that doesn't necessarily mean that we need the name. Generally, it's better to use a brief description (e.g., *a union leader, two office workers, a local woman*) in the lead to set up the actual name(s) for early in line two:

SET UP

NAMES FOR

LINE TWO: Police have arrested an unemployed truck driver
for yesterday's robbery at the Jones Trucking
Company. Police say John Smith went in to see
his former employer armed with ...

SET UP

NAMES FOR

LINE TWO: A man charged with robbing, raping and then
murdering a local teenager went on trial today.
David Jones sat silently ...

In both the previous examples the lead described the subject of the story, but the actual name—the detail of the name—didn't appear until line two. This helps keep the lead shorter and tighter.

Save the Day and Date for Later

Don't start the lead with the day or date unless it's the critical part of the story. Always have the date somewhere in the story, usually in the lead sentence, but remember that almost all stories we report happened *today*—that's not news.

No: This morning, dozens of police officers called in
sick in what's believed to be the latest attack of
the "blue flu."

YES: Dozens of police officers called in sick this
morning, in what's believed to be the latest attack
of the "blue flu."

Sometimes, especially in the morning news, at noon and in the late news, we want to emphasize the time of day to demonstrate how timely the story is. "This morning" might work at the top of a story or two in the morning or noon news, and "tonight" might work at the beginning of a story on the late news. But if story after story starts that way, then the impact is lost.

Update Leads

Update leads whenever possible. Frequently, the future effect of an earlier action makes a lead sound more timely and interesting.

OLDER: The city council last night voted to increase property tax rates.
UPDATED: Property tax bills will be going up.
OLDER: The fire that began at an industrial complex yesterday continues to burn.
UPDATED: The smell and smoke from tons of burning plastic continue to blanket the south side.

Responsibility

If you're unsure whether to use a clever lead, a delayed lead or anything other than a main point lead—don't. A lot of tasteless journalism has been on the air because someone picked the wrong time to try to be clever or cute. You'll never go wrong with a well-written main point lead. You may have missed an opportunity to do something a little different, but you won't embarrass yourself or your news organization. If the lead doesn't demand something a little different, proceed with caution.

NEVER: The two sides are practically killing each other over whether a woman has a right to an abortion.

You can get the attention of the audience by either shouting or whispering. Shouting is easier, but it isn't nearly as riveting.

Above All . . . Get It Right

How you express information makes little difference if you screw up the facts.

WRONG: A yearly survey on global terrorism ... shows Iraq is a main sponsor.

That sentence, which recently went on the air on a top 50 market TV station, is tight and straightforward. The only real problem is that it's wrong. The survey said that *Iran* is the main sponsor—not *Iraq*. There's just no excuse.

●●●●●

Types of Endings

Not only do broadcast stories need to start strong, they need to end that way, too. We bring them full circle; we wrap them up. We are, in the end, telling the audience stories, and a good story always has a beginning, a middle and an end. Think about how you're going to wrap up the story at the same time you think about how you're going to start. In television, where stand-up bridges in recorded packages are recorded at the scene, reporters really need to figure out, at least generally, how they're going to structure the whole story even as they're covering it.

Future Ramification Close

Probably the best ending—and one of the most common—is the *future ramification* close:

```
    Smith says they'll appeal the decision to the
state Supreme Court.
```

This kind of ending tells us where the story goes from here. If the facts you're dealing with include that kind of information, this will almost always be the strongest ending.

```
    Jones says no matter what the council decides,
he'll never give in.
```

Part of what makes the future ramification close so strong is that there's almost never any doubt that you've wrapped up and ended the story.

Summary Point Close

The *summary point* ending restates, in different words, what the story is all about:

```
    What it all means is that food prices are likely
to stay just about where they are.
```

This kind of ending is particularly useful in a complicated story in which at least some of the audience might have gotten lost in the data.

Frequently, a story started with a soft main point lead because of its complexity will work best with a summary point ending. Just make sure, in restating the sense of the lead, that you change the exact wording.

> All the legislators we talked to said schools
> should expect lean times and layoffs for the
> foreseeable future.

Information Close

Some endings close the story with a new, related bit of *information:*

> The airline carries more than a million passengers
> a month.

The information ending tends to add some general perspective to the story. But be careful in an information ending that you don't raise new questions instead of closing the story.

> **PROBLEM:** This is another in a series of problems the
> airline has had all year.

Ending a story like that will drive the audience crazy, wondering about what those other problems have been. Bring the story to a clear conclusion; don't raise new issues.

Opposition Point of View Close

The *opposition point of view* may end a story:

> But opponents argue that the new law won't work
> and will only make things worse.

Be careful with this kind of close, too. Because you're leaving the audience with a different point of view than you focused on for the story, you may elevate a minor point to undeserved prominence. If the story is long enough, it's generally better to raise opposition points inside the story. Above all, be fair, and don't use this kind of ending as a means of furthering your own point of view.

Punch Line

The last type of ending is the *punch line*. A story that uses a *delayed* or *suspense* lead always ends with a punch line. The punch line—the last line—is typically the unexpected twist in the story that puts everything into perspective. See the delayed lead and ending earlier in this section on pages 128–129.

● ● ● ● ●

Summary

The broadcast lead is like the newspaper headline; above all else, it must capture the attention and interest of the audience. There are four main point leads: hard, soft, throwaway and umbrella. The two other types of leads are delayed or suspense and the question lead. To figure out the lead, figure out what the story is really about, what's new and focus on people and local. Put some form of locator in the lead. Don't use names of people who aren't well known in the lead. Because all broadcast stories must come to a close, the ending is the second most important line in the story. The five types of endings are future ramification close, summary point, information, opposition point of view and the punch line.

● ● ● ● ●

Key Words & Phrases

main point lead . . . hard lead . . . soft lead . . . throwaway . . . umbrella lead . . . delayed or suspense lead . . . question lead . . . start with new news . . . focus on people . . . focus on local . . . put location in the lead . . . save the name for later . . . future ramification close . . . summary point . . . information close . . . opposition point of view close . . . punch line.

● ● ● ● ●

Exercises

A. The following lead sentences have errors and/or words, phrases or means of expression not acceptable for broadcast writing. Make them into acceptable broadcast leads. Again, for the sake of this assignment, you're in Springfield.

　1. Janice R. Hennessy, Associate State Commissioner of the State Liquor Commission, has called for a new crackdown on underage drinking.

　2. The mayor said that, "I think it is counterproductive to have the state take away funding from urban renewal programs here when it is clear that the benefits of the program, in producing new tax revenue from buildings formerly costing the city money in upkeep and now generating dollars by being in private hands, clearly outweighs the cost."

　3. An extremely serious car accident last night resulted in 6 injured and 2 dead.

4. A low interest loan by Samuel J. Clarke to a member of the County Commission that for the past 3 weeks has been considering his request for a zoning variance appeared today — when information about the loan was first released — to raise questions of propriety and ethical behavior and jeopardize his already-questionable zoning variance request in more uncertainty.

5. The Fire Department's arson squad head says the severity of last Tuesday's fire at the Smith General Store, Incorporated, in which 3 customers were hurt and 1 fireman died, has been traced to a broken sprinkler system in the building.

6. Last evening, not long following the unsuccessful negotiations with the city council broke off, local city workers voted then to begin striking against the city this morning.

7. FBI agent Mary Smith said this morning that the Union Bank and Trust, Incorporated, of 200 West University Ave., lost $2500 to burglars some time around 4 a.m. in the morning.

8. In it's regular weekly session this afternoon, the Long Beach City Council discussed in a heated manner what would become of the Westminster Nursing Home project.

9. There was a lot of activity last night if you were a Springfield fireman. A house fire on the east side left two families homeless tonight in a fire that took firemen 2 hours to control, while near downtown, three families lost their homes and a fireman collapsed and was taken to the hospital.

10. Three innocent bystanders and a member of the U-S. House of Representatives were shot by an unidentified man with a gun at a campaign rally for the Congress person this morning in front of the entrance to the Colorado State Park. The bystanders all died, and the Congress member is in critical condition.

11

•••••

TV: Story Forms

•••••

Story Forms

A television newscast is made up of a mix and match of five basic TV story forms.

- The *reader*, in which the anchor appears on the screen reading the story, with or without graphics.
- The *voiceover* (*VO*, pronounced V-O or VOH), which typically starts with the anchor on camera reading the first line or two of a story and then continues with the anchor reading live over video, with natural sound under.
- The *VO/SOT* (sometimes spoken as letters, V-O-S-O-T, and sometimes pronounced as VOH-soht), which typically starts, as with the VO, with the anchor on camera reading the first line or two of a story and then continues with the anchor reading live over video, with natural sound under, and then goes to a bite (SOT: sound on tape). Variations can include going to VO again after the bite or starting with SOT, then going to voiceover and perhaps then going back to SOT.
- The *package* (or pack), a prerecorded report normally with reporter narration over video, a stand-up and bites. If the package is introduced by the reporter live on location, the internal package stand-up may be omitted.
- *Live*, in which a reporter or anchor broadcasts live directly from the scene of a story, often wrapping around a package or including voiceover video either shot earlier or live.

Readers

Readers are basically radio reports read on TV, and the writing style and approach are exactly the same—with one exception. If graphics accompany a reader, usually in the form of an over-the-shoulder box showing a picture or symbol, then the writer needs to structure the story in such a way that the words make clear what the audience can see in the graphic box. If the box includes a word or phrase, then that word or phrase should be included at the same general time the box appears. If the box appears with the anchor at the beginning of the story, then the lead should include that word or phrase. You can't make the graphic clear somewhere later in the story; it must go with the lead. For example, if you're using a picture of someone—or a picture and a name—on the screen with the anchor, you can't wait until well into the story to identify or talk about the individual. If the story starts with a graphic, then sentence one of the story must reference it in some way.

Anchor
without
gfx: City officials are scrambling to meet a Monday deadline for a court-ordered plan to integrate a south side housing project.

Anchor
with gfx
(mayor): Mayor Dan Smith and members of his administration are scrambling to meet a Monday deadline for a court-ordered plan to integrate a south side housing project.

Anchor
with gfx
(housing project): City officials are scrambling to meet a Monday deadline for a court-ordered plan to integrate this south side housing project.

Without graphics you write the story exactly as you would for radio. With graphics you must incorporate whatever the audience sees in the graphic into the writing.

Voiceovers

Most anchor *voiceovers*, or *VO* stories, are read live by the anchor, with the accompanying video started on cue. That means that the video (sometimes called b-roll) can easily start just a little early or a little late. Most voiceover copy should not be written so pointedly that it will not make sense if the timing isn't perfect with the visuals. The two best ways to avoid the problem are to have the anchor who will be reading the VO on air to read through and time the copy before it's edited and to have anchors who can keep an eye on the monitor and know whether to speed up, slow down, or just ad lib a bit. Live voiceover narration that *points* to the picture works well if you have the anchors who can do it. Phrases like *as you see here* and *watch the upper left of your screen* really help focus the audience attention on the story and get people to pay extra attention to the TV.

NARRATION: An armed man charged into the store ... you can see him there, in the upper left of your screen ...

Phrasing like this works every time to bring the casual viewer back to the screen. But few things look worse on TV newscasts than having an anchor say . . . *as you see here* . . . and there's something else on the screen because the timing was off—or, as happened to a weekend network anchor a number of years ago, there was nothing there at all because the video didn't run at all.

VO/SOT

TV stories that are constructed for the anchor to read voiceover pictures leading into a bite (VO/SOT or VO/SOT/VO) must be written with particular care. The slightest error will result in either the anchor talking over the start of a bite or what will feel like an interminable pause between the anchor lead-in and the start of the bite. Two procedures help to minimize the chances of error. First, have the anchor time the voiceover copy carefully to calculate the amount of video to run before the bite starts. Second, the less voiceover copy before the start of a bite, the more likely that the anchor's timing will be correct. Conversely, the more copy to be read VO before the bite, the greater the chances that the anchor will read faster or slower than expected or stumble in the copy and run well behind the video.

The best way to hit the SOT cleanly in a VO/SOT or VO/SOT/VO is to have the bite separate from the video voiceover material that precedes it. That way, the video with the bite isn't run until the anchor is at that spot in the script, minimizing the chances for mistiming. That's how it's most often done today.

Packages

Packages, because they're prerecorded, allow maximum use of the medium. Because the material is prerecorded, lots of natural sound and many short bites can be used, and sound and picture can be layered on top of each other. The challenge is for the TV reporter to write and structure a story as it's being covered.

STAND-UPS. Stations expect a reporter to do an on-camera *stand-up* somewhere in the piece. Stand-up opens are now rare except in live reports, and most stations don't encourage stand-up closers either, although networks and some stations still use them. Most stand-ups are now internal bridges. Because the stand-up must be recorded at the scene of the story, the reporter needs to calculate in the field how the piece will work and how it will be put together. Some reporters record more than one bridge, allowing an option in case one doesn't work well, but that involves a time luxury that's not often available.

What a reporter needs to do is assess a story quickly and write in the mind. The stand-up section(s) should be scripted—mentally if not in writing. Some reporters are quick studies and memorize their stand-ups; most use or memorize notes and ad lib. A reporter who relies too heavily on notes on a pad, tablet or cellphone isn't making good eye contact with the audience. If you can't remember what you want to say in the stand-up, maybe you're trying to say too much. The only notes you should need to rely on at all for a stand-up are names or numbers. Generally, stand-ups work best within a package when:

- available visuals are the weakest, particularly background material in a story
- the story requires a transition from one aspect to another, or
- the reporter can actually demonstrate or point out part of the story

Regardless, the setting for the stand-up must be appropriate. A stand-up that could have been shot anywhere probably shouldn't have been shot at all.

ANYWHERE

STAND-UP: The robber then ran from the store, firing shots at people walking by and passing cars, and then disappeared in nearby woods.

That's just a recitation of facts and could have been shot anywhere.

BETTER

STAND-UP: The robber then ran from the store, right by where I'm standing, firing shots at people walking by and passing cars, and then disappeared in those woods over there.

Now we're using the location to help tell the story, and we've built in some movement on the part of the reporter to help the audience understand what happened.

Live

Live reporting includes a number of different scenarios. It could just be a reporter on camera live on location. It could include the reporter, live, talking over edited video shot earlier or live pictures. Most often, it involves a live open and close with a prerecorded package in between.

●●●●●

Putting Packages Together

Because packages are prerecorded, they can be precise. Before writing anything, the reporter should see what visuals are available and think about how those pictures will tell the story. Pick out the natural sound bridges that should be interspersed throughout the story to give the audience a better feel for the characters and setting. Select the best bites and figure out whether they should be toward the beginning, middle or end. Write the script based on what the pictures say, what they don't say, and the most logical sequence for telling the story. At the same time, you want to intersperse throughout the story the bites that you got from the people you interviewed and the natural sound that you collected.

Pacing

Pacing is critical, and long stretches of narration are boring. Generally, start your package with natural sound full or a strong, short bite. After that, keep the narration short before hitting the next bite or sound bridge. Think in terms of 8 to 12 seconds at the most from the package start to the first bite or nat sound full. Shorter is better. That means you need to resist the temptation to start stories with background and history. Those things may be important for the story, but:

■ they're probably the least interesting part
■ they're not why the story is on the air today
■ it's far better to intersperse that material here and there throughout the package

The package will be much more interesting if you keep it moving back and forth between natural sound full, reporter track and bites.

After recording a voice track, that track and the natural sound full and bites to be used are put together. The pictures used to cover the narration (with natural sound under) can then be edited precisely to coordinate with the script so that the audience sees what you're talking about. Generally, place edits at logical pauses in the script.

It probably surprises most people that Steve Hartman edits his own stories at CBS. He obviously doesn't have to; that's his choice. "So much of writing is about editing," says Hartman. "I lay the soundbites out on the timeline . . . and then once I have that skeleton, then sometimes I'll even start to lay in the video for different sequences that I want . . . and then I'll start to write." And rewrite. "I'll put down these shots, and I'll realize that for this sequence to work, this sentence needs to be a second shorter. So I'll rewrite it."

Don't Outdate Packages

Reporters must also be careful about putting potentially dated material in prerecorded packages. Think about what might change between the time the script is tracked (recorded) and when it will go on the air. In any kind of accident or disaster the number of dead and injured can easily wind up wrong by air time as more bodies are discovered, some of the injured die or numbers get corrected in the aftermath of a chaotic situation. People sought by police could be arrested; people lost can be found. Before you record anything, think about what could easily and quickly change, and reserve that material for the live portion of a report or the anchor lead-in.

If new information seriously outdates a package, the package shouldn't go on the air. A package that has to be corrected at the end should never have been broadcast. That's like lying to the audience. Given the difficulty of filling that much air time at the last minute, it's critical that the dilemma be avoided completely. Don't *ever* prerecord potentially dated information.

● ● ● ● ●

Live Reporting

More and more reporting careers are made—and lost—on the basis of *live reporting*. The audience expects up-to-the-minute information, and they like the immediacy and feel of live reports. That's why there are so many of these, even if there is no longer much going on at the scene.

In live reporting, the typical structure involves some variation of an anchor lead-in to live reporter. Generally, the station starts on the anchor, then goes to a double box, where we see the anchor on one side of the screen and the reporter on the other side. Then the reporter starts talking, and we switch to the reporter full screen at the live location.

Depending on the situation, the reporter may present the whole story on camera (usually because the story just broke and the reporter and crew just got there) or will start and end on camera with video in the middle. That video could be live pictures, video shot earlier or an entire package recorded earlier. Frequently, live reports end with anchor–reporter question and answer (Q & A).

VIDEO	AUDIO
Mike (anchor) CU	((Mike)) The state Environmental Protection Agency has been out on the south side today, surveying a smoldering mountain of tires — the aftermath of yesterday's fire. :08

2-box with Mike left/Jane right	Reporter Jane Smith has been trudging through the debris with the inspectors. Jane, do they think there's any danger? :06 <center>((Jane))</center>No, Mike, they don't.
Jane full screen live super: Live Jane Smith Reporting South Side	Although water samples still need to be tested, officials tell me there's no evidence of any danger. But there is a very smelly mess out here. :08
take sot (package) full	((————————SOT————————)) Natural sound full of officials going through debris. :04 ((————————VO————————)) <center>((Jane))</center>The fire department has been standing by all day ... just in case there are any more flare-ups. :05 ((————————SOT————————)) Natural sound full of firefighter yelling to another firefighter. :02 ((————————VO————————)) Firefighter Dan Jones says it's been one of the longest nights — and days — of his career. :05 ((————————SOT————————))
super: Dan Jones City Firefighter	"The problems aren't just the smoke and fire ... it's the smell. It's almost impossible to breathe out there. I can't tell you how glad I'll be to get home, whenever that is." :12 ((————————VO————————)) <center>((Jane))</center>Now that the fire is under control, the city has to figure out what to do with the estimated 50-thousand tires out here. :06 ((————————SOT————————)) Natural sound full of bulldozer moving tires. :03 ((————————VO————————)) Tire Resale filed for bankruptcy protection two months ago, so the

city will pick up the clean-up
tab ... at least for now. :06
((——————SOT——————))
"What choice do we have?
The company isn't going to do
anything, so we have to. Taking
them to the landfill is the best
we can do." :09
((——————VO——————))
((Jane))
Not according to the state E-P-A.
Officials there say they've
already taken the city to court
to get the landfill shut down
because it's overloaded. :07
((——————SOT——————))
"The city needs to come up with a
plan. We'll try to work with the
city, but I can't make any
promises." :08
((——————on camera——————))
((Jane))
The E-P-A says it should have an
answer for the city in about
three days. If the E-P-A says no,
the city will have to look at
other landfills — at a much higher
cost. Mike. :09
((Mike))
Jane, what kind of money are we
talking about? :02
((Jane))
If the city can use the local
landfill, the cost is expected to
be about a hundred thousand
dollars. If the mess has to
be shipped somewhere else, it
could come to five times that
much. :10
((Mike))
And what about the results of
those water tests the E-P-A is
running? :04
((Jane))
I'm told to expect those on
Wednesday. But again, officials are
not expecting any problems. :05

super: Mary Cooper
City Mayor

super: Steven Small
State EPA

Jane full screen live
super: Live
Jane Smith Reporting
South Side

2-box—Mike left/
Jane right

1-shot Jane

2-box—Mike left/
Jane right

Note that the story starts *not* with the reporter live, but with the anchor lead-in, which should say that the reporter is live at the scene. Note also that the lead-in to the reporter contains meaningful information about the story, and the introduction goes right to the heart of the critical question: Is there any danger? Different stations may set varying time constraints on stories, but the above structure and times are reasonably representative.

The anchor lead-in runs 8 seconds before the double box and another 6 seconds afterward for a total of 14 seconds. The reporter then talks for 8 seconds before the video runs. That 8 seconds includes the scripted *very smelly mess out here* which is the cue for the director to start the prerecorded package. The total video time is 1:07. Note that within the package, the longest single continuous element is a bite that's 12 seconds long. The longest single stretch of the reporter track is only 7 seconds, but that hasn't stopped the reporter from including plenty of information on the story. There are three nat sound full bridges in the story—all of them in between sentences rather than splitting sentences apart. The reporter live close is 9 seconds, followed by 21 seconds of Q & A, all worked out in advance. The entire story, from anchor lead-in to final answer, is 1:59.

Planning

The key to live reporting is planning. Some reporters are such quick studies that they can write out a script and memorize the material almost instantly. Most reporters cannot rely solely on memorization. Still, you can't leave the report to chance. Plan what you want to say. Make notes—one or two words if possible on the points you want to raise—in the order in which you want to report them. If a particularly good phrase occurs to you when you're sketching out your notes, write it down. Just the act of writing something will help you remember it.

Glancing down occasionally at a notebook or tablet or smartphone is fine, but simply reading won't work. And if you've got a phone in one hand and a mike in the other, gesturing is going to be pretty difficult.

As in the example above, recorded packages inside a live shot should start and end with natural sound full or a bite. Those front and back sound bridges mask the different sound of the reporter live in the field versus the reporter's voice track prerecorded at the scene or in a sound booth at the station.

Crosstalk

In live reporting, probably the greatest opportunity for foot-in-mouth disease comes in the live crosstalk between the anchors and the reporter after the story. Whenever possible, crosstalk should be scripted at least to the extent of what question(s) will be asked or subject(s) covered.

Everyone's credibility is on the line. Anchors who ask questions that have already been answered in the report look like they haven't been paying attention (probably because they haven't been paying attention). A reporter who can't answer an unexpected question looks inept. Producers should determine whether there's going to be Q & A after the report, and the reporter should go over with the anchor and producer what that Q & A should include and not include.

Perhaps some better planning would have prevented this bizarre—but real—example of *live* phrasing:

Terrible: Now, Lou and Michelle, I'd be lying to you if I said there were absolutely no problems.

Lying? What kind of brain fade would have a reporter even suggesting that as a possible approach in reporting? Then there's the time that an anchor in a top 10 TV market asked the live reporter whether he agreed with a jury's verdict of guilty in a murder trial. Save that kind of editorial viewpoint for private discussion off the air. Fortunately, in that case the reporter had better sense than the anchor and managed to dance around the question.

Live reporting is both so important and so potentially hazardous that good reporters regularly study the recordings of their live reports to assess strengths and weaknesses—and improve.

Live Look

Stations also use what they sometimes call *live look* or *look live*. As the name implies, this isn't live at all. What's typically involved is a recorded open and close from the scene, introing a package and tagging it out. It looks live, but because it's prerecorded, there's no crosstalk. And the reporter should not be introduced as being live.

●●●●●

Golden Rules

■ Reporters sound far more articulate when they're scripted than when they're off-the-cuff.

■ Reporters never sound as articulate off-the-cuff as they think they do.

●●●●●

Summary

TV newscasts are made up of 5 basic story forms: reader, voiceover, VO/SOT, package and live. Packages, because they're prerecorded, can be the most complex and sophisticated story form. Packages generally include reporter track, video (b-roll), bites, nat sound full (and under) and a reporter stand-up. Because live reporting plays to TV's strength of immediacy, packages are frequently introduced and ended with reporters live in the field. Generally, start packages with nat sound full, hit the first bite or nat sound full bridge within 8–12 seconds, don't start a package with history and don't outdate a package by prerecording changeable information. Preplan crosstalk so no one is embarrassed.

● ● ● ● ●

Key Words & Phrases

basic TV story forms . . . reader . . . voiceover or VO . . . VO/SOT . . . package . . . live . . . stand-up . . . bridge . . . crosstalk

● ● ● ● ●

Exercises

A. Watch a morning newscast (half an hour), a 6 p.m. newscast and a late (10 p.m. or 11 p.m.) newscast. Make a short list of each story covered and what form it took. How many packages were in each newscast? How many included a reporter live on location? Did any start with a reporter live in the newsroom or on the set? If so, why do you think it worked that way? What do you notice about the mix of story forms?

B. Record a local TV package and break it down by individual elements. Did it start live with the reporter on the scene? How long did that run? Could you tell what the roll cue was to start the prerecorded video? How did the package start, and how long did each element go: reporter track, bites, stand-up, nat sound full, etc. Note also what the reporter was trying to get across in each element of the story. Do you think the story was effective? Why or why not? Were there elements of the story that you think the reporter could have left out? What and why? Were there things left out of the story that you think the reporter should have included? What and why?

C. Prepare a 20–30 second "live" intro to a prerecorded package, and deliver it—without notes—to the rest of the class. How did that go? How did the class think it went?

12

• • • • •

TV: Working with Pictures

• • • • •

The Power of the Visual Image

Working with Strong Pictures

The most critical thing to understand in writing for TV is the power of the visual image. Long after the story ends, the impression in the viewer's mind is likely to be a strong picture—not the spoken word. Given the nature of the beast, TV tends to seek out the visual story, and to the extent that pictures tell a story, the writer or reporter is best advised to get out of the way.

VIDEO	AUDIO
Anchor CU	((Mike)) Today's high winds nearly turned deadly for some construction workers on the west side.
Take eng/nat sound full super: West Side	((————————SOT————————)) Natural sound full of wind swirling debris at site :03 ((————————VO————————)) ((Mike)) Just after noon, gusts of up to 30 miles an hour jolted this concrete wall ... sending heavy blocks tumbling down just a few feet from workers on their lunch break. The men told us that just minutes before, they had been up on what's left of this scaffolding ... and down below ... right in the path of the falling blocks.

Note that the story is written for the available video and clearly refer-ences what the viewer will see. In this story, the words help add detail and clarity beyond what the audience can plainly see.

Working without Strong Pictures

On the other hand, many of the stories reporters cover use only weak visuals—pictures whose use would be mystifying if not for the words. Obviously, in that case, the pressure is on the script.

VIDEO	AUDIO
Anchor CU	((Sarah)) Testimony started today in federal court here in a trial that will determine the future of Smith Park.
Take eng/nat sound Full	((————————SOT————————)) Natural sound full :03 ((————————VO————————))
super: East Side	((Sarah)) Work at the park has been stopped after a lawsuit filed by the state contractors association. The group says too many contracts went to minority firms ... although the U-S Supreme Court struck down a law setting aside a minimum percentage of business to go to minority-owned companies. The city argues that it has removed minority requirements for future work ... but the contractors group wants the city to re-open bids on current work. The city wants the court to lift a restraining order so park construction can continue.

In a story like this, because federal courts will generally not allow cameras, the only possible meaningful visuals involve the construction site. That means the story has to be structured so that those pictures make sense right at the start of the story. Then, having made sense of the pictures from the park site, the script can move away to other parts of the story for which there aren't worthwhile pictures.

• • • • •

The TV Balancing Act

Television is a balancing act. Telling viewers what they can plainly see wastes their time and misuses the medium. But words that have no relationship to the pictures will surely confuse the audience—hence the balancing act.

Former NBC correspondent Don Larson says that once you've focused on what the story is really about, you need to *prove* your story with video and sound. If you're talking about how hard someone works, the audience needs to see that. "Allow your viewers to experience the same surprise, alarm, joy that you experienced when you first discovered your story," says Larson.

Use Pictures and Words for What They Do Best

Use pictures for what they can do better than words: convey feeling, emotion, action. Use the script to handle what the visuals don't: details, facts, background. As simple as this sounds, it's really the key to writing for television. It also means that if you're going to do this well, you need to know what your pictures are—and what story they can tell—before you start writing the script.

VIDEO	AUDIO
Anchor CU	((Steve)) Students at Smith Elementary School walked the picket line today — and school officials were glad they did.
Take eng/nat sound full	((——————SOT——————)) Natural sound full :03 ((——————VO——————)) ((Steve))

super: Smith Elementary School North Side	Armed with posters and banners and led by the school's drill team — about 500 kids took to the streets around the school to show the community they won't give in to drugs.
	    They also urged others to stay drug free ... and promoted the school's anti-drug DARE program.
	((——————SOT——————))
	    "Give me a D–D, give me an A–A. Give me an R–R. Give me an E–E. What do you have? Dare." :09

((—————————VO—————————))
((Steve))
The idea for today's parade
actually came from Smith
Elementary's Parent Association.
Many of them marched, too.
((—————————SOT—————————))

super: Pat Green
        Parent

"This is great. This is about
kids and families taking
responsibility for their own
actions and asking others to do
the same. It's about positive peer
pressure and having kids feel
better about themselves." :12
((—————————VO—————————))
((Steve))
Organizers say they'll all be
back out later this month ...
during the city-wide anti-drug
march slated for downtown.

Note that we started with natural sound full, setting the scene for the march. We start the voiceover script explaining what the audience can see: lots of kids with posters and a banner, led by a drill team. Then the script explains what may not be obvious from the pictures: why the kids are marching. Then we go back to natural sound and then to background. Notice that we're well into the story before we do that. Note also that this section of the script and the last section relate to the video but only indirectly. No one will be confused, however.

Use Natural Sound and SOT

Natural sound (nat sound) can make or break a TV story. Natural sound is real life. It's what would have happened even if the cameras weren't there. Always look for it, and to the extent that you've got it, use it, write to it and let the story breathe. Notice how it's used in almost every story in this and other chapters.

Always use natural sound under anchor and reporter voiceover. The far greater feel given to the story is incalculable. The same, by the way, is at least as true in radio packages. Hardly anything heightens the sense of "being there" as much as natural sound under. However, we generally do not run natural sound under a bite. Usually, the technical recording of the bite isn't strong enough to handle the competition of natural sound. Besides, the bite itself should provide its own ambient background.

For some reason, the use of nat sound seems to separate weaker, small-market news operations—that frequently don't use much nat sound—from larger-market stations that do. But nat sound is available to everyone. Use it.

Write TV Loosely

Write television loosely. That doesn't mean you can write sloppily, but you don't need to fill up every second with narration. In radio an absence of sound means an absence of news. In TV there's always the picture, and picture with natural sound can carry a story on its own. How long a story can go without narration depends on what's happening. A poignant picture may tell part of a story so well that voiceover narration would only detract from the moment.

VIDEO	AUDIO
Anchor CU	((Tina)) People on the city's south side say their neighborhood sounded like an airport runway this morning. Just listen to this:
Take eng/nat sound Full	((—————SOT—————)) Natural sound full :03 ((—————VO—————)) ((Tina))
super: South Side	The roar was actually a high pressure gas line that the gas company started emptying at six A-M. The company is re-routing almost a half-mile of gas line near the intersection of Main and Oak because of development in the area. The company says it decided on the dawn reveille in order to get the job done in one day with minimal service interruption.

Here we point not to a picture but a sound. We'll also see what's making the noise, and so will the people tuned to the news, because this type of introduction is guaranteed to get people to pay attention. Having gotten their attention, we're going to tell them what it is. Then, as the pictures of the scene continue on, we move to the details and background of the story.

Coordinate Words and Pictures

You must not write copy that fights with the pictures. If there's a clash between what viewers see and what they hear, confusion becomes the only product. The trick in TV is finding the middle ground where the words neither duplicate nor fight with the pictures.

One technique that works well here is to coordinate the words and pictures at the beginning, then let the words move away to discuss related material while the pictures continue. That's exactly what we did in the scripts above. This way, visual scene changes make sense even as the script covers other, related ground. You can't move the script so far away that the words and pictures fight with each other. But if you start together and return periodically, you have plenty of freedom.

VIDEO	AUDIO
Anchor CU	((John)) The city said no at first, but it now looks like officials will come up with a pile of money to make up for what appears to be a wet mistake by the fire department.
Take eng/nat sound Full	((————————SOT————————)) (Water rushing along yards) :03 ((————————VO————————)) ((John))
Super: West Side	Officials suspect a fire department employee didn't follow regulations last night while flushing out some hydrants in the 14-hundred block of Smith Avenue. Big mistake. The water backed up ... breaking underground lines ... and flooding yards and basements in 10 homes. When neighbors were told they'd have to pick up the tab for repairs, they complained to the mayor and called the media. And that got just the response they wanted. ((————————SOT————————))
super: Kelly Watts Homeowner	"It was outrageous. The city created this disaster, and then they wanted us to pay for it. Well, we got together and said

```
               we'd fight this for however
               long it'd take. And we said
               we'd sure remember this in the
               next election. That's when
               things turned around." :14
         ((——————VO——————))
                    ((John))
               Damage is expected to come to
               about 12 thousand dollars. As
               of an hour ago, fire and water
               officials were still wrangling
               over which would come up with
               exactly how much of the repair
               money.
```

Again, we start the story writing to the video, then move away to give related details of what took place.

Visualizing the Story

Obviously, TV's strength lies in visual stories. Because news refuses to limit itself to visual stories, the real challenge in the business involves imagining and creating video for a nonvisual story. If a picture-poor story can be handled well in a reader, that may work the best. But a complicated—and therefore longer—story will need pictures. Think about what visuals are or might be available. Would a slightly different approach to the story make it more visual? Can you compare the issue to something that *is* visual and then move to the specifics of the story at hand? Could stills be used, inserting movement by the camera (zooming in or out or panning left or right) instead of the subject providing the action? Think about any graphics that might make a story easier to understand or more visually interesting. There are some amazing data visualization programs out there that may help you demonstrate the story.

The writing in a nonvisual story must be that much better to compensate for the visual weakness. The answer is never avoiding the story. A reporter's job is to make every story interesting—including the nonvisual one. After all, you probably don't need a reporter to tell a compelling visual story nearly as much as you need a good photographer.

"We're more like the Ford Company assembly line these days than we are storytellers," says retired NBC national correspondent Bob Dotson. "If the story itself is compelling, we're home free, but we spend tons of time trying to get the live truck up but not a whole lot of time during the day working to tell the story correctly."

Find time to do it right.

• • • • •

Picture Cautions

Use Meaningful Pictures

Although a TV story sometimes gets told in a certain way or sequence because of available pictures, there's no excuse for running video that detracts from or obscures the main point of the story. Video wallpaper—meaningless video for its own sake—adds nothing to a story. As obvious as that seems, look at how many times stations insist on running worthless video of the front door of a bank, for instance, that was held up some time earlier in the day. Nothing to see, and the doors look like any other bank, but the station took pictures of it, so it goes on the air. Why would a producer think the audience would rather see that than the highly paid, popular anchors?

Today's Pictures

It's understood that in the absence of a super to the contrary, video used on the air was shot for that particular story that day by that station. File footage that might in any way be misinterpreted should be noted on screen with a super, and any footage supplied from outside the station (or affiliated network) should also be identified.

Watch Your Supers

TV pictures allow some shortcuts in script writing. Information like geographic location, names and titles can be supered instead of written into the script. This can help move the story along, all but eliminating, for instance, the weak video of someone sitting at a desk while being introduced. But make sure all the appropriate identifiers are in the story, and don't keep the audience guessing. Late supers disorient and distract the audience.

• • • • •

CARE about the Story

Reporters generally do not get to choose every story they work on, and journalists must respond to events in the news. So you need to care about those events and the people involved, but you also need to find your own special stories to cultivate.

"You always have to have one story you're working on that you're passionate about," says Larson. If you are passionate, then sooner or later, you'll get to do it. And don't be afraid to take chances. It's hard to be really good without, occasionally, being really bad.

When you first start out, you're unsure of yourself, and you can't afford to fail. "But to be really good," says former KCBS radio's Mike Sugarman, "you have to be bad sometimes, because you're experimenting, you're pushing the envelope, and you have to do that."

Larson says the first critical mission for every reporter is to find a way to care about the story. "If *you* don't care," Larson says, "no one else will."

It is as simple—and as difficult—as that. If you don't care about your story or the people in it, you'll never make the audience care. That caring starts with the job itself.

Part of great reporting is doing something special in every story, something that separates your effort from everyone else's. If you can't articulate what it is that made your story special . . . then it's probably not.

Dotson says the key to doing that is figuring out ways to reclaim the bits of wasted time everyone has through the day. That's how you find the time to make a good story great.

Larson says that too many reporters confuse the need to be objective with "a lack of empathy and a lack of passion." Reporters need to be more passionate and more empathetic, he says. "There should be stories on a regular basis where reporters finish writing them and start to cry because they care so much."

KGO-TV reporter Wayne Freedman tells people to look away from the action. "Your best story may not be the fire," he says. "Once you get the flames, look away." Look at the people watching those flames.

"The smallest, least powerful voice frequently holds the most powerful story," notes Larson. "Think big, but then search in the smallest of places."

"When I end a story," says CBS' Steve Hartman, "I want there to be some purpose for my telling it. I don't want it to just be some candy that people munched on and didn't get any nutritional value from it. I'd like people to be left feeling something . . . or better yet, having learned something . . . not necessarily about the world but, better yet, about themselves."

● ● ● ● ●

Strong Stories Have Central Characters and a Plot

"Television is at its best when it lets the viewer experience," says Dotson, and the easiest way to get the audience's attention is to start with someone affected by the issue—as opposed to just starting with the issue.

As an example, Dotson says reporters should spend less time at city hall talking to the usual officials and more time in the neighborhood.

"Find someone who's got the problem," says Dotson. "Put the information from city hall into a visual story that reflects the day to day lives of people who are watching TV."

"I call it a quest," says Larson. "What is the quest? Whose quest is it? Great stories begin and end with people, even when you think they're not there."

Freedman tries to hook people at the beginning by finding a main character and developing a little theme. "It's basic storytelling," says Freedman. "Beginning, middle, ending and a main character. And I've added the simple truth." That "simple truth" could be the moral of the story, or it could just be a human observation. Hartman calls it a "life lesson."

●●●●●

Prove Your Story

This is another concept that's simple enough to explain but much harder to execute. Once you have your focus, your story concept and main character, you need to use the detail and sound that you've collected to prove the point you're trying to make. You do that not by telling the audience what to think or how to feel but by picking sound and bites that demonstrate the point and enable the audience to feel on their own.

"Attention to detail allows the audience to experience truths," says Larson. "You have to ask questions that go to the heart of the matter; you have to listen for poignant telling detail which will enlighten and move the audience, details which might illuminate or show the complexity or reveal the simplicity of a story. That's the craft of being a good reporter."

Larson says reporters need to listen and pay attention for the right detail: the forgotten birthday, the patron saint, a nickname. "Keep sifting details until you find a way to care," says Larson, "and then allow your viewer the same opportunity."

A number of years ago, Freedman did a story about a woman named Pam who freeze-dried her newly-departed dog, Beast, because she couldn't bear to be apart from her pet. Making fun of the woman would have been easy, but the story went beyond that. Freedman let you see the woman in the telling details he always finds. Beyond the large portrait of the dog on the wall, the general Beast decorating motif, Pam's computer opened with Beast's bark. She tended a garden of artificial plants arranged among artificial rocks. Near the end of the story, when Freedman notes that, "It's both amusing and sad," he's telling the viewer that it's okay to be confused. "If you don't understand you never will," the script reads, "and Pam wouldn't care anyway because sometimes, even in death, a pet provides comfort." That's the simple truth Freedman searches for in his stories. At the very end, we see Pam cradling the stuffed dog in her arms and petting it. Freedman asks, "Aren't you ever going to get another dog?" "There will never be another Beast," she says and pauses. "Besides, I already have a dog."

●●●●●

The Element of Surprise

Larson says that powerful stories must surprise the viewer. Not shock or stun, but "reveal something with power."

Larson says that surprise could be uncovering the truth in an investigative piece or the simple telling detail of how a mother misses a lost son. Most likely, it's what surprised you as reporter or writer when you first explored the story. It's what you learned that you didn't know, it's the surprise ending or a peculiar twist or turn along the way.

Dotson notes that if viewers can sense what's going to happen right from the beginning, then why should they watch? So he tries to add in something they didn't expect in every story he does.

Dotson once covered a "nothing tornado story"—no one hurt, limited damage. As they're shooting, they focus on an older man who keeps picking through debris.

Dotson edited the story in such a way that the audience knew he was looking for something, but he didn't find it until the last scene in the piece. Then the old man reaches down into a pile of rubble and pulls up a hunk of pink goo and puts it up right next to his face. He opens his toothless mouth and says, "Well, it got my teeth, but it didn't get me." "Now you have a piece that people are there for the last frame," says Dotson. "They notice it; they talk about it."

●●●●●

Connecting with Truths

"The simple truth is just whatever connects the viewer to the storyteller and the person in the story," says Freedman. It's the concept that you find a story about life in the news of the day. Something the viewer can relate to.

Larson speaks of universal themes, calling them echoes. "What it means to be alive," says Larson.

Sometimes we may miss the simple truth because it's so obvious. Freedman struggled with a follow-up story on some of the worst fires the San Francisco area had seen in years. Working on the story, watching emotionally drained people stare and sift through charred possessions, Freedman thought that he couldn't write this story—didn't have the right to write this story—because he hadn't suffered as they had. "That struck me as being true," says Freedman, "and I wrote it down and used it in the story: 'No one can appreciate what these people are going through unless they have done so themselves,'" the script noted. A simple truth.

Freedman says he frequently puts the simple truth in the story in the same place where it occurred to him. If you can find a story with a universal truth—or find a story's universal truth—the audience may remember it forever.

"I think that fairness and unfairness are human variables," says Deborah Potter, "Whether it's affecting one person or thousands of people, these are stories that are just automatically going to connect."

Connecting is something that Larson says we really don't do well—or often. Think of the top 10 news stories of the year in your city or state, he suggests. An election, a major local crime, a scandal in government, perhaps. Then think about the 10 most important things in your own life.

Larson says that if we were really honest, our own list would be about the birth of a son or the fear for an aging parent or the concern about breast cancer or the insecurity about employment—critically important personal truths. And yet, so often, those aren't the stories we concentrate on in TV news.

"There was always a life lesson," Hartman says, referring to his Everybody Has a Story series on CBS. "Those life lessons often focused on faith and family . . . something that really matters to a lot of people but goes unreported for the most part on network or local newscasts . . . as opposed to the coverage of crime and murder and politics which is really irrelevant to our daily lives."

If you want to be a better journalist, Larson says pay attention to the "personal truths, fears, loves, ambitions." That's what people care most about, share with each other, and most understand. And what journalism too seldom explores.

● ● ● ● ●

Summary

People tend to remember powerful pictures more than words, and if pictures tell a story, a good reporter should get out of the way. When video is more limited, you need to find relevant pictures, and structure the story around what's available. Use pictures for what they do best: convey feeling, emotion and action. Use the script to fill in what the pictures don't: details, facts and background. Natural sound is real life; use it throughout stories. Coordinate pictures and words. The real challenge in reporting is making the nonvisual story interesting. Don't use video wallpaper. The best reporters find a way to care about every story they do. Good stories have a beginning, middle and end . . . and characters that we care about. The pictures and sound should prove your story. Stories will be more memorable—even everyday stories—if you can find the universal truth in them.

●●●●●

Key Words & Phrases

power of the visual image . . . what pictures do best . . . what words do best . . . natural sound . . . video wallpaper . . . caring . . . central characters and a plot . . . stories have a beginning, middle and end . . . story focus . . . story concept . . . prove your story . . . life lesson . . . connecting with truths

●●●●●

Exercises

A. Come up with three workable television story ideas. The first one should be a strong visual story for TV. The second should have a strong audio element (not bites but strong natural sound). The third should emphasize content but should specifically be a weak video story. Explain why each story is strong or weak visually or audibly and/or why it would be easy or hard to do on TV.

B. Do enough research on each story so that you can write out how the story might work on TV. You can actually interview people so you can write out exact quotes or you can envision what someone might say for the story. The goal here is to construct on paper how these stories *might* look and sound. How are you going to get out of the way of the strong pictures? How are you going to feature the strong audio element(s)? How are you going to visualize the story that isn't inherently visual?

C. Research, record and edit the stories for real. What worked out as you expected? What didn't?

D. Which stations in your area use one-man-bands, and how much do they use them? Note the categories of usage in the chapter, and make a list of the stations in your market area and where each falls in the list.

13

•••••

Producing News on TV

Producing is what brings order out of chaos. A television news program is, at its core, simply a collection of news stories along with specialized segments. A well-produced show brings some measure of coherence and logic to what are otherwise unconnected bits of information.

Viewers frequently remark that one station's news looks much like another. Given a reasonably consistent definition of news, the more hard, breaking news events on any given day, the more likely that competing stations will look alike.

Most days, however, there are relatively few "must run" stories. So slow news days tend to highlight the different approaches that at least some stations take.

Many stations have an explicit news approach and philosophy. It might be an emphasis on consumer, investigative, crime, standing up for the underdog stories; it might be "live and late breaking"; it might be something else. What's typically at issue is a general approach to news and the kinds of stories that a station especially seeks out. Some stations take a harder edge, some put music behind stories, while others would never allow that. Some stations handle most significant stories with a live element; some stations frequently bring reporters on the set or live in the newsroom; some stations work at giving their video an edgier, gritty feel.

It's useful for everyone in the newsroom if the station articulates a news philosophy so that everyone understands what the station is trying to do and how it plans to accomplish that goal.

•••••

Overview

The average television station produces more than five hours of local news every weekday. Stations will commonly run two or three hours in the morning before the network morning news programs start at 7 a.m. That means starting local news at 4:30 or 5 a.m. Or earlier. Then there are local "cut-ins" during the network morning news shows. Many stations run news for a half hour at noon. Some run more. Then afternoon news starts at most stations by 4 or 5 p.m. (sometimes earlier) and commonly runs to 6:30 p.m. or 7 p.m. Depending on time zone, tradition and/or philosophy, the network news usually comes on for a half hour at 5:30 p.m. or at 6:30 p.m. Then stations commonly run 30–35 minutes of news at 11 p.m. in Eastern and Pacific time or 10 p.m. Central and Mountain time.

Those are typical times for stations that run news and are affiliated with ABC, CBS or NBC. Fox affiliates are most likely to run news an hour earlier than the late news: 10 p.m. in Eastern and Pacific and 9 p.m. in Central and Mountain. That newscast might run for either half an hour or an hour, depending on market, news tradition, competition or other factors. The number two news time for Fox affiliates is in the morning, followed by early evening.

Almost all (96–99 percent) of the stations affiliated with ABC, CBS, Fox and NBC run local news. But more and more stations actually get their local news from another station. While more than 80 percent of ABC, CBS and NBC stations produce their own news, only 41 percent of Fox affiliates produce their own local news.

Considerably fewer CW or independent stations run local news, but if they do, they tend to follow a schedule similar to Fox affiliates.

Along with the 705 local stations that originate local news (and have their own newsrooms), another 357 stations—mostly Fox, CW and independents—also run local news that they get from one of those 705 stations. Over the last decade, the number of TV newsrooms has slowly but fairly steadily decreased, and the number of stations getting news from another station has steadily gone up.

Currently, the biggest growth in local news is actually among Spanish-language stations, generally affiliates of Telemundo or Univision. Hispanic stations tend to run news early and late evening, but schedules and amount vary considerably.

Obviously, the cable news channels run news all day long. In addition to the national channels—CNN, Fox, MSNBC and CNBC—there are a number of regional and local cable news channels running news 24 hours a day, and there are a few local, independent TV stations that run a huge amount of local news each day.

● ● ● ● ●

Audience

The audience available for each newscast varies by time of day, and how they watch the news varies as well.

The biggest growth area in TV news is in the morning. That's been true for several years, and overall, morning news is rapidly becoming the top time for TV news. Less clear is how the audience watches morning news. The presumption is that people turn on the news in the morning and go about their business—more listening than watching, much like radio news. The research isn't definitive yet, and audience behavior may also be changing.

The noon audience is primarily made up of three groups: retired, unemployed and housewives and stay-at-home parents. Overall, the audience tends to be older (because of the large number of retired people watching), and the audience tends to sit and watch the news rather than doing a mixture of other activities.

The blending of other activity and news tends to be the norm in the early part of the afternoon newscasts. The time before the 6 p.m. news tends to be busy in most households with kids returning from school or play, dinner preparations and so on. Newscasts in the afternoon tend to skew female. At 6 p.m., the news audience jumps as a lot more people return home, turn on the news and focus more on it, and the audience is more balanced by gender.

The late news audience is again balanced male-female (although some research suggests it skews male) and, at the end of the day, viewers tend to focus more on the newscast (rather than doing other things along with watching). For many stations, this is the most important newscast of the day. That's not because of content but because of money. Even though the 6 p.m. news usually has more people watching, the late news tends to have a younger audience that more advertisers want to reach, so the late news tends to have the most expensive local news advertising rates of the day and to bring in the most money (per minute) for the station.

Audience Flow

Never underestimate the power of inertia. Even with the remote control, the channel people have been watching has the advantage as people move from one half hour of viewing to the next. Lead-in is critical.

That also means that whatever channel people were watching when they went to bed is the one that comes on automatically in the morning, although that's not the case with some cable systems. People may well change the channel, but the late-night winner has a leg up in the morning.

A popular game show will bring a large base to the noon newscast (the *Price Is Right* is tough competition), and popular talk shows in the afternoon provide a boost to the first afternoon newscast. The late news follows network prime time, so whichever network is particularly strong (or weak) in that last show before the news determines the potential base for the late news. Each network has particular strength on different nights, and different entertainment programs tend to deliver more or fewer men versus women, older audience versus younger. Generally, NFL football delivers the highest audience, which is why there's so much of it on TV on an increasing number of nights.

Why can't people just switch channels? They can, and they do. But whatever prime-time program people are watching determines which news promos they see, so the late news on that channel has an extra shot at convincing people to stay with the channel they're on. Then there's inertia.

What about people using a DVR (digital video recorder) to record and watch news when it's more convenient? The latest figures (Nielsen 2015) show that 50 percent of U.S. homes have a DVR, but the amount of TV viewing from DVR has changed little. And given the short shelf life of news, few people record and watch news through the DVR.

●●●●●

Newscast Structure

All newscasts contain news and weather, and that news includes a blend of stories and story types (see Chapters 2 and 11). Sports and special segments appear in select newscasts.

Early morning newscasts (before the morning network news) frequently skip sports unless there's something unusual, and special morning segments tend to be limited to large and major markets. Stations will run local, national and international news, and weather. Traffic, too, if it's a big enough city. The morning news is actually a series of mostly repeated newscasts. Depending on the station and market, the news cycle could be 20, 30 or even 60 minutes, largely repeating with some updates and minor changes after each interval. Since few TV stations have more than one or two reporters (at most) working in the early morning, much of the local news is actually from the night before.

Once the morning network news starts, the local station will simply supply local cut-ins: roughly five-minute newscasts each half hour with just local news and weather and maybe traffic.

In the afternoon, before 6 p.m. or the network newscast, local stations will generally run a mix of local, national and international news along with weather and, if applicable, traffic. Generally, there will be no sports, but expect to see health news, which tends to be especially popular with women.

The 6 p.m. news is commonly the local newscast of record. Expect to see local news, weather and sports. It would be unusual to have national or international news, since the network newscast is on right next to this newscast (usually just before).

The late-evening news summarizes, overall, the news of the day, so you'll see local, national and international news, weather and sports.

News, Weather and Sports

In a typical day, when there is not extraordinary local news, the audience is probably most interested in weather, then news, then, way back, sports. Generalizations are risky and not without exceptions, but that's the way it works.

So why don't stations start with weather? Well, sometimes they do. If the weather has been—or is expected to be—exceptional, stations will almost always start the newscast with weather. If the weather is ordinary, then stations start with news, as much to tell the audience that "this" (whatever the top story is) is the most important local news that it has. In some measure, it's a reassurance that the world is largely the way we left it when we last checked the news.

Note that the first commercial of the newscast doesn't usually come until at least eight or nine minutes after the start of the newscast. Note also that the weather almost always comes shortly after the quarter hour. Note, too, that sports almost always comes at the end of the newscast. Television is way too researched for accidents. This is programming for ratings.

Television station ratings are conducted primarily by the Nielsen Company and are tracked in 15-minute intervals, although people meters are likely to change that eventually. If you take a look at a ratings report, you'll see that stations get a rating for 6 p.m., for instance, then 6:15 p.m. and then 6:30 p.m. and so on. In order for a station to get credit for 15 minutes of viewing, someone (or, technically, the household) must watch the station for at least 5 minutes of the 15-minute block of time. On a theoretical basis, that means the same person could show up as audience for three different stations. In practice, it doesn't work that way.

The reason a station runs its longest block of news at the top of the show is that a viewer is unlikely to change channels while the news itself is on. Once a station goes to a commercial, at least some people may hit the remote and check out the alternatives. Or turn off the TV. As long as that first commercial comes after at least 5 minutes, the station will get credit for the 15-minute viewing block.

Weather comes shortly after the quarter hour because stations know that it's another major draw for the audience. Stations run weather just after the quarter hour in order to get credit for another 15 minutes of viewing.

Sports comes at the end where it won't do much damage. Considerably fewer people follow sports, and a few stations have dropped sports as a defined unit in the newsroom, having regular reporters handle specific sports stories just as they handle other news. Part of the thinking behind dropping sports, or at least cutting it back, is that sports fans have so many other options for getting information, like ESPN, that they no longer need the sports segment of the news. On the other hand, while the sports audience is relatively small (except in some markets), it tends to be rabid, so dropping sports completely could be a risky venture. My research on this (I ask the question periodically as part of the RTDNA Surveys) suggests that there's no mass movement to cut back on sports, but it's certainly not a growing area in local TV.

Special Segments, Franchises and Features

Along with the standard news, weather and sports, many stations run special segments. In a large city, traffic reports are common in the morning and afternoon newscasts. They might be delivered by the anchor, a reporter at a traffic center or a helicopter reporter.

Probably the most common beats that stations assign to reporters include health and consumer (and education, which doesn't usually translate into special segments). Many stations run health reports in the 4 p.m. and 5 p.m. newscasts. Some of those are done by the station itself; others are purchased from one of the several companies that supply health news either for a fee or in exchange for the station running ads that the company supplies or both.

A lot of stations run a consumer feature, although placement varies from one station to the next. Those segments are usually done locally with a particular reporter specializing in that area.

Some stations also produce regular features on child or pet adoption, food, gardening, entertainment reports and reviews, and a wide variety of specialty areas that stations have developed. Some of those run daily, some weekly, some in between.

Stations also purchase a variety of special interest segments that they use to fill out newscasts. "Mr. Food" is a common noontime feature. *Consumer Reports, Better Homes and Gardens* and some other publications and companies produce TV features. There are even companies that produce special series for use during sweeps (ratings periods).

Story Repetition

Chapter 2, "News," notes that stories have a life cycle that ends within 24 hours unless there are new developments. But as stations run more and more news and add more and more newscasts, there's a growing tendency to "re-rack" stories from earlier newscasts. This is especially true on the weekend, where thin staffing leads stations into replaying complete packages one or even two days after their original broadcast. Networks aren't immune to this, either. Some networks have filled much or all of the second half of their weekend newscasts with stories lifted in their entirety from earlier news programs.

● ● ● ● ●

Building a Local Newscast

From a structural or form standpoint, the newscast producer has a mix and match of readers, voiceovers, VO/SOTs, packages and live shots (see Chapter 11). Chapter 2 discusses story types from an assignment perspective.

From a news standpoint, anything is possible. Keep in mind that, as noted earlier, certain newscasts contain only certain elements.

We have trained the audience to expect the top story at the top of the newscast. Barring staggering major national or international news, that's going to be a local story, regardless of the newscast. The strongest story should get the audience's attention; it sets the tone for the newscast, and it introduces the anchors. Many stations also start with what's called a "cold open." That means that the beginning of the newscast starts with natural sound or a bite from the top story, followed by the anchors talking about the story and, perhaps, introducing a live report. Then what?

First, let's back up. Newscasts are broken up into blocks, separated by commercials. The exact number of blocks of news and other information tends to vary by both newscast and station—determined, ultimately, by the number and placement of commercials. Some stations number the blocks—typically four or five in a half hour—some use letters (A, B, C, etc.). The first block includes the top story, usually includes the most meaningful events of the day and is the longest block. Remember, it has to go eight or nine minutes to capture audience and ensure rating credit. The second block, a much shorter one, also contains news, commonly contains station franchises (like health or consumer stories) and promotes the weather coming up. The second block also varies depending on events and the time of day. For instance, in the late evening news, the second block might well concentrate on national and international news. The third block is primarily the weather. Weather is ultimately local, so a local events calendar or local arts or music events might go well there; or severe weather from elsewhere around the country; or a lighter local news story. The fourth block is primarily sports. Because sports appeals to a relatively small part of the audience, it might be useful to add into that block some stories that might have a wider appeal, especially ones with strong and promotable pictures. The fifth block may contain the kicker (a light story run at the end of the newscast) and a look ahead to the next newscast. The kicker should be a highly promotable story—preferably local and with video—that helps keep the non-sports audience through the sports. After the first three blocks, there's a bit more variety in approach from station to station.

So in putting together a newscast, it's not just an open pit into which stuff gets poured. There's a prescribed outline into which the day's events must fit, and good producers think about where each story might go when the assignments are set in the morning meeting (see Chapter 2).

There's been a trend away from starting the newscast with a traditional newscast open, promoting the anchors. More and more, stations start with the top story in order to grab the attention of the viewer. The old newscast open frequently runs later in the block. Also to attract interest, stations tend to try to start each block with a strong video story—rather than a simple reader.

Determining flow within each block depends on the events of the day. Are there stories that logically flow out of or somehow connect to the top story? If the top story is a strike at a major local business, do you have other local business/labor news to go afterward? You also need a strong lead for the second block, so think about what will go there. Promotion for blocks three and four concentrates on weather and sports, respectively.

As producer, you also need to pay attention to story form. Reporter packages tend to slow down the pace of a newscast because a package means a lot of time, relatively speaking, on one story. Readers and voiceovers tend to pick the pace up because they're usually shorter. So you need to spread out different story forms so that you don't run package after package after package and then reader after reader after reader. Some stations like to have what's called a "high story count." Doing that requires fewer and shorter packages. That means you should have given all of this some thought when stories were assigned earlier in the day.

The producer also determines which anchor will read which story. Generally, in a dual anchor situation, the producer will have each anchor read about the same number of stories, although many stations have a "lead" anchor who will typically read a little more and is more likely to lead the show and introduce the top story. Note that many producers don't have anchors simply alternate stories. That would create an annoying ping-pong effect in news delivery.

Just to give you an idea, here's what a newscast lineup might look like:

6 P.M. Newscast

00:00–00:08	intro
00:08–00:25	anchors lead in to reporter at the airport
00:25–02:25	reporter live at airport . . . leads into news package on an emergency landing . . . reporter live out of package . . . crosstalk with anchors
02:25–03:05	anchor VO/SOT follow-up to opening report
03:05–03:27	anchor VO (fatal accident)
03:27–04:43	anchor introduces reporter live from south side traffic tie-up . . . reporter package . . . reporter live tag
04:43–05:16	anchor VO (new state law on sex offenders)
05:16–05:30	anchors intro story and go to reporter on set
05:30–05:40	reporter on set intros story
05:40–08:10	package with voiceovers (child molestation)
08:10–08:34	reporter on set wraps up package
08:34–08:53	anchor intros story and goes to reporter in the newsroom

08:53–10:03	reporter intros story and does voiceover for video (teen-age bank robber)
10:03–10:14	tease: reporter promos upcoming story with stand-up
10:14–12:19	commercial break
12:19–12:36	anchors intro story and go to reporter
12:36–12:41	reporter intros story (development in neighboring county)
12:41–14:28	package with voiceover
14:28–14:33	reporter tags out
14:33–14:37	tease: weather
14:37–16:49	commercial break
16:49–19:27	weather
19:27–19:32	anchors toss to sports reporter
19:32–19:49	tease: reporter previews sports report
19:49–20:21	bumper: stock updates (visual, no voice)
20:21–22:38	commercial break
22:38–26:12	sports . . . including sports reporter live in the field
26:12–26:45	evening weather update
26:45–26:50	good-bye

11 P.M. Newscast

00:00–00:08	intro
00:08–00:29	anchors intro lead story (three dead in shooting) and toss to live reporter
00:29–02:58	reporter live intro into package . . . live tag and crosstalk with anchors
02:58–03:20	anchor VO on suspect at large
03:20–03:32	anchors intro story and toss to package
03:32–05:13	package (battered women shelter)
05:13–05:34	reporter tags out live from the newsroom
05:34–05:57	anchors VO follow-up (drunk driving)
05:57–06:22	anchor VO (radio fraud)
06:22–06:48	anchor VO (voting machines)
06:48–07:02	anchor VO (politician's father dies)
07:02–08:39	anchor VO (3 quick national headlines)
08:39–09:10	anchor voiceover (health franchise)
09:10–09:44	tease: what's to come
09:44–12:00	commercial break
12:00–12:17	anchor intros story and tosses to reporter
12:17–13:46	package (new kind of Catholic prep school)
13:46–13:57	reporter tags story out from newsroom
13:57–14:40	anchor VO (air traffic control)
14:40–15:39	reporter VO (convenience store robbery)
15:39–15:54	tease weather
15:54–17:54	commercial break

17:54–18:12   anchors toss to weather
18:12–21:12   weather
21:12–21:29   anchor VO (former President Bush appearance)
21:29–21:45   tease: preview of upcoming sports
21:45–22:00   bumper: lotto numbers (visual, no voice)
22:00–24:32   commercial break
24:32–28:02   sports
28:02–28:05   tease: coming up later
28:05–31:07   commercial break
31:07–31:12   good-bye

The 6 p.m. newscast (pp. 173–174) runs a total of 26:50 (after subtracting commercials just before and just after the newscast). Of that, 12:56 is news, 3:34 is sports, 3:01 is weather, :45 goes to intro, teases, bumps and close, and 6:34 is commercial time.

The 11 p.m. newscast (pp. 174–175) runs a total of 31:12 (after subtracting commercials just before and just after the newscast). Of that, 13:16 is news, 3:30 is sports, 3:00 is weather, 1:36 includes intro, teases, bumps and close, and 9:50 is commercial time.

The newscasts (above) came from different stations, and you can see some differences in approach to commercials and teases.

Chapter 21, "TV Script Form and Supers . . . Glossary," includes notes on standard newscast abbreviations and a typical format for newscast supers.

Determining the newscast lineup isn't the end of the job; it's really just the beginning. The stories in the lineup are there based on what you, as producer, think they're going to be. Stories change, and that may affect their placement. Your lineup, determined hours (preferably three and a half to four hours) before the newscast, assumes that news won't break out between then and airtime. News has a pesky way of breaking out whenever, and a good producer has to be ready to completely change a newscast in order to respond to events of the day—even at the last minute.

Then there's the flow within the newscast. Reporters and writers should put together each story in the best way possible. In the end, those stories also have to flow one after the other as well as possible, and it's up to the producer to ensure that flow. That commonly means rewriting story lead-ins so that they *logically* flow from the previous story. *Logically* flow. If they don't or can't flow logically, just move on. A forced "transition" that basically says the next story has nothing to do with the previous one is a waste of time. See also "Transitions Between Stories" in Chapter 4, pages 45–49.

Newscasts these days tend to be all about live reporting. Audiences have indicated that they like live reporting, and even while many people in the business feel that they too often go live for live's sake—from a site where nothing has happened for hours—the audience seems surprisingly forgiving where live is concerned.

Live reporting increases the producing challenge because it clearly offers an opportunity for problems and surprises. Technical problems could kill a live shot; events could make a live shot dangerous or inappropriate; a live camera is an idiot-magnet for spectators who have too little happening in their own lives, and there's no telling what someone may do in the background or to the reporter; and then there's simply controlling the total time spent in reporter talk and/or reporter-anchor crosstalk.

● ● ● ● ●

Teases and Promos

Teases are those things at the end of news blocks designed to convince the audience to stay through the commercials because what's coming up is worth waiting for. They're written much the same as *promos*, which are free-standing program elements—run like commercials within entertainment programs—intended to get people to watch or listen to the news. Don't confuse either with journalism. Teases and promos are designed to get people to listen to or watch the news, and they're written in the same basic style as news. But they're not news, and, in fact, they usually fail if they have real news value to them.

Why cover them, even briefly, in a book about writing news? Two reasons: First, news people write almost all news teases, and news people are commonly called on to write or approve news promos. Second, the flagrant disregard for responsibility and the audience in teases and promos contributes heavily to the negative perception many people in the audience have about the broadcast news business. We'd be in a lot better shape if we wrote teases and promos better and more responsibly.

● ● ● ● ●

Promotion

Stations seem to view teases and promos as anything from among the most important products on the air—hiring people specifically to write them—to the least important—letting interns and production assistants handle the load. More often than not, the task falls to the newscast producer. At least some studies show that promos—especially in TV where some run in prime time—can make a big difference in the size of the audience. The more interesting the news program looks or sounds, the more likely people will watch. Teases can do the same thing. Later in the newscast, when people may be more likely to tune out—either because of the time or because they're not interested in sports—teases can make the difference as to whether the audience is still there.

● ● ● ● ●

Tease . . . Don't Tell

The most common mistake in teases and proms is telling the audience what the news is:

No TEASE: Coming up next, Mike tells us about the beautiful weather we have in store for our area.

No TEASE: Coming up next, two favorites of Cincinnati Bengals fans lose their jobs this Labor Day. John Smith and Jim Jones are among the latest players cut. We'll tell you why ... when we come back.

No TEASE: All the trouble on the University of Oklahoma football team has cost the job of their winningest coach. John has sports ... next.

There's really no reason for the audience to stay through the commercials to hear about any of those stories. The writers have already told the audience what the news is.

The key to successful teases is telling the audience just enough to get them interested—but not so much that they don't need to stay tuned. Take a look at how those three teases, which went on the air (with names changed), could have been improved to do what they're supposed to do:

BETTER

TEASE: You're going to like what's coming up next. Mike with the weather ... when we come back.

BETTER

TEASE: Coming up next, two favorites of Cincinnati Bengals fans lose their jobs this Labor Day. The latest list of who's been cut ... when we come back.

BETTER

TEASE: The winningest coach in college football loses his job. John has sports ... next.

These revised versions give the audience a reason to keep watching or listening. In the first case it's fairly obvious that we're going to get a nice weather forecast, but the audience can't like what they don't hear. They'll be there. Both the second and third examples are designed to pique the curiosity of even the most marginal sports fan.

Note also that although these teases are designed to get people's attention, they also do nothing to irritate the audience by either promising something that can't be delivered or delaying information that might be considered critical to someone's safety and well-being.

• • • • •

Make Them Care

Another common problem in teases is that they're simply not compelling or not of wide enough interest. Too many teases are greeted with an indifferent "who cares?" attitude on the part of the audience:

WEAK
TEASE: The Logan Elm school district will have to cut its budget. We'll have a report.

WEAK
TEASE: A little extra sleep may help you. Dr. Jane Smith will explain on Health News.

The first tease will only work—if at all—with people in the Logan Elm school district. Even then, it's pretty dry. Worse, Logan Elm is a relatively small school district outside the core city, so its strongest appeal is to a tiny portion of the total audience.

Most people would grab a little extra sleep if they could, so the second example isn't much of a tease either. Neither gets the audience to care. Rewrite them to broaden the interest and raise a question the audience will want the answer to:

BETTER
TEASE: What happens to school districts when voters say no? We'll take a look at some of the tough cuts facing one system.

BETTER
TEASE: Is extra sleep good or bad? Dr. Jane Smith has the answer on Health News.

The first rewrite on the school system attempts to broaden the appeal to make the story a possible answer to problems that every school district might face—and to write the tease in a more compelling fashion. The second tease raises a question to which most people are likely to want the answer.

While questions in news stories are almost always inappropriate, questions in teases and promos make sense. In news stories we're supposed to be answering questions, not asking them. In teases and promos we're specifically *not* answering questions. We're commonly raising questions that require the audience to watch the news to learn the answers.

Here are some teases that went on the air that worked:

Good

TEASE: Just ahead, the naked truth about snowmen ... and the people who build them.

Good

TEASE: What's warm and fuzzy and now a part of the police force? We'll have the answer ... when we come back.

Good

TEASE: Up next ... a marriage where the groom got cold feet ... and cold hands ... and cold arms ... and we'll tell you about it ... right after this.

Good

TEASE: When we come back, a dying woman loses her money, her car, and her home. She says people she hired to take care of her ripped her off.

Good

TEASE: What do dogs and coffee have to do with our government? Coming up at five ... the strange studies being funded with our tax dollars.

These work because they're tightly written; they're cute, clever, intriguing or compelling; and they make you want to stay to find out exactly what they're talking about. Short and clever, the first example above makes a strong case for something worth seeing. The second and last use questions that are just peculiar enough to pique our curiosity. The third one sounds like a fun, oddball story. The fourth one says we're going to see a strong human story. All of them promise something that will get the audience's attention.

● ● ● ● ●

Going Too Far

Although some teases and promos don't work because they either tell us too much or don't get our attention, a bigger problem comes with telling people things we shouldn't.

■ Don't say *coming up next* if it isn't. At the least, if you use that phrase, make sure the story is in the next block—preferably, the first story up. If you're going to promote a story for the end of the newscast, tell the audience that it's *coming up later, still to come,* or something of the sort. We're in the news business; never lie to or mislead the audience.

■ Don't promise what you can't deliver. If you promote a story as *compelling,* make sure it's compelling. If it's not, do the story better, don't promote it or don't exaggerate in the promotion. People feel cheated if what they get isn't what you promised. Quite a few years ago, a large-market TV anchor told the audience that coming up, there were 10,000 dead in some small town not too far away. The dead turned out to be chickens. Think how amusing that story was for all the people who had friends and family in that town. Think about what station they *won't* turn to tomorrow. And if you're promising great pictures, make sure you can deliver. Again, don't lie or mislead.

■ Don't tease audience safety or well-being. If you really have a story that affects the safety and well-being of the audience, tell people what it is; don't blithely tease that you'll tell them the information later. If the story is that strong, tell people what it is, and tell them that you'll have more information coming up. If the story is real, they'll tune in. *Not* giving the audience information that's truly a matter of public safety makes clear that you care about the audience only as a commodity. You would never treat someone you cared about that way; don't do it to the audience.

● ● ● ● ●

Summary

In the end, the producer's primary job is to get on the air on time, get off the air on time and run all the commercials in between. Those are not optional. Everything else is potentially up for grabs and remains that way until the newscast is over.

For some, producing a newscast is seven hours (or so) of normal news work, a half hour of panic, and a half hour of chaos. The more productively those seven hours are spent, the less likely you'll face either panic or chaos.

Producing is what brings order out of chaos. The average television station produces more than five hours of local news every weekday. Different newscasts appeal to different audiences and, therefore, contain different elements, although news and weather are in all newscasts. Newscasts generally start with the top story, and a newscast is divided into blocks, each of which contains certain material. The length and timing of the blocks are designed to achieve maximum ratings.

Teases run at the end of news blocks to convince the audience to stay through the commercials. Promos are free-standing program elements intended to get people to watch or listen to the news. Neither involves journalism. Good teases and promos get the audience interested without telling them exactly what's coming up. Don't tease real safety issues. If the public's safety is at stake, just give them the news.

●●●●●
Key Words & Phrases

producer . . . newscasts . . . ratings . . . blocks . . . franchises . . . audience flow . . . newscast structure . . . teases . . . promos

●●●●●
Exercises

A. Record a half hour or hour of a morning TV newscast. Write down all the stories, elements, story forms and which anchor reads each story or lead-in in the newscast. Note when the station went to commercials (and for how long). What can you tell about the thinking that went into the producing of the newscast? Did the producer work to tie stories together? Did the producer mix up the different story forms?

B. Record another half hour newscast (5 p.m. or 6 p.m. or late news) and compare that one with the morning show. How are the shows different in terms of content? Can you see different approaches to the producing itself?

C. Take the material in one of the newscasts you recorded and see whether you can rearrange the material in a way that improves the newscast. Why do you think it's better?

D. Using any edition of your local newspaper, assemble a half hour local newscast based on the material available in the paper. Explain why you did what you did.

14

• • • • •

Radio/Audio: Story Forms and Working with Sound

Not so long ago, when we talked about audio, that meant radio. Today, radio is simply one aspect of the audio storytelling spectrum. Audio is now a standard part of information websites. More than 60 percent of radio websites include audio, and even more include streaming audio. But it's not just radio websites. More than half of TV websites include audio (56 percent), and 39 percent include streaming audio. More and more newspaper websites include audio as well, and more and more slideshows are cut to audio.

Regardless of whether we're talking about websites or radio, the basic principles of working with sound remain the same.

• • • • •

Radio Story Forms

Television divides stories based on the technical aspects of the construction, but radio generally divides its stories based on a mixture of technical construction and the origin of sound:

■ The *reader*, as in TV, simply involves the newscaster/anchor/announcer reading a script with no outside sound.

■ *Actualities*, which are radio's version of TV bites, are the "actual" sounds of a news event or newsmaker. This can include chanting protestors or comments from the mayor.

■ *Nat*, *natural* or *ambient* sound (among other names) includes the "natural" or general sound of a meeting, traffic, playground—whatever the news event is about. Some consider the sound of chanting protestors (listed above as an actuality) to be nat sound, but it's probably better to distinguish the two on the basis of function. Actualities involve the use of words to be understood, and nat sound creates a feel for a part of a story, serves as a sound bridge between story elements or serves as an audio bed under the reporter in a wrap.

- *Voicer* is a radio report that includes just the sound of a reporter reading a story, most often limited to 20–30 seconds in commercial radio and a little longer in public radio.
- *Wrap* or *wraparound* is a voicer that includes one or more actualities. These are most often limited to 30–60 seconds in commercial radio but can be considerably longer in public radio, especially with the added use of nat sound.
- *Live* or *ROSR* (radio on scene report) is a live report from the scene of a story.

●●●●●

Drawing Radio Pictures

The Words

In many respects, radio is the most visual of all the media. Television pictures are limited to the number of diagonal inches on the screen, but radio offers the opportunity for limitless images in the mind's eye. The price of that opportunity is the precision and storytelling ability necessary to evoke those images.

Unlike television, radio allows no shortcuts, no easy way out. Names and details cannot be supered on the screen. Charts and diagrams and animation cannot make clearer what the words do not. Poignant pictures can carry the television writer; radio writers must draw those pictures from scratch.

Using Nat Sound

There is some help available, although it's frequently not used. Natural sound can do for radio what pictures do for TV. Natural sound can give us the "feel" of being there. We may not be able to see the scene, but, properly done, we should be able to feel it and fill in the visual details coupling well-drawn words with listener imagination.

Nat sound is available for most stories. We don't get it for two reasons: 1) We don't think about it enough, and 2) We aren't there to get it. Radio's ability to gather news inexpensively via the telephone also contributes to its mediocrity. It's hard to gather nat sound over the phone. You can get actualities from anybody you can reach, but you can't get the sound—and feel—of being there. Cost factors will always limit our ability to get out and gather the news in person. It also means that we shouldn't miss local opportunities to collect nat sound.

Other than straight interviews, everything offers ambient sound. It's not just the obvious such as stories on racing and protest marches; even meetings have sound to them. Traffic, children at play or in school, factories, sporting events and lunch counters all have special sounds that can help give the audience the feel of going on location. One of the first things a radio reporter should do out on a story is to listen and record the natural sounds of the event. Frequently called a *wild track*, this sound is used either full (nat sound full) or as background under the track of a reporter's story or wrap. The effect makes all the difference between having the listener merely informed about an event and having the listener transported to it.

Weave the nat sound in and through every report you can. Natural sound bridges used full volume can also help change the mood or location of a story or presage new information not yet delivered. Critically, it continuously sets the scene and reinforces the credibility of the report. You cannot get that sound without being there.

"You have to have a passion," says Mike Sugarman, whose work at KCBS radio in San Francisco earned him perhaps more local, state, regional and national awards than any other local commercial radio reporter in the country.

Sugarman says he gets really excited about good sound. "I remember coming home once doing some story where I was at a bowling alley, and my wife said, 'Some reporters go to Sarajevo and get really excited. You get to the back of a bowling alley, and that's what you get excited about.' Because it was great sound; I just loved it."

Sugarman says he looks for that kernel, that little bit that he finds interesting or important or fascinating. "If *you* think it's dull," says Sugarman, "then it's going to be dull."

Listen to the Sound Quality

Be careful about the quality and clarity of both nat sound and actualities. First, remember where your audience is. A lot of radio listening takes place while people are doing other things—commonly getting ready for work or driving in the car. That means you're competing with the distractions of other things, including other people, road noise and the general obligations of paying attention to driving. It also means that actualities must be sharp and clear to be understood. A great actuality is worthless if the audience can't make it out. Don't depend on someone turning up the car radio and straining to hear. It won't happen.

Although you can run nat sound under a reporter track recorded cleanly in the studio, you normally can't run nat sound under actualities. Most aren't done under technical conditions good enough to handle the competition. Besides, the actualities should include their own ambient sound.

Putting It All Together

Watch the weaving of words and sound to create a feel for the story:

Intro: About 24-thousand people here are expected to be without a home at some point in the next year. For most of us, that's pretty hard to imagine. But as reporter Bob Smith found out for this special series on homelessness, it's a harsh reality growing at an alarming rate. :15

MAN AT SHELTER CALLING OUT NAME: "Jones ... Jones ... is Sam Jones here? :04 ... *fade nat sound under: man calling names*

SMITH: If you sign up early enough ... if you wait in line long enough ... you might get a bed. But even if you can't, usually there's still space. On a couch ... in a chair ... a patch of floor. :10

NAT FULL: people talking :03 ... *fade nat sound under*

SMITH: Just over half the area homeless will spend the night in a place like this ... one of eight emergency shelters in the city. :06

NAT FULL: street sounds/traffic full :03 ... *fade nat sound under*

SMITH: The rest? Well, some stay in cheap hotels ... a few with friends or family ... some will make camp under a bridge ... some will just be on the streets or in cars or shacks — like Shorty. :10

SHORTY: *(voice sounds old, shaky and with a hint of alcohol)* "I got no place to go. The only thing I got is gettin' cans. Copper and brass and stuff like that. That's all I got." *(fade voice under)*:08

SMITH: He's 46 years old ... but he looks and sounds twice that. He's bundled in layers of tattered cloth. Blood from a large cut on his forehead has dried where it flowed. :10

SHORTY: "When you're living by yourself like this, sometimes you need to get your mind off things." *(voice trails off ... under)*:06

SMITH: Shorty looks down at an empty bottle of vodka on the dirt floor of his shack ... a home of discarded wood and cardboard. :07

SHORTY: "Quite often I get depressed. But it's one of the things I have to overcome, you know? I'm the only one that can do it. I get depressed ... get lonely ... and lonesome. *(pause)* But I have my cat. *(cat meows)* My cat keeps me company." *(cat meows)* *(nat sound outside under)* :16

SMITH: Less than a week later, Shorty died. His real name was L-D Beeler. The autopsy report says he died of natural causes ... mostly alcohol. He's in the city morgue now. :11

NAT FULL: sound of people in bar :03 ... *then under*

SMITH: A group of his friends at the West Broad Street bar are trying to raise the money to bury Shorty.

:05 *(cross-fade nat sound under from bar to slight wind outside)* If they can't ... and no one claims him ... the city will have the body cremated. Eventually, Shorty's remains will be buried with 60 others in a single grave. :09 *(start bringing music up under)* Anonymous dust in a pile of ashes. :03 ... total: :17

GROUP AT SHELTER SINGING: "Amazing Grace, how sweet the sound that saved a wretch like me." *(sound under)* :14

SMITH: Back at the shelter, there's almost always a good turnout for prayers and singing as supper time approaches. :06

GROUP: prayer of thanks: :04 ... *and under*

SMITH: This is the story of the city's homeless ... and the many different groups — and people — that includes. Tomorrow ... day-to-day survival ... life in the shelter. I'm Bob Smith. :10

At 2:28 tape time, this is a long radio story—more attuned to public radio than commercial radio—but there's no inherent difference in technique. Notice the similarity in technical approach and pacing to a television package. There's one 16-second actuality, but most are just a few seconds longer than the many natural sound bridges that help to give a feel for the story. Notice the physical description—the audience needs to "see" Shorty. Notice also that the narration is broken up into short bits, mostly 6–10 seconds. The one long one of 17 seconds has two natural sound changes or bridges within it. Note also the use of a strong central character to help tell a story. In this case, Shorty is a vehicle to tell a larger story of one segment of a city's homeless population. We commonly attempt to humanize stories this way. It's easy for a story about the homeless to seem distant and one-dimensional. A story tends to have a lot more meaning when we bring it down to the level of a single human being or family. It's about getting the audience to care. By the way, the story—and names, other than the reporter—are real.

Former NBC correspondent Don Larson complains about all the "empty people" in the news. He says there's no dimension to many of the people we cover, and so there's no reason for the audience to care. "It's like there's been a vampire that runs through the news every day and sucks the blood out of every possible human being," says Larson.

Notice also the detail in the homeless story—like the description of the shack, the clothing, the bottle. NPR's Susan Stamberg believes details tell the story, and she works to draw strong visual images for her radio audience. That attention to detail is one of Stamberg's favorite parts of the writing. Listening and watching and making notes are critical, Stamberg says, "observing the bits and pieces that help tell the story and draw the images."

Sugarman calls it painting or cooking. "It's whatever you can use to make it tastier, make it interesting," says Sugarman. It could be a weird fact, a sound, or part of an interview, or an observation. It could be anything.

"The art of what we do," says former NBC correspondent Bob Dotson, "not just the craft—but the art—is being able to select the right stuff for the story. Not only so that the words and pictures don't fight each other, but more importantly, that they are compelling and create an experience."

"I want people to feel something," says CBS correspondent Steve Hartman. "Laughter and tears are pretty closely tied, and sometimes we think a story has to be either a funny story or a serious story. But really, when the story is both, that's when it's best."

●●●●●

Summary

The principles of audio storytelling remain the same, regardless of the medium. Radio divides its stories based on a mixture of technical construction and the origin of the sound. Those six story forms include reader, actualities, nat or natural sound, voicer, wrap or wraparound and live or ROSR. Many if not most commercial radio stations involve newscasts with an anchor reading a series of stories, possibly punctuated with some nat sound bridges. Non-commercial radio, especially National Public Radio and NPR-affiliated stations, tend to place more of an emphasis on reporting and the use of sound.

●●●●●

Key Words & Phrases

reader . . . actualities . . . nat or natural sound . . . voicer . . . wrap or wraparound . . . live or ROSR . . . NPR

●●●●●

Exercises

A. Listen to the major radio stations in your area.

1. How many of them run local news?
2. How much news do they run and when?
3. How long are the newscasts?
4. Do those newscasts include any sound? Are there actualities and/ or natural sound?

5. Was all the sound gathered on the phone, or did the station send a reporter out to gather interviews and/or natural sound?

6. How many radio stations in your area actually have reporters who go out to cover news?

7. Are there any all-news stations in your area? If so, do they cover the news differently from other stations?

8. Are there any news/talk stations in your area? To what extent are they news versus talk? How do they cover the news?

9. Are there any public radio stations in your area? How do they cover the news?

B. Write and record two different radio newscasts for two different radio stations in your area. Explain why the newscasts were written and put together differently. Who do you think is the primary audience for each station? Back that up with concrete evidence.

C. Listen to *Morning Edition* or *All Things Considered* on National Public Radio. How are the stories on those programs different from the ones you hear on most of the local commercial radio stations? Working either individually or in pairs, report, write and record a local story in the same style as you hear on NPR.

D. Compare the audio stories on radio, TV and newspaper websites. What similarities and differences do you notice? What are the similarities and differences you notice between those audio stories on the web and the stories you hear on the radio?

15

•••••

Online News

There are plenty of bright people who are absolutely convinced that the future of news is online. That may be so, but as Chapter 20 will make clear, the future isn't now—nor is it all that clear. The web as replacement for TV would also represent a significant departure from history. Over the years, as new technology has come along, older media have been forced to change and evolve. But none has disappeared. Complicating the question further is that TV is in the online business, although for a variety of reasons—explored more fully in Chapter 20—TV stations have not put the effort or emphasis into online news that they could.

However, the web does offer a new dimension currently unavailable to any other medium, and it's the primary source of news for younger people, especially 18 to 34 year olds. So it's an increasingly important part of traditional media's news and information offerings.

More and more, stations break news on the first, best available medium, and that's commonly mobile, social media or the station website. In addition, TV stations now report that 27 percent of web content is only on the web—not on air. Logically, that number should be shooting up year after year. In fact, it's changed little in the last few years. Even so, more and more stations are really starting to understand that the web isn't simply an extension of the on-air brand. It's a lot more than that.

•••••

Some Basic Terms and Concerns

It's not a big deal, but there's a difference between the internet and the World Wide Web (or web). The internet is the infrastructure that allows computers to communicate with each other. The web is the network (or web) over which that communication takes place. Email is not a part of the web—even though you probably access your email via the web. Email is, however, sent over the internet.

The URL is the address of a web site. It stands for "uniform resource locator." The end of the basic address—after the period but before any slashes—is the domain. The domain indicates either the type or the purpose or the geography of the web site.

.com is commercial or business

.edu is education

.gov is government

.int is international

.mil is military, the U.S. Department of Defense

.net is networks (as in internet network, not TV)

.org is short for organizations—usually non-profit, but it doesn't have to be

Sites that end in .gov are official U.S. government websites. That doesn't necessarily make the information correct. Government and government agencies can be self-serving and just plain make mistakes, but at least you have a source that should be worth citing.

Sites that end .edu are education sites, like a university. But many schools make their system available to faculty, students, staff and alumni. A site marked .edu might be an official university site or the personal site of a clueless freshman.

Sites ending in .org are often owned by nonprofit organizations, but that's not a requirement, and a number of for-profit businesses operate .org websites. And nonprofit doesn't necessarily mean unbiased or authoritative, anyway. Many nonprofits are also advocates for a variety of interest groups. Again, this is useful information to know, but nothing about a .org at the end of a URL guarantees accuracy or unbiased information.

Sites ending in .com are commercial sites. But that doesn't mean those sites can't contain good, unbiased information. Most news sites—newspaper, magazine and broadcast—are .com sites because they sell online advertising.

As the internet has grown, so have the online suffixes. Many are additional commercial endings, and many denote country of origin, or at least licensure, like .ca for Canada, .mx for Mexico and .au for Australia. Then there's the relatively new domain, .vegas.

●●●●●

Research and the Web

The internet has certainly revolutionized news. Start with research and news gathering. A staggering amount of material that was once available only in reference books or courthouses is now readily available to everyone online. Census data, health statistics, proposed legislation and legal rulings are examples of such factual material. The federal government, states, counties, cities and even towns and villages are all making much of their data available online. Keep in mind, though, that older material hasn't always been digitized, and organizations and governments frequently don't make all current data available online, either.

Unfortunately, the widespread democratization of the web means that anyone and everyone can make information available online. The greatest research challenge today remains separating accurate, reliable data from random, self-serving opinion. Or even spoof sites. Fake news. You can't be too careful about where information comes from, and, given the potentially anonymous nature of the web, that's even more true for online material than other sources.

In 2016, the Woolshed Company, based in Australia, released a video showing that it had produced at least eight fake videos to "explore the phenomenon of 'viral videos and shareable content.'" Those fake videos were viewed 205 million times, and made it onto countless news websites and on air. The videos showed amazing feats and fascinating encounters. But they were all fake.

The internet is a great tool, but it's not a substitute for critical thinking, checking with sources and other research. Research generally involves collecting information, locating people, and confirming information you already have. There are search engines (like google.com), subject directories (like yahoo.com) and restricted subject area search tools (like findlaw.com). The quality of your research depends on where you go, the quality of your questions and the evaluation of both your information choices and the material itself.

Through email, the internet also allows journalists to conduct interviews online. Be cautious. First, there's no substitute for a face-to-face interview. You get to see the person you're talking to, you get to know if there's anyone else present during the interview who might influence the answers, you get to see the body language of how that person reacts to you and your questions, you get to hear the nuances of how someone answers a question, and you get to know with reasonable certainty that the person you're talking to is the person you think you're talking to.

Most of those things are lost in email interviews—starting with the certainty of whom you're interviewing. Consider email interviews as a last information-gathering resort, and note in the story that you received the answer via email.

Still, it's a great way to follow up with someone you interviewed in person or on the phone to get quick clarification on a point. Again, face-to-face is always first choice; phone contact is second choice, but email can be a useful way to reach a hard-to-pin-down, busy person. It's a great way to set up an interview. It may also be your only choice to reach someone far away. And having a paper trail of information can be useful. Just recognize the drawbacks and act accordingly.

● ● ● ● ●

Content Management System (CMS)

At its core, a content management system (CMS) is a computer program that allows digital content to be created and modified by multiple users who are operating on the same user interface. It's the backbone of how stations create and manage their website.

Just as consolidation has hit the media ownership business, it's also hit the CMS business. Lakana is one of the biggest media CMS systems. Lakana came about from the merging of several CMS companies by owner Nexstar Media Group. The system is now widely used by both broadcast and even some print companies. Sinclair Broadcasting expanded its station holdings by buying out a variety of broadcast companies, thereby inheriting a variety of CMS systems. Instead of consolidating down to one of the systems, Sinclair built its own, and all of its stations now use that proprietary system. WorldNow, which was one of the biggest broadcast CMS players, was bought out by digital messaging company, Frankly. A number of broadcasters defected, but WorldNow still handles a bunch of stations. Some station groups, and almost all public broadcasters, use open source content management systems. Mostly that's Drupal with most of the rest using Wordpress.

Does any of this matter to you? Sure. The system you use determines how you as a producer of news convey that news to people online, on social media and on a smartphone. While all the systems do the same general things, they all do them just a little differently. Just as with newsroom software, it's another bit of technology that must be learned for each place of employment.

● ● ● ● ●

The Information Website

All television stations and almost all radio stations (99 percent) have websites. All television websites include local news (assuming the station runs local news), and 80 percent of radio websites run local news.

Among TV websites, virtually all include news video, still pictures and text. More than three-quarters of the sites include live streaming of news and events, live newscasts and a calendar of events. About two-thirds of the TV sites include mobile-related material, user-generated content and live cameras. About half have audio. In the optional extra category—about one-third of TV websites—we find streaming audio, recorded newscasts and blogs. Podcasts are now found at under 10 percent of TV websites, and their number has actually been dropping in TV (although it's been going up modestly at radio websites).

Generally, the bigger the market, the more complex the station website is likely to be.

At radio stations, only text, still pictures, streaming audio and audio passed the 50 percentile mark, although an event calendar came close. Podcasts, news video and recorded newscasts all came in at around one-third of radio websites.

The biggest push at station websites has involved more, better and/ or special content. That's included more news, more material exclusive to the web, more video, more weather, more investigative work, specialized reporting, polls and even mini-newscasts for the web or mobile. That's topped the list for the last few years. Right behind that is streaming. That's involved an increasing emphasis on streaming live events and breaking news and, to a lesser extent, sports.

Stations have also made big efforts with social media (see Chapter 16). And stations have worked at better coordination of their websites and their mobile apps, they've instituted more guidelines on who posts on their sites and how often that posting takes place; they've upgraded the CMS and backbone of their websites, and more and more stations have hired people specifically to work on or coordinate efforts on the web or social media.

Web Design

As you wander through the web, notice that there are no hard-and-fast rules for much of anything. From site to site, design varies from minimalist to frenetic, and the fact that so many information websites continue to be redesigned so often is testament to the continuous but unfulfilled search for the perfect information website structure and organization.

Little within the sites is standardized either. Some sites use graphics for navigation; some sites use hypertext; some use both. Some sites work hard at not forcing the user to scroll down the page; some sites force the user to scroll forever. Click or scroll?

It's a relatively new medium, so it shouldn't be a surprise that there are more questions than answers. We are, in essence, still defining what the web is. It looks like a TV, but you read it from 18 inches away, on a screen that shows much less text than we see on the printed page.

Complicating the production further, news is most commonly generated by people whose background and orientation is either print or broadcast, and it shows in most news websites.

News on the Web

Start with how people use the web: They don't just read, they scan, surf, scroll, chat and click. It's activist sitting. In between, they check email, answer landlines or mobile phones, and they commonly have the radio, a CD or television on in the background. Or the foreground. It's a multimedia experience even before people do anything.

Despite the ease with which people declare what news on the web should look like, there's remarkably little good research on what users really want. For instance, it's really hard to imagine that most web users want a news home page that makes the Las Vegas strip seem placid by comparison. But take a look at some of the news websites, complete with scrolling, flashing and assorted animation, and busy to the point of tawdry comes to mind. Perhaps part of the problem is the pull between content people—who seem to want to put every story on the home page, along with links to everything they have ever produced—and sales people—who appear to want to sell every sliver of white space with blinking, moving and flashing ads. Then there are the pop-ups and unwanted video rolls. Less is frequently more, but you'd certainly never suspect that based on many if not most news websites.

Part of this is probably also the result of the news media not knowing how to deal with a loss of control. For television and radio—newspapers and magazines, too—the producers of news determine order and priorities. On the web, the user is in control. So the typical news website seems to respond by adding more material and special features in hopes that something will appeal to someone. And then there are the ads, polls, games and so on.

Sometimes these overarching principles seem to get lost, but there are two key points to keep in mind when putting together stories for the web:

1. The user is in control. Here the model is closer to newspaper. Editors can put whatever they want on page one, but nothing prevents the reader from starting with sports or the comics. In broadcast, the producer determines the sequence, and there are no changes allowed. On the web, users will decide what captures their attention and where to go. Users enter a news website from countless different entry points. Some come from the website home page; some come from non-news websites; many come from a news aggregator; more come from social media sites or a link from a friend. Facebook (coupled with Twitter to a much lesser degree) probably supplies more users than anything else. So the web is really unlike any medium that precedes it. Theoretically, a newspaper reader could skip to the end of the story and might well randomly look at pictures or charts, but, at its best, the web user is in full control. The user can start wherever and go wherever, deeper and deeper in one narrow direction, perhaps never returning to the broader story or any part of it. Or, more commonly, glance at headline after headline until something appeals enough to click.

2. Web information remains linear. Web consumption is driven by the audience, and while the experience itself is nonlinear, that doesn't mean that the information itself is nonlinear. In fact, the information website is constructed as a series of short, linear information experiences. What's nonlinear isn't the information—or the packets or chunks of information that make up the website or pages of a website. What's nonlinear is the user's opportunity for consumption.

Readers can take varying paths through a website, with each experience different from the next.

There are also divergent philosophies among information websites about what news to emphasize. Some information websites are all about local. National and international news can be accessed on demand, but everything featured on the home page is local. Some information websites routinely include some of just about everything. Some vary, reacting to the day's (or hour's) events.

Not surprisingly, the philosophy of the operation determines at least some aspects of the content.

Newspaper websites are likely to use photographs and picture galleries. Television websites are more likely to emphasize video. Not surprisingly, radio websites tend to include more audio. Web news producers tend to favor what they know based on their own background—and what their organization is most likely to produce, or produces best.

In fact, the web experience potentially includes everything traditional media provide—and more. It offers headlines (print), still photos (print), moving pictures (TV), audio (radio), photo captions (print), slide shows—with and without audio (presentation media), lists and bullet points (print, TV and presentation media), tables, graphs, charts and maps (print, mostly, and TV and presentation media, too), sidebars (print), letters (print), summaries (print), animation (TV occasionally), surveys (newspaper and TV), data visualization (presentation media), message boards, hypertext, live chats, weblogs (blogs), databases and games (all mostly web devices).

Constructing Web News . . . Headlines

Straightforward headlines work best. In many cases, the headline may be the only thing a user sees in order to decide whether to click on it and take a look. A cute or humorous headline may just puzzle the user.

Problem headlines:

- Supreme Court: Smith Can Proceed With DTF Hearings
- Honda Leads List of Top 10 Most Stolen Cars
- Diabetes, Erectile Dysfunction, Heart Disease Share Common Link
- Witnesses Decry Horse Doping in House Testimony

Headlines need to be clear instantly, and they need to attempt to grab the user's attention. The first example, above, has two problems. First, it doesn't make clear that it was the *State* Supreme Court, and, second, it uses initials that aren't widely and instantly recognized (Drug Task Force). The second example says too much. Better to tell people that there's a new list of the 10 most-stolen cars. People will check to see if theirs is on the list. The third example is much too long and involved. In the last example, "decry" is a short, but almost never-used term, and "in House Testimony" can be read multiple ways and is confusing. Keep it simple.

Utilitarian headlines:

- U.S. Judge Blocks Oil, Gas Drilling in Wisconsin
- Two Injured in SW Las Vegas Shooting
- Jeep Recalls More Than 650,000 SUVs
- Report Cites Abuses by Mexican Military

These are all simple and straightforward. Notice that most are shorter than the first group. This is especially important for the rapidly increasing number of people who first hear about news on a mobile device. As a general rule, keep headlines under 70 characters, including spaces. That's about where Google truncates headlines in a search, and Google remains one of the two dominant players in how people arrive at a website.

Better headlines:

- Wounded Officer Battles for His Life
- Car of the Future Not So Far Away
- Iraq Handing Out Cash to People on the Street
- Rapist Gets 25 Years and a Little Mercy

Still short, all of these are more interesting, more compelling and more likely to have users click on them—which, after all, is what the headline is supposed to accomplish.

Remember that the user is frequently scanning for information rather than reading.

There's also increasing—and well-founded—concern that more and more web headlines are written less with the idea of informing an audience and more with the idea of SEO (search engine optimization) and pandering to what Australian journalist Mel Campbell calls "lurid clickability."

Constructing Web News . . . Leads

Because web stories have headlines and maybe subheads, the lead of the web story doesn't need to fulfill the same role as in broadcast. Generally, the web story starts with something akin to newspaper's inverted pyramid—a sentence that generally tells what the story is about. After that, it's kind of a free for all. Newspapers tend to produce web stories that look like shorter versions of traditional print stories. They move from the traditional lead through a traditional print-type story. There is a tendency for a more casual writing style—like broadcast—but that's not consistent. Not surprisingly, broadcasters tend to model their stories more like broadcast, with a hard main point lead and shorter stories.

As you go through website after website, it's generally easy to tell whether it's a newspaper- or broadcast-based site just by reading the lead.

Broadcast website leads (with names altered):

- Three North Dakota teenagers are in the hospital this morning after an overnight crash in Jones County.
- Smithville Power says its residential customers will be paying 22 percent more for electricity this year than last year.
- Authorities have charged the son of state Rep. John Jones in connection with a shooting that left another man wounded.
- Smithville police said a man trapped in a collapsed tunnel for over four hours has been pulled out.

Note that all of those examples are hard, main point leads, just the way you might run them on the air.

Newspaper website leads (with names altered):

- Some Smithville residents are supporting a new district proposal to dredge and remove vast amounts of bulrushes, cattails and other vegetation that has grown thick along the lower Jones River, choking the open water and narrowing the channel.
- Gov. Brown ordered an additional 2,000 National Guard members to help battle California's blazes Friday, the same day President Obama announced plans to survey the damage.
- In a move that signals the state's newly deregulated auto insurance system is making the market more competitive, Smith Insurance Conglomerate, the nation's largest insurance company, will soon start selling auto policies in North Carolina.
- After studying 21 years' worth of traffic fatality statistics, researchers say there may be a positive correlation between high gas prices and road safety.

As with broadcast website leads, the newspaper website leads are really fairly traditional print leads. All these leads are serviceable, although the first and third are far more complex and contorted than they need to be. Note that the broadcast website leads are far more conversational—clearly a result of their origin. Also clear: we haven't arrived at a consensus on exactly how web news stories should begin.

Constructing Web News . . . Chunks

Most of the stories we post on the web are relatively short and straight-forward. They might have a picture or, preferably, video, but they're certainly not complicated or in-depth.

What's different about the web is that stories can go so far beyond that. For special stories or in special circumstances, we do more. But to make the information more user-friendly, there's a tendency to break up information into chunks. This involves splitting a story into its major components, each of which is largely self-contained, and each of which constitutes a chunk. Don't confuse chunks with paragraphs. A chunk is likely to include a number of paragraphs. The key with the chunk is that all the material within the chunk is related to one element of a story or to an overview of the story. Many websites also routinely add space between paragraphs to improve the appearance and break up the text.

Let's look at an example – starting with where we might come up with a story idea.

Every year, the American College Health Association releases what it calls the National College Health Assessment . . . looking at the physical and mental health and habits of American college students. The material is online and readily available; the organization is involved in advocacy and education programs along with its research.

It's the kind of material that seldom makes it into the news media unless the organization itself releases some finding of consequence. But almost any time you have access to *data over time*, you can find a news story. What you're looking for is change. It doesn't matter whether something is changing for the better or for the worse—any change is potentially newsworthy. Obviously, for a news story you want to report not simply the change but why the change is taking place (if possible) and what the implications are—positive or negative.

Looking through the data, there's been a slow but fairly steady increase in the percentage of students who reported feeling "overwhelming anxiety" within the last 12 months. For TV, it's easy to see that you could put together a reader, VO/SOT or even a package pretty easily on this. You have the data saying that American college students are apparently feeling more and more anxiety, and that provides the story. It's easy enough to find students at a local school who will support that finding; you can interview one or more mental health professionals about what they're seeing or signs to watch for and advice on coping; b-roll is readily available. What could a website do with the story, and how could it be chunked?

The study itself was straightforward and could be handled in one chunk, which should definitely include a chart showing the increase and the difference between men and women (since the difference is significant). Another chunk could include signs and symptoms to watch for in terms of anxiety. There are medical sites you can link to for issues like symptoms and treatment. It would be possible to put together video or audio on a question and answer with a physician, and it would be possible to put together a video, audio or slide show story on coping with anxiety and how to relieve stress. None of these things is hard to do or takes much time.

How to chunk information involves evaluating the characteristics or characters of a story. What kind of story is it? What are the different aspects or divisions of a story? How can you divide it by subject area? How can you divide it by technology? Think about the audience. Who is it? Who is it supposed to be? Who else might be interested? Is there a target audience?

Those chunks of information must each be largely self-supporting, because there's no telling which, if any, chunks the consumer has read prior to reading any other. But they also can't be so repetitious that the user who has read other material won't learn anything. It's the same kind of quandary facing the producer of the late news. In many cases, half the audience watched the station's 6 p.m. news, and half did not. Simply repeating material from 6 p.m. to 10 or 11 p.m. will bore those people who saw the earlier newscast, but leaving out the material potentially eliminates important news. The key, then, is emphasizing important points without sounding like you're repeating.

Information provided as bullet points, charts, graphs, tables, graphics and so on works especially well on the web because people can take in that information—or ignore it—quickly and easily. So look for material that lends itself to those presentation forms.

A simple chart could look like this:

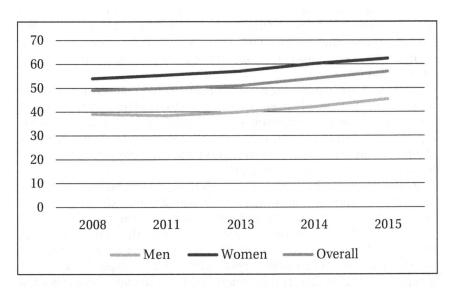

Figure 15.1 Percentage of college students who have felt "overwhelming anxiety" in the last 12 months. Source: National College Health Assessment.

That chart is a simple example of *data visualization*. Data visualization is just the visual representation of information—something that can help people quickly understand material both online and on air.

A bullet point list on the story could look like this:

ANXIETY: Emotional symptoms to look for:

■ Worrying constantly
■ A feeling of helplessness, that you can't do anything about it
■ An inability to stop thinking about the things that make you anxious
■ Not being able to cope with uncertainty, a need to know what's going to happen
■ A feeling that things just won't work out, a sense of dread

You could also construct or link to lists of physical symptoms and behavioral symptoms. This is also a great topic for audience engagement, feedback and participation.

Constructing Web News . . . Style

Most news websites have moved away from the extensive internal links throughout every story, but it varies. *The New York Times* (nytimes.com) still uses internal links. At this writing, the *Washington Post* (washingtonpost.com) uses fewer, and other papers, like the *Los Angeles Times* (latimes.com) and most TV news websites also have fewer internal links. There's some thinking that those are distracting. It may make more sense to include links in a separate box or at the end of each chunk or at the end of the story. Again, there's little consistency here.

Because there's no telling what the user has read before or where the user will go next, people in stories will have to be identified within each area, and initials and acronyms must either be introduced right at the top or more than once. Attribution appears to be more often at the end, like print, but that's not consistent, and a lot of websites work hard at using present tense, as in broadcast.

Interestingly, in the examples of web leads above, taken from actual print and broadcast websites, both groups are mixed on the use of broadcast's present tense versus print's more common past tense.

Theoretically, the web has the ability to provide the best of what both print and broadcast can offer. Obviously, it can offer words and information—and it can even exceed print in total volume if warranted. It can offer moving pictures and audio. While newspapers can run a few pictures, the web can run a gallery. While newspaper or TV can run a chart, the web can do that along with a searchable database of information that can answer questions about each user's zip code, local school district or neighborhood. It can take a newspaper's depth of coverage to new levels. It can provide the animation that television is capable of but rarely uses. And it can be as immediate as radio.

The value of hypertext is the ability to go deeper, further and wider than ever before. The downside, for the news producer, is the loss of control on news consumption. From a user's standpoint, this is a dream come true. It's no different than someone hearing or reading a story and wondering about some related point—except that, with the web, the person can go there instead of just wondering about it.

Those links can also allow a reporter to provide the detailed evidence to support statements written in the story, documents the story may refer to, side issues, background and older articles in the archive. Each of those areas involves depth that most readers won't want but at least some may find interesting.

The writing style that's developing for the web appears to be a cross between print and broadcast. It's tighter and more conversational—like broadcast. But it tends to have more detail—like print. In some cases, stories appear to be print stories, written in broadcast style. In these cases, more attention is given to tight, short, declarative sentences, active, one idea per sentence, logical flow of information. At some sites, there appears to be a trend toward more use of humor or opinion. Or snark.

A number of journalists (especially print ones) describe the web style as a reversion back to the inverted pyramid. But Jonathan Dube, formerly of AOL and CyberJournalist.net, suggests that a better visualization would be the "Model T." In this system, the lead is a long horizontal line, conceptually like the print lead, summarizing the story and telling why it matters. But the vertical line, according to Dube, can be a range of structures depending on the information and the approach. It could be a traditional inverted pyramid (like newspaper), or it could be a narrative (more like TV), an anecdote, or something else.

Some argue that the complete essence of a story must be told within the first four paragraphs. Part of that reasoning is so that people who leave the story will have gotten the gist of it. Others argue to make the first paragraph inclusive and tight because more and more people are expected to receive the material via phone, and a phone screen will display limited text at one time.

More and more, stations are taking the view that they need to get information out as fast as they can on the first and best medium for it. That might be breaking into programming for a live report, but mostly it's getting the news out on the station website or to mobile users. Generally, it's website first with other efforts pointing people to the website.

Online Writing Rules

Seven rules for writing online:

1. **It's still journalism.** Do it right. Speed is helpful; mistakes are not.
2. **Think about the medium.** What different techniques can you use to tell different parts of the story—or, perhaps, the same parts in different ways?
3. **Think about readers or users.** They're sitting 18 inches from a monitor with lots of choices, and even as they read, they're holding a device (the mouse) to make new choices. What will capture their attention? What do they want to know? What might some of them want to know? Use quotes. Build in surprises. Appeal personally (like broadcast). Think about how you'll grab the attention of the scanning user.
4. **The headline needs to provide concrete information.** In many cases, users may be faced with a choice simply based on the headline. Think about whether they'll know enough to make a choice. The lead/opening paragraph needs to tell the overall story tightly and succinctly. Remember that every sentence determines whether the next sentence will be read. Every choice provides alternative ways to go. Make sure there's a clear geographic identifier in the headline, subhead or lead.
5. **The experience may be nonlinear, but each element of the information is linear.** And each of those elements needs to be self-supporting. Stories are a collection of short linear pieces that could very well be consumed in a random, nonlinear manner. Use links to split long blocks into multiple pages.
6. **Think interactivity.** Think about what you can present or include that can get the user involved. That could include the ability to personalize the data for each user or a variety of multimedia tools.
7. **Try new things.** There's still a lot we don't know about using the web. Experiment and learn.

Other Issues

The nature of the web and its 24-hour news cycle also offer the opportunity to amplify the biggest problems in the media. Mistakes can live forever in the system unless media develop and follow up on a comprehensive plan to correct stories, including those already archived.

It's clear that there's a lot more "point of view journalism" on the web than we see in traditional media. That raises questions about whether anyone does or should care about your opinion . . . and whether "point of view journalism" is really journalism.

The web offers a competitive world much more like TV than newspaper. In most communities, there is one paper, take it or leave it. There are almost always choices in television. Even more so on the web. That kind of intense competition can energize reporters and editors. It can also lead to bad choices resulting from inadequate thought. And because the web is potentially even more immediate than television, it can amplify TV's potential for speed ahead of facts, accuracy and context.

Video

It's becoming increasingly clear that reaching people online needs to include video. More on this in Chapter 16, "Social Media and News." but Facebook, by far the dominant player in social media, has recently changed its algorithm for "news" distribution, and two things appear clear from this: 1) Material from friends and family will take precedence over material from news organizations; 2) Video trumps other sharable information. That should be good news for TV since video is TV's trademark product.

Podcasts

A podcast is a digital audio file designed to be downloaded from the internet to a computer, tablet or smartphone for consumption whenever the person who downloads it wants to listen.

Podcasts can be a one-time thing or a regular (or irregular) series. They can be free or available at a charge.

Research conducted in 2016 by Wondery and comScore found that most internet users knew what podcasts were but had either not listened within the past half year or had never listened to one. Overall, 35 percent of internet users said they had listened to a podcast at least once, but a third of those hadn't listened in six months or more. Of those who had listened in the previous six months, only about half listened at least once a week.

National Public Radio has made it clear that it's betting on podcasts to help reach elusive millennials (roughly 18 to 34 year olds). NPR has found that while millennials are not big news consumers, in the first quarter of 2016, they were the fastest-growing group of listeners, and NPR attributes at least some of that growth to podcasts.

The use of podcasts has been slowly increasing in radio—but decreasing in TV. One thing that might be holding podcasts back involves audience measurement. It's easy to quantify downloads, but it's not easy to quantify listening: when, how much or even whether listening takes place at all. So while ad spending for podcasts is increasing, the long-term future remains unclear.

●●●●●

Hyperlocal News

Just like it sounds, hyperlocal news is simply news about a much smaller community than we commonly see covered. Most often, hyperlocal means geography—coverage of relatively small communities within the larger market. That could be anything from a defined neighborhood to a small town. Hyperlocal could also be defined by a common or shared area of interest, like a school district. The web is the vehicle of choice for hyperlocal news distribution.

As this is written, a number of the hyperlocal news sites that I noted in the last edition of this book are now gone, and what remains is a shell of what had been. Patch, the largest collection of hyperlocal news sites around the country, was spun off from AOL, and a much slimmed down Patch is now separate and owned mostly by Hale Global. The company says it operates just over 900 sites in 23 states with about 125 full time staffers. That's stretched pretty thin, a fraction of the employees who once populated Patch.

There are still a variety of efforts at hyperlocal news, but so far the business models have simply not been able to self-support what is an inherently people-intensive industry.

Hyperlocal frequently translates into backpack journalists working out of a car and home rather than an office. But the model and (business) future of hyperlocal news is very much up in the air at this point. Hyperlocal also tends to reflect a blending of traditional news and more broadly defined information, like community bulletin boards.

●●●●●

Multimedia

Most of what news organizations put on the web isn't multimedia—it's multiple media. Text with pictures or video or audio isn't multimedia; it's just two media put side by side. Real multimedia—the true integration of text, information graphics (with animation, rollovers and so on), video and slideshows is really reserved for special stories done by a handful of larger (mostly newspaper) websites.

Mostly, news organizations use the web as another platform for what they have always produced. TV websites mostly include the same video that they have or will put on the air along with text that they or AP or other services generate.

Newspaper websites run mostly text, although many have gotten better about not just dumping newspaper text onto web pages. They run more still pictures, including photos which the newspaper never could have handled before. More and more, they're also using video, which too often looks painfully amateurish. Some have attempted audio/still slide shows, which usually demonstrate a complete lack of understanding about how to edit audio and pictures together.

Almost all information websites have gotten much better about expanding their news coverage, offering more varied elements (video, audio), and even providing for at least some user interactivity, although that's mostly comments on news or blogs or sending in pictures.

Few broadcast websites have moved into real multimedia. In past editions, I've suggested a variety of newspaper websites and some of the best of their multimedia stories. But most of those excellent examples are now dated, many have disappeared, and they have not been replaced by the same volume or quality of new multimedia efforts. Apparently, it's simply too people-intensive (in other words, costly) to produce that material.

There are some efforts at *The New York Times* (nytimes.com), but mostly there's just a scattering of material done here and there for some special projects.

One outstanding local TV example comes from WXIA-TV in Atlanta. The Tegna (formerly Gannett) station did a four part investigative series called *Inside the Triangle*. It was a six-week investigation into heroin use and overdose among young people in the affluent suburbs of Atlanta. In its first week or so, it had almost four million page views—based on promotion almost entirely through social media. First release was only online, TV to follow.

Multimedia presentations take time, and they're not applicable for the fleeting news of the day. But for ongoing stories, for significant institutions or issues in a given community, it can be a real demonstration of what the web can do.

●●●●●

Data Journalism

Data journalism involves the use of numbers to convey information. It could involve things like school test scores by school district or even individual school. It could involve crime statistics by neighborhood. It's not that you couldn't do data journalism within a variety of media, it's just that online can do it so much better than any other.

Data journalism online requires three skill sets: coding, design and journalism. ProPublica's Scott Klein wrote on the NICAR listserv, reprinted by Nieman Lab, a series of steps for a small- to medium-size newsroom to take to establish a data journalism team. Among his excellent tips: it's all right to start small; recruit people who can do at least two of the three needed skills and teach the third; have each person be owner of a project (rather than trying to create an assembly line of people each handling a separate aspect of a project); treat members as journalists, not "data monkeys"; make sure they report to news, not IT.

● ● ● ● ●

Summary

Online news has become a critical part of virtually every traditional news outlet, although even the most successful information websites produce only a small fraction of the revenue of the station (or newspaper). The internet opens up tremendous possibilities for researching news stories, but it's not without potential problems. There are clearly no firm design standards for news websites. The nonlinear aspect of the web means that the user is in control, but stories on the web still involve linear chunks in a nonlinear environment. There are seven rules for writing online: 1) It's still journalism; 2) Think about the medium; 3) Think about the users; 4) Use short, concrete headlines; 5) Online involves linear information in a nonlinear environment; 6) Think interactively; 7) Try new things.

Video is key online and in social media. Podcasts are growing in radio but not TV. Hyperlocal news is no longer a growing phenomenon as the business model remains hazy. True multimedia is still more of a promise than a reality—especially at broadcast websites. Data journalism remains a mostly unfulfilled promise, especially on broadcast websites.

● ● ● ● ●

Key Words & Phrases

world wide web . . . internet . . . URL . . . domain . . . research on the web . . . search engines . . . subject directories . . . restricted subject area search tools . . . information websites . . . web design . . . nonlinear . . . chunks . . . podcasts . . . SEO . . . hyperlocal news . . . multimedia . . . data journalism

● ● ● ● ●

Exercises

A. Compare the website for your local newspaper with the website of one of the major local television stations. How are they different, and how are they similar? Compare how each handles a major local news story that both are covering. Which does a better job on local, national and international news? Support your views with concrete examples.

B. Compare the websites of the local television stations within your market. How are they different, and how are they similar? Compare how each handles a major local news story that both are covering. Which does a better job on local, national and international news? Support your views with concrete examples.

C. Using the story scenarios at the end of Chapter 4 (Stories), develop a multimedia online plan for the handling of each of the stories. List all the possible elements that you could include for each of the stories, including elements that would require additional reporting.

D. Based on the discussion in the chapter, evaluate which local information websites do the best job of real multimedia reporting. Pick out the three best, local multimedia stories, and explain why you think so.

16

Social Media and News

Social Networking

The newscast on the KSNV-TV in Las Vegas ends with:

```
That does it for News 3. But remember, our
conversation doesn't end with the show. Share your
stories with us online ... send us your story ideas
and comment on what you've seen on our Facebook and
Twitter pages.
```

At Scripps' KERO-TV in Bakersfield, California (market 126), news goes on the web first, then social media and push alerts. With few exceptions, on-air newscasts are at the end of the line.

"If we worry about the competition knowing what we're doing [because we put it out online first], then we're failing our viewers," notes Crosby Shaterian, the station's Director of New Media.

Eric Galvan, who's the Executive Producer for the morning show at KERO, says his work day begins by checking social media to see what's going on, locally and everywhere else. Then he checks what the station has and sends out push alerts and posts to Facebook and Twitter. And that's before the morning show starts at 4:30 a.m.

Every reporter and anchor at KERO is required to have a station Facebook page and post to it and Twitter at least once a day. And along with a couple of people full time on digital, every reporter—all of whom are MMJs—rotates through a "digital day" once a week. It's exactly what it sounds like.

Aubrey Clerkin, Digital Executive Producer at KSNV-TV in Las Vegas, oversees the station's social media and online efforts. She estimates that a quarter of her time involves fixing copy from others before it gets posted. She also doesn't have to guess where their online traffic comes from and which stories are most popular; it's on a big monitor in the newsroom for all to see. Anchors and reporters can also see how their posts are doing in popularity compared with others at the station and others in the market. At KSNV, most web traffic comes from mobile, and Facebook supplies more users than all others combined.

Clerkin estimates that she sends out six to 10 push alerts per day, and all of them involve content. Nothing just promotes a program.

The importance of social media has made the social media manager probably the fastest growing position in TV news today. The issue certainly isn't whether social media is important, the question is how to handle it. Some stations and media companies are handling their own social media efforts, and some are using software specifically designed to deal with social media. Probably the most widely used service comes from a company called Social News Desk.

Newsroom computer systems have also reacted to the increasing need to post material on multiple platforms. Today's newsroom computer systems operate on what they commonly call a story-centric basis. The idea is that newsroom material is being produced for on-air as well as online and social media, and the computer system works to make it relatively fast and easy to post and format material for the various platforms in use.

TV consolidation has also meant that stations have access to more and more material than ever before. They always had access to feeds from their network (assuming they're an affiliate) and from news services like CNN and AP (assuming membership), but now they have a huge supply of material from other stations within their company (like Nexstar and Sinclair) and easy access to material anywhere online as well.

More and more, the notion in the industry is that everyone needs to be involved with social media. That's part of what the 2016 RTDNA/Hofstra University Survey found. When asked what they were doing that's new in social media, the number one answer from TV news directors was organization and strategy. More and more, that involved laying out specific guidelines on minimum posting requirements, especially by anchors and reporters.

Social media involves a station reaching out to members of the audience. That reaching out could include efforts at gathering news and information, such as pictures or news or crowdsourcing, or it could mean promotional efforts to boost newscast or website audience, or it could mean efforts at building a dialog with the audience to bring them into the decision-making process.

A lot of the time, reporters find that when they post to social media about a story they're working on, potential sources find them and help supply additional perspectives and information that they might not otherwise have picked up.

It's not simply that television and radio stations are doing more with social media these days, it's also that—at least in the case of TV—they're doing something different. At least at TV news operations, social media is about connecting with and having conversations with the audience. Radio, in contrast, looks more like television did a few years earlier, where most of the efforts really are just promotional.

In 2016, Pew found that 62 percent of U.S. adults get at least some news on social media; 18 percent say they often get news on social media. That doesn't mean they get most of the news on social media, but it does mean that social media is a critical gateway for information—frequently sending people to media websites—or media Facebook sites. At the top of the list: Reddit at 70 percent followed by Facebook at 66 percent, Twitter at 59 percent, Tumblr at 31 percent, Instagram at 23 percent, YouTube at 21 percent, LinkedIn at 19 percent, Snapchat at 17 percent, and Vine at 14 percent. Those are the percentages of users of each of those social media sites who report getting at least some news on the site.

But if you take into account how many people use each social media platform, then Facebook is the overwhelming winner—and the only platform reaching more than half of U.S. adults (67 percent). YouTube actually comes in second at 48 percent. Relatively few people get news on YouTube, but lots of people use it, so it scores fairly high. Pew also found that, overall, people mostly get news on social media by chance rather than seeking it out.

And chance is likely to happen less often because of a change in policy by Facebook. The company altered its algorithm so that what people see in their News Feed will be determined primarily by what friends and family post . . . rather than news from publishers (like stations). That will make it harder for news media to make the cut, and it's less likely that news will make it into most people's News Feed. To try to cope with that change, it's also likely that news media will adjust what they send out to people to increase the odds that recipients will repost to others. We'll probably see more cute or bizarre video and less hard news. Breaking news posts may take on an even more urgent tone, but the accidental information that has made it through the filter will likely diminish.

In any case, the changes will make the job of social media manager even harder. If social media is where people learn about news—even accidently—then stations need to be there to supply that information. And since so many social media users are younger than the typical news audience, social media becomes a way to expand the reach of news to younger people.

That's what NBC's "Meet the Press" has been doing with Facebook Q&As between host Chuck Todd and the audience. The show has also been experimenting using Facebook Live. The result has been a huge growth in the Facebook following of the show.

Some stations use Facebook Live to run events and news conferences, provide mini-reports from the field or just show a reporter setting up gear. Some are even using Facebook Live to operate a virtual live TV channel on their Facebook pages, showing news and sports events (and other things) that the station was unable to broadcast because of on-air programming commitments. So now stations are live streaming on two platforms: Facebook Live and their own website. Increasingly, it's the same material on both sites. The live streams may come from the regular field cameras the reporter or photographer uses, but it's even easier to live stream from a smartphone.

Digiday reports that NPR has learned several things experimenting with Facebook Live. First, don't go live just because you can. "Hovering around" has no meaning; showing something with real content does. Second, the audience has a real interest in meaningful live reporting. Third, while video quality is important, it's less important than strong content. Fourth, whatever you do should be about engagement and deepening the loyalty of the audience.

●●●●●

Social Media, Branding and the Reporter Workday

The web and social media have had a profound effect on how reporters spend their time. Reporters that I spoke with gave staggeringly large ranges for the amount of time they spend doing social media each day. Many said that creating web versions of stories and posting to social media probably added one or even two hours to their day. Since most stations clamp down on overtime, that one to two hours comes out of time that used to be spent on just creating news for TV. Some solve that time problem by doing some of their social media postings from home before or after work. Other reporters say the extra time spent on social media comes to maybe 10 to 15 minutes a day. Clearly, it's going to vary by newsroom, by reporter and by inclination.

It's also important to understand that part of what anchors and reporters are doing is creating a brand for themselves. That's something that ambitious reporters and news people should be doing starting in college. Branding is about creating extra value for a news person, and that extra value makes a difference in getting and keeping a job; it makes a difference in job opportunities; and it makes a difference in salary. It's a different world than in used to be. . . . for better and worse.

●●●●●

Facebook

Facebook is, by far, the most important social media outlet for broadcast stations. In the 2016 RTDNA/Hofstra University Survey, every single TV station that produces local news had a Facebook page. Many had more than one. In contrast, 92 percent of radio stations had at least one Facebook page. The concept is simple enough: if that's where people are spending an increasing amount of their time, then that's where stations need to be. Still, what stations are doing there—and whether it's accomplishing anything—varies a great deal.

For many stations, it appears that they're on Facebook because they feel that they should be. Typically, stations post photos of talent and events, upload videos of recent stories, promote upcoming stories, newscasts and events, run discussions and so on. That's much the same material that stations also put on their websites, and in that sense, the Facebook page is frequently another extension of the web.

For many stations, Facebook is more helpful at locating people for news stories than providing a lot of other tangible benefits.

Facebook Live should result in significant changes in how stations use social media, with more and more converting what has been a largely promotional effort into a Facebook page that looks a lot more like the station website. Or maybe even a station.

● ● ● ● ●

Twitter

Howard Kurtz reported my favorite line about Twitter from CNN's Tom Foreman: "It's as if you could just parachute into diners around the country and listen to what people are saying."

But you do need to remember that the people in that diner may not be representative of the larger population. While 19 percent of the U.S. adult population has a Twitter account, Pew found that 36 percent of those users actually check into Twitter on a daily basis. Other statistics find that nearly half of Twitter's registered users have never even sent a single tweet.

Is the TV newsroom actively involved with Twitter? 2016

	Constantly	Daily	Periodically	No
All TV	67%	27%	6%	<1%
Market				
1–25	87	10	3	0
26–50	83	14	2	0
51–100	78	18	4	0
101–150	52	39	8	1
151+	39	50	11	0

Is the radio newsroom actively involved with Twitter? 2016

	Constantly	Daily	Periodically	No
All Radio	22%	22%	17%	40%
Market				
Major	48	30	0	22
Large	32	24	21	24
Medium	21	20	16	44
Small	8	21	21	50

Twitter use has steadily expanded in TV, but its growth in radio has been much slower.

In a number of respects, Twitter could actually be extremely important for a station. Almost all TV stations participate in the 140 character (per tweet) universe, commonly sending out breaking news information, promotion on specific stories coming up on air or online and sending out links to stories and video posted on the web. Probably more critical for stations, Twitter allows a station to monitor what's going on in the community to be able to respond quickly to potential news stories. The assignment desk and reporters (and others) should be monitoring the various community news, tipsters and columns that you can find almost everywhere these days.

Twitter is a great way of communicating with a segment of your audience. But no one likes constant chatter; be selective. Not everything is breaking news. Always include links to stories. Most experts are now saying that you're better off posting news to the web first, and then linking to it in Twitter rather than tweeting the information first.

Although stations tend to use Twitter more for distribution (sending out material, promos, information and links), it's also a great news search tool and aggregation tool.

● ● ● ● ●

MMJ, Backpack Journalists and One-Man-Bands

There are those who envision the new television landscape as one more and more populated with the super-journalist who can do it all: cover a story for television, post an expanded version on the website and maybe even write 15 column inches for a newspaper. Call them one-man-bands (admittedly old school), multimedia (MMJ) or backpack journalists—their use has been growing over the last decade.

Percentage of TV Newsrooms Using One-Man-Bands—2016

	Yes, Mostly Use OMBS	Yes, Use Some OMBS	Yes, But Not Much Use	No, Do Not Use
All TV	50%	33%	11%	6%
Market size:				
1–25	25	45	20	10
26–50	21	50	14	14
51–100	42	39	15	5
101–150	67	22	5	5
151+	83	15	2	0
Staff size:				
51+	18	52	20	10
31–50	54	34	10	2
21–30	71	18	5	5
11–20	93	3	3	0
1–10	80	15	5	0

Certainly we're seeing the rise of the backpack journalist equipped to do it all. Although some people are ready to pronounce this the era of the backpack journalist, it's too early to be sure. Even the much-discussed rise of the use of one-man-bands in TV news really isn't backed up by actual numbers nearly as much as anecdotal stories. Generally, the use of MMJs has increased at the rate of about 2 to 3 percent per year. That's meaningful, but it's not overwhelming. The biggest jump is actually in larger markets which have gone from no one-man-bands to some. Smaller stations always had reporters who operated as one-man-bands. Regardless of gender.

There has always been a widespread expectation in the industry that new hires would know how to shoot and edit, especially if they wanted to be reporters. What's really new is a rapidly expanding expectation of web skills and, especially, social media skills.

In television, three-quarters of TV news staffers have at least some web responsibilities; in radio, it's about 82 percent. Even in the biggest markets, 60 percent of TV staffers and 76 percent of radio staffers help on the web.

Mark Christian is Chief Photographer at KERO-TV. Since the station is heavily a beginner's market—especially for reporters—and has such a major commitment to digital, Christian put together what he calls an "MMJ Success Guide":

Each day you should have about three stories to pitch in the morning meeting that are already researched and vetted. The most common pitches are stories from the paper, the competition and station emailed stories. However, it is best to think out-of-the-box and not just follow the competition. If they did a story the day before, think of how you can further the story with a different angle.

Enterprise stories: This is accomplished by being active in the community. 1) As you drive around town be story-minded every day. This includes while you are off when you are at the store, Starbucks or anywhere else when you engage the public. Chances are, if it's interesting to you it's interesting to our viewers. 2) Hand out your business card to everybody you meet and tell them to inform you about something they think is newsworthy. 3) Join or follow local community social media groups and stay up-to-date with recent posts that you can turn into a story.

Make every effort to contact people before the morning meeting to see if they are willing to speak with you on camera before you pitch the idea in the morning meeting.

Always think web first. Once you are assigned a story, write something quick for the web. When you are at the story location, shoot video, take cell phone pictures and get your interviews. Then do a 30 to 45 second Videolicious. Write your web story and send it back including the cell phone pictures. 3 to 6 pictures is a good rule of thumb.

Communicate with the desk often during the day and inform them of your progress. Write your package, either in the field or back at the station. If you are feeding your PKG from the field for the 5, make sure it is FTP'd [File Transfer Protocol is a system for sending computer files] *before 4:45 p.m. If you are on the 6, then 5:45 p.m.*

That's the concept of how the day works for the MMJs in Bakersfield.

●●●●●

Beyond Facebook and Twitter

Facebook and Twitter are the best known—and most used—social media tools, but there are plenty of other programs that stations use as well. Here's the latest (alphabetical) list of social media in use at stations, as of 2016:

- *Banjo* is a website and app that allows users to see what's going on in the world in real time.
- *Burst* is a mobile video platform enabling users (reporters or viewers) to capture and upload video to the cloud and then integrate it for social media, web or broadcast.
- *Flickr* is an image and video hosting website used for sharing those photos and videos. It's owned by Yahoo.
- *Google+* (or Google Plus) is a social network, akin to *Facebook* (and well behind *Facebook* in subscribers). The future of Google+ is unclear.

- *Hootsuite* is a social media management system that works to coordinate many of those other software programs.
- *IFTTT* is a web based system allowing the user to create conditional automated distribution of messages or postings. The name stands for *If This Then That*.
- *Instagram* is used for online mobile photo and video sharing and social networking. Instagram is owned by *Facebook*.
- *LinkedIn* is a business-oriented social networking service.
- *NPR One* is an audio app that allows the user to stream NPR stories and podcasts.
- *Numerous* tracks and updates all the numbers you tell it you care about (e.g. birthdays, anniversaries, etc.).
- *Periscope* is an online live video streaming service (app). It's owned by *Twitter*.
- *Pinterest* is a "visual discovery tool" to help people find and save creative ideas.
- *Rdio* was an online music streaming service. *Rdio* went into bankruptcy, and many of its assets were purchased by *Pandora*.
- *Slack* is a cloud-based messaging app for teams.
- *Snapchat* is a video messaging app.
- *SoundCloud* is a global online audio sharing platform which can be used for uploading and recording audio.
- *Storify* allows people to use social media (like *Facebook*, *Twitter*, etc.) to create stories and timelines.
- *Tagboards* are included within websites to allow people to see and leave messages without registering.
- *Tumblr* is a social networking and microblogging platform. It's owned by *Yahoo*.
- *TuneIn* is an online service allowing access to thousands of radio stations, programs and podcasts.
- *Videolicious* is a software program that enables users to create, edit and publish videos just using an iPhone. Android software is in the works but not available as this is written.
- *Vine* is an app used to create and share very short videos. It's now owned by *Twitter*.
- *YouTube* . . . you know what *YouTube* is, a video-sharing website. It's owned by *Google*.

Obviously, not all stations are using all of these tools, or even any of them. In television, 73 percent of news directors said they're using social media beyond just *Facebook* and *Twitter*. And 77 percent of that group made *Instagram* the easy winner. For *Instagram*, most stations said they were using the software for branding, mostly behind-the-scenes pictures, reporter pictures, sharing content, weather updates, re-sharing user generated content, Friday night high school football, visual promotion of stories, pictures of events, promotions, short videos, and to interact with the audience.

Well behind *Instagram*, at 20 percent, came *Periscope*. News directors noted they used it for behind the scenes pictures, streaming, teases, and live events.

After that came *Pinterest* at 16 percent. News directors said they used it for pictures.

Also at 16 percent is *Snapchat*. News directors noted using it for a personal side of the newsroom, weather pictures and sports.

Then a tie between two Google properties: *Google+* and *YouTube*, each at 9 percent. *YouTube* was used for videos, interviews and uploading stories. News directors didn't mention how they were using *Google+*.

Videolicious came in at 2 percent and was being used for teases, according to one news director.

Other software just got single mentions: *Storify*, *Vine*, *Slack*, *Numerous*, *Banjo* and *Tagboard*.

Generally, the bigger the market and the bigger the staff, the more likely a TV station was using social media beyond just *Facebook* and *Twitter*.

In radio, almost 32 percent of news directors and general managers listed various software other than *Facebook* and *Twitter* that they're using. That *other* list turned out to be *Instagram* and other. In radio, *Instagram* was mentioned 50 percent more often than all the other (non-*Facebook* and *Twitter*) software combined. Everything else was in single digits, starting with *Periscope*, then *YouTube*, then *Snapchat*, then everything else. A number of the NPR affiliates mentioned *NPR One*.

● ● ● ● ●

Mobile

Overall, the biggest change in media consumption over the last few years has been the steadily increasing time spent on smartphones, and much of the change and increasing emphasis on social media is designed to reach those smartphone users. Nielsen reports (2016) that 81 percent of Americans use a smartphone regularly, and they spend an average of one hour and 39 minutes online per day via those smartphones. Only TV use exceeds smartphone use.

Today, a reporter with a mobile phone and Facebook Live (or other software) can be on social media and connecting with the audience from just about anywhere in a matter of moments.

Couple Facebook Live with Instant Articles, and at least some stations are posting more and more of their content on Facebook, specifically aiming to reach the large and growing mobile market. The tradeoff is control. After all, a station is providing content via Facebook rather than its own website. Then there's the question of money: Who will get how much revenue from advertising that reaches those mobile eyeballs?

More and more, stations say their online traffic comes primarily from Facebook rather than Google, and that switch is because of the increasing use of mobile. A study by Parse.ly Network in 2016 found that Facebook, at 46 percent, followed closely by Google, at 40 percent, supplied a combined 86 percent of referral traffic to station websites.

●●●●●

Apps

Apps—short for applications—generally involve software programs designed to run on mobile devices—phones and tablets. At this writing, the percentage of TV stations that have apps is up to 93 percent. The bigger the staff, the more likely that the station has one or more apps. The typical station had 2 apps, and, in TV, almost all apps are free.

The percentage of radio stations with apps remains just under half at 49 percent. Smaller groups, smaller newsrooms and, especially, smaller markets keep the number down. Noncommercial stations were more likely to have apps than commercial stations, but noncommercial stations tended to have fewer apps per station than commercial stations.

Note that there's sometimes a fuzzy dividing line between the information covered in this chapter and that in Chapter 15, "Online News."

●●●●●

NewsON

NewsON is a new business (as of 2016), backed by several of the largest TV station owners to make local news more widely available on smartphones, tablets and connected TV devices like Roku. Given that the players include Nexstar, ABC, Cox Media Group, Sinclair, Hearst and Raycom, the app should allow the viewing of local news on most of the TV stations in the U.S. (that run local news). The app is free; the service is ad-supported. It's too new to know what the impact will be on local TV news.

● ● ● ● ●

The Bottom Line

Facebook and Twitter and the various other social networking tools all have potential value. But the best people in the business will tell you that the best way to get people to your station and website is to produce the best content, and then let people know in as many ways as you can. Try new things. "If we're not creating and innovating," notes Crosby Shaterian at KERO, "if we're not experimenting, then we're failing the industry."

One thing to also keep in mind: 15 percent or so of American adults do not go online at all.

● ● ● ● ●

Summary

Stations' use of social media is steadily increasing. Most stations use Facebook and Twitter, TV much more so than radio. Station use of social media is changing, especially in TV, where more and more stations are using social media to conduct conversations with their audience. Radio tends to lag in this area, where most use remains promotional.

● ● ● ● ●

Key Words & Phrases

social media . . . social networking . . . Facebook . . . Facebook Live . . . Facebook News Feed . . . Twitter . . . Reddit . . . crowdsourcing . . . YouTube . . . LinkedIn . . . Pinterest . . . Instagram . . . backpack journalists . . . Banjo . . . Burst . . . Flickr . . . Google+ . . . Hootsuite . . . IFTTT . . . MMJ . . . NPR One . . . Numerous . . . one-man-bands . . . Periscope . . . Rdio . . . Slack . . . Snapchat . . . Sound-Cloud . . . Storify . . . Tagboards . . . TuneIn . . . Videolicious . . . Tumblr . . . Vine . . . NewsON

● ● ● ● ●

Exercises

A. Compare the Facebook pages for your local newspaper with those of one of the major local television stations. How are they different, and how are they similar? Compare how each handles a major local news story that both are covering. Which does a better job on local, national and international news? What differences do you see in terms of philosophy or approach to social media? Support your views with concrete examples.

B. Compare the Facebook pages of the local television stations within your market. How are they different, and how are they similar? Compare how each handles a major local news story that both are covering. Which does a better job on local, national and international news? What differences do you see in terms of philosophy or approach to social media? Support your views with concrete examples. How are they different from the station websites?

C. Examine the various websites and Facebook pages for the stations in your market to determine what other social media the stations are using and how they're using them. Make a list for each station, note specific examples, and evaluate the effectiveness of what they're doing. Which station seems to be on top of the technology race? How does that compare with the ratings race and station viewership?

●●●●●

The Radio-Television Digital News Association (RTDNA) Social Media and Blogging Guidelines*

In 2010, RTDNA's Ethics Committee and Al Tompkins, the Broadcasting and Online Group Leader for The Poynter Institute, developed the following guidelines for social media and blogging.

Social media and blogs are important elements of journalism. They narrow the distance between journalists and the public. They encourage lively, immediate and spirited discussion. They can be vital news-gathering and news-delivery tools. As a journalist you should uphold the same professional and ethical standards of fairness, accuracy, truthfulness, transparency and independence when using social media as you do on air and on all digital news platforms.

Truth and Fairness

■ Social media comments and postings should meet the same standards of fairness, accuracy and attribution that you apply to your on-air or digital platforms.

■ Information gleaned online should be confirmed just as you must confirm scanner traffic or phone tips before reporting them. If you cannot independently confirm critical information, reveal your sources; tell the public how you know what you know and what you cannot confirm. Don't stop there. Keep seeking confirmation. This guideline is the same for covering breaking news on station websites as on the air. You should not leave the public "hanging." Lead the public to completeness and understanding.

■ Twitter's character limits and immediacy are not excuses for inaccuracy and unfairness.

■ Remember that social media postings live on as online archives. Correct and clarify mistakes, whether they are factual mistakes or mistakes of omission.

■ **When using content from blogs or social media, ask critical questions such as:**

  – What is the source of the video or photograph? Who wrote the comment and what was the motivation for posting it?

  – Does the source have the legal right to the material posted? Did that person take the photograph or capture the video?

  – Has the photograph or video been manipulated? Have we checked to see if the metadata attached to the image reveals that it has been altered?

■ Social networks typically offer a "privacy" setting, so users can choose not to have their photographs or thoughts in front of the uninvited public. Capturing material from a public Facebook site is different from prying behind a password-protected wall posing as a friend. When considering whether to access "private" content, journalists should apply the same RTDNA guidelines recommended for undercover journalism. Ask:

  – Does the poster have a "reasonable expectation" of privacy?

  – Is this a story of great significance?

  – Is there any other way to get the information?

  – Are you willing to disclose your methods and reasoning?

  – What are your journalistic motivations?

For Discussion in your Newsroom

When an Army psychiatrist killed 13 people at Fort Hood, Twitter messages, supposedly from "inside the post" reported gunfire continued for a half hour and that there were multiple shooters. Journalists passed along the information naming Twitter writers as the sources. The information proved to be false and needed to be corrected. If one or multiple shooters had been at large, withholding that information could have caused some people to be in harm's way. The nature of live, breaking news frequently leads to reports of rumor, hearsay and other inaccurate information. Journalists must source information, correct mistakes quickly and prominently and remind the public that the information is fluid and could be unreliable.

Questions for the Newsroom

– What protocols does your newsroom have to correct mistakes on social media sites such as Twitter and Facebook?

– Does your newsroom have a process for copyediting and oversight of the content posted on social media sites? What decisionmaking process do you go through before you post?

– What protocols do you have for checking the truthfulness of photographs or video that you find on Facebook, YouTube or photosharing sites? Have you contacted the photographer? Can you see the unedited video or raw photograph file? Does the image or video make sense when compared to the facts of the story?

– Who in the newsroom is charged with confirming information gleaned from social media sites?

Accountability and Transparency

■ You should not write anonymously or use an avatar or username that cloaks your real identity on newsroom or personal websites. You are responsible for everything you say. Commenting or blogging anonymously compromises this core principle.

■ Be especially careful when you are writing, Tweeting or blogging about a topic that you or your newsroom covers. Editorializing about a topic or person can reveal your personal feelings. Biased comments could be used in a court of law to demonstrate a predisposition, or even malicious intent, in a libel action against the news organization, even for an unrelated story.

■ Just as you keep distance between your station's advertising and journalism divisions, you should not use social media to promote business or personal interests without disclosing that relationship to the public. Sponsored links should be clearly labeled, not cloaked as journalistic content.

For Discussion in your Newsroom

1. Your consumer reporter at a major electronics show wants to give a glowing blog review of a new digital camera. When the company makes the splashy announcement, the reporter Tweets the news. The message virals fast and wide. Your station will be running ads for the camera as part of the company's national advertising campaign. How will you tell the public that you have a business relationship with the camera company?

2. Your political reporter has been covering the challenger in the mayor's race. On his personal Facebook page, your reporter says, "I am covering another candidate who is dumber than dirt." The candidate's press secretary calls to demand that the political reporter be

"taken off the campaign." Your reporter's defense: "What I say on my own time on my own website is my business. Plus I didn't name names."

How will you respond? What should you tell the public about the complaint and your decision?

Image and Reputation

■ Remember that what's posted online is open to the public (even if you consider it to be private). Personal and professional lives merge online. Newsroom employees should recognize that even though their comments may seem to be in their "private space," their words become direct extensions of their news organizations. Search engines and social mapping sites can locate their posts and link the writers' names to their employers.

■ There are journalistic reasons to connect with people online, even if you cover them, but consider whom you "friend" on sites like Facebook or "follow" on Twitter. You may believe that online "friends" are different from other friends in your life, but the public may not always see it that way. For example, be prepared to publicly explain why you show up as a "friend" on a politician's website. Inspect your "friends" list regularly to look for conflicts with those who become newsmakers.

■ Be especially careful when registering for social network sites. Pay attention to how the public may interpret Facebook information that describes your relationship status, age, sexual preference and political or religious views. These descriptors can hold loaded meanings and affect viewer perception.

■ Keep in mind that when you join an online group, the public may perceive that you support that group. Be prepared to justify your membership.

■ Avoid posting photos or any other content on any website, blog, social network or video/photo sharing website that might embarrass you or undermine your journalistic credibility. Keep this in mind, even if you are posting on what you believe to be a "private" or passwordprotected site. Consider this when allowing others to take pictures of you at social gatherings. When you work for a journalism organization, you represent that organization on and off the clock. The same standards apply for journalists who work on air or off air.

■ Bloggers and journalists who use social media often engage readers in a lively give-and-take of ideas. Never insult or disparage readers. Try to create a respectful, informed dialogue while avoiding personal attacks.

For Discussion in your Newsroom

1. Edgy Facebook and Twitter postings create more traffic, so you urge your newsroom to get online and be provocative to get more attention. How will you respond when your anchor poses holding a halfempty martini glass on her Facebook site? How will you respond if your reporter's Facebook profile picture shows a bong in the background? What would your response be if a producer, who identifies herself as "conservative" on her Facebook page, Tweets her opinions during a political rally?

2. A news manager "friends" a neighbor he meets at a block party. A year later the neighbor decides to run for mayor. The news manager gets an indignant call from the incumbent mayor's press secretary suggesting the station coverage will be biased, since your news manager supports the challenger. Does the news manager have to "unfriend" his neighbor to preserve the appearance of fairness? Could the manager make things right if he "friended" the mayor, too?

*RTDNA Social Media and Blogging Guidelines,
adopted in 2010. Reprinted with permission.

17

•••••

News, Weather and Sports

•••••

Why News, Weather and Sports?

That's the triumvirate we think of when we think about TV newscasts, and that tradition goes back right to the beginning of local TV news. Note that all newscasts do contain news and weather, but not all newscasts include sports.

Research today tells us that, on an average day, more people are interested in the weather than any other single news story. That explains why weather is always a part of TV newscasts and why, if the weather is unusual, stations will frequently lead with the weather. Absent unusual meteorological conditions, stations generally use weather as the main draw for the second quarter hour of the newscast (see more on this in Chapter 13, "Producing News on TV").

It's not that more people are interested in the weather than in the news itself; it's that weather is more likely to be of more widespread interest than any single news story. Major breaking news changes that equation.

Sports is more complicated. Research tells us that sports is of interest to a minority of the audience, and the most serious sports fans now get their sports news from a myriad of options, including online, mobile or cable/satellite/telco.

Because of all those alternatives in sports information, some stations have dropped sports as a regular part of the news. Most of those efforts have been rescinded. As this is written, there are a few stations that have no sports anchor and simply cover sports the same way they cover any news story. But most have returned sports to the primary newscasts (early and late evening), and there is no evidence that sports is disappearing as a part of TV newscasts.

Still, because sports appeals to a smaller segment of the audience, virtually all TV stations run sports at the end of the newscast, so that if people tune elsewhere or turn off the TV, that desertion won't harm the station's ratings (see more on this in Chapter 13).

• • • • •

Reporting Weather

Few topics interest people as much as the weather. Weather and time are the two most important bits of information the morning radio audience wants, and weather shows up as the number one item in most television markets. But the audience doesn't want all of the data available.

First and foremost, people want to know the current sky condition, the temperature and whether anything is going to fall from the sky. Next, they want the short-range forecast. In the morning that means what it's going to be like that day, including sky conditions and temperature. Around noon that means what it's going to be like that afternoon and evening. In the early evening it's the forecast for that night and tomorrow. In the late evening it's the forecast for overnight and tomorrow. Commonly, we give the audience three day parts. This is what a typical morning radio weather forecast might sound like:

```
In the weather forecast, we'll have partly cloudy
skies today with a high around 55. Tonight, mostly
cloudy skies, with lows in the mid-30s. Tomorrow,
overcast skies and light rain expected, with highs
in the upper 40s. Right now, we have partly cloudy
skies and 41 degrees.
```

Next in interest tends to be the longer-range outlook: three to seven days. The audience knows (or should know) that it isn't terribly accurate, but they want it anyway.

Notice all the weather conditions *not* in the previous forecast. Generally, most members of the audience don't care about barometric pressure (since most don't know what it means, anyway). Other than boaters, people don't care about the winds unless they're going to be really noticeable.

Few care about humidity unless it's going to be markedly different from usual or it's high in the summer. High humidity readings in the summer strike the same kind of endurance chord that the wind chill does in the winter. We do like to know when we've endured really bad weather. Tides are relevant for a relatively small number of people right on the coast.

Severe Weather

Nothing sends people to radio and TV faster than the threat of severe weather. A severe weather warning (meaning that the severe weather condition definitely exists) should be broadcast as soon as it's known and repeated at regular intervals. Generally included in this are tornadoes, hurricanes, tropical storms, severe thunderstorms or other conditions and flooding. Severe weather watches (meaning that the conditions are right for the development of the severe weather) should also be broadcast. It is important that you make clear what the condition is, the geographic area involved, the duration of the watch or warning, what the watch or warning means and what action, if any, people should take.

● ● ● ● ●

Defining Weather Terms

blizzard: A winter storm with winds of 35 mph or more, lots of snow falling or blowing and visibility near zero.

Celsius (centigrade): The temperature scale of the metric system, based on 0 degrees as freezing and 100 degrees as boiling (at sea level). To convert temperatures to Celsius, subtract 32 from the Fahrenheit reading, multiply by 5, then divide by 9. Unless your station insists on using Celsius readings along with Fahrenheit, don't use Celsius. Americans have clearly shown that they neither understand nor care about Celsius readings. See also *Fahrenheit.*

chinook wind: A warm, dry wind occurring along the Rocky Mountains, sometimes reaching speeds of 100 mph.

climate: The average of weather conditions *over time.* Just because it's really hot doesn't mean that it's climate change—although climate change could be making it worse. And just because it's cold doesn't disprove climate change. Don't confuse *weather* with *climate change.*

coastal waters: Waters within about 69 miles of the coast.

cold front: The leading edge of a cold air mass advancing on a warm air mass. In the summer, thunderstorms can form a squall line in front of the edge. In the winter the result is often a cold wave.

cyclone: A storm with strong winds rotating about a moving center of low atmospheric pressure. Not the same as *tornado.* See *hurricane.*

degree–day: An index that is used to determine the amount of heating or cooling required to maintain constant temperature. The calculation assumes no demand for heat or cooling when the mean daily temperature is 65 degrees. To determine heating degree days, subtract the mean (average) temperature for the day from 65. If the high for a day is 56 degrees and the low 32 degrees, the mean is 44, resulting in 21 heat degree days. Cooling degree days also lead to a calculation of the energy required to maintain a comfortable indoor temperature—using the same formula except subtracting 65 from the mean temperature instead of the other way around.

dew point: The temperature at which the air is saturated with moisture and dew starts to form. When the dew point is below freezing, it's called the frost point—and that's what you'll get.

drought: An abnormal dry period lasting long enough to have a serious impact on agriculture and water supply.

dust storm: Blowing dust of 30 mph or more with visibility one-half mile or less.

earthquake: Involves a shaking of the earth's crust, the release of built-up stress caused by portions of the earth's crust grinding against each other. Commonly measured on the Richter scale. Minor earthquakes occur frequently; a reading of about 2.0 on the Richter scale can be felt by people. Each full point increase represents a doubling of strength. There is no upper limit to the Richter scale, although the highest ever recorded is 9.5 (Chile in 1960). Anything above about 4.5 can cause considerable damage. The Richter scale measures an earthquake's strength. The less commonly used Mercalli scale measures the earthquake's intensity in a given area. On a 1 to 12 scale, 1 means hardly felt, and 12 means total damage.

El Niño: A warming of the tropical Pacific Ocean—starting along the coasts of Peru and Ecuador—that can cause disruption in the world's weather systems. Major El Niño events occur every 5 to 10 years.

equinox: When the sun is directly over the equator. The autumnal equinox is usually September 23 (sometimes the 22nd); the vernal equinox is usually on March 21 (sometimes the 20th). The astronomic starts of fall and spring.

Fahrenheit: The temperature scale that is in common use in the United States. Freezing is 32 degrees; boiling is 212 degrees at sea-level. In the unlikely event that you need to convert Fahrenheit to Celsius, subtract 32 from the Fahrenheit reading, then multiply by 5, then divide by 9. See also *Celsius*.

flash flood: A sudden, violent flood, usually after heavy rains or considerable, rapid melting of snow.

flood: Streamflow in excess of a channel's capacity. Remember that reporting how high a river or *the water* will crest is meaningless without some comparison—particularly height above flood stage.

fog: A stratus cloud with its base at ground level, reducing visibility to less than 0.62 mile (1 kilometer). *Heavy fog* means visibility is down to one-quarter mile (0.4 km) or less.

freeze: When the temperature remains below 32 degrees long enough to damage crops. *Hard freeze* and *severe freeze* are synonymous and mean that the freezing conditions are expected to last at least two days.

freezing drizzle, freezing rain: Both terms mean that the precipitation will freeze on contact with a cold object or the ground, resulting in a coat of ice called glaze. See *ice storm.*

frost: Normally, *scattered light frost* is the term used. It is the freezing of dew on the ground.

funnel cloud: A violent, rotating current of air that does not touch the ground. If and when it touches the ground, it becomes a tornado.

gale: Usually, gale force winds, meaning sustained wind speeds between 39 and 54 mph.

heat index: A calculation of what the combination of heat and humidity feels like. Given as a "temperature," it's based on the idea that when the humidity is high, the temperature feels even hotter than it is. Sometimes called the *misery index.*

Relative Humidity	Air Temperature (Degrees F)						
	80	85	90	95	100	105	110
40%	79	84	90	98	109	121	135
50%	80	86	94	105	118	133	
60%	81	90	99	113	129	148	
70%	82	92	105	122	142		
80%	84	96	113	133			
90%	85	101	121				

When the Heat Index Is:	Here's the Possible Reaction:
80–90 degrees	Fatigue with prolonged exposure and physical activity
90–105 degrees	Sunstroke, heat cramps and heat exhaustion
105–130 degrees	Sunstroke and heat cramps likely, heat stroke possible
130+ degrees	Heat stroke highly likely with continued exposure

heavy snow: Generally, 4 or more inches of snow within 12 hours or 6 or more inches of snow within 24 hours.

high winds: Generally, winds of 40 mph or more for at least an hour.

humidity: The amount of moisture in the air. *Relative humidity* (the term more commonly used in weather forecasts) is the amount of moisture in the air as a percentage of the amount of moisture that air of that temperature can hold.

hurricane, typhoon, cyclone: A tropical storm with a warm core and wind speeds of at least 74 mph. Hurricanes that drop below that wind speed are downgraded to tropical storms. Hurricanes start east of the international dateline; typhoons start on the west; cyclones occur in the Indian Ocean. Otherwise, all three are identical.

hurricane season: When hurricanes are most likely to take place. In the Atlantic, Caribbean and Gulf of Mexico, that's June through November; in the eastern Pacific, it's June through November 15; in the central Pacific, it's June through October.

ice storm: When rain falls through a thin layer of below-freezing air at the earth's surface, causing the rain to freeze on contact; glaze.

Indian summer: An unseasonably warm spell in October or November. Purists insist that you can't have Indian summer until after a cold spell or frost.

jet stream: A narrow band of strong wind, normally 6 to 9 miles up, that influences the development and path of weather conditions.

knot: Used for offshore wind speed and the speed of boats and ships. Because *knot* means one nautical mile (6,076.1 feet) per hour, it's redundant to say *knots per hour.* To convert knots to approximate miles per hour, multiply knots by 1.15.

Northeaster: Strong, steady winds from the northeast—along with rain or snow—associated with a strong low pressure system moving northeast along the east coast of North America. Also called a *Nor'easter.*

offshore waters: Generally, from 69 to 288 miles off the coast.

relative humidity: See *humidity.*

sandstorm: Same as dust storm, but for sand: blowing sand of 30 mph or more with visibility one-half mile or less.

Santa Ana wind: A warm, dry wind blowing west into southern California from the high desert plateau to the east, associated with very high temperatures, dust storms and fires.

seasons: Meteorologically, spring is March, April and May; summer is June, July and August; fall is September, October and November; and winter is December, January and February.

severe blizzard: Same as *blizzard* but with higher winds (45 mph or more) and temperatures of 10 degrees or colder.

severe thunderstorm: Intense thunderstorms with high winds (58 mph or more), heavy rainfall, hail, flash floods and/or tornadoes.

sleet: Formed from the freezing of raindrops or refreezing of melted snowflakes into ice pellets 5 mm or less in diameter.

smog: Commonly used to describe polluted air that reduces visibility, especially common over large cities.

snow avalanche bulletin: Issued by the U.S. Forest Service for appropriate areas of the western United States.

snow flurry: A light, on-and-off snow shower.

snow squall: A heavy but short snow shower.

solstice: The summer solstice usually occurs on June 21 (sometimes the 22nd) when the sun is right over the Tropic of Cancer; the longest day of the year in the Northern Hemisphere and the astronomical start of summer. The winter solstice is usually on December 22 (sometimes the 21st), when the sun is over the Tropic of Capricorn; the shortest day in the Northern Hemisphere and the astronomical start of winter.

squall: A sudden increase of wind speed by at least 16 knots and lasting at least one minute.

stockman's advisory: Public alert that livestock may require protection because of a combination of cold, wet and windy weather.

tidal wave: Popularly used to describe an unusually large and destructive wave that reaches land.

tornado: The most destructive of all atmospheric phenomena—a violent rotating column of air that forms a funnel and touches the ground. Not the same as *cyclone*.

travelers' advisory: Alert that difficult road or driving conditions exist over a specified area.

tropical depression: A tropical cyclone with surface wind speed of 38 mph or less.

tropical storm: A warm-core cyclone with sustained wind speeds from 39 to 73 mph. See *hurricane*.

tsunami: A seismic sea wave, generally caused by an underwater earthquake.

typhoon: See *hurricane*.

urban heat island: The higher temperatures in urban areas caused by the burning of fossil fuels and the absorption of heat by pavement and buildings.

UV (ultraviolet) index: An index that measures the exposure to ultraviolet rays on a scale of 0 (least exposure) to 15 (extremely high exposure).

Index Value	Exposure Level
0 to 2	Low
3 to 5	Moderate
6 to 7	High
8 to 10	Very High
11+	Extreme

warm front: A front created by warm air moving into an area of colder air.

warning: Generally means the existence or suspected existence of whatever the condition is that's being warned about.

watch: Generally means the possibility of or correct conditions for whatever is to be watched.

wind chill: A calculation of what the combination of temperature and wind feels like on exposed skin. The lower the temperature and/or the higher the wind, the larger the wind chill factor or index—and the more miserable and cold we feel.

Wind Speed	Air Temperature (MPH) (Degrees F)													
Calm	40	35	30	25	20	15	10	5	0	−5	−10	−15	−20	−25
5	36	31	25	19	13	7	1	−5	−11	−16	−22	−28	−34	−40
10	34	27	21	15	9	3	−4	−10	−16	−22	−28	−35	−41	−47
15	32	25	19	13	6	0	−7	−13	−19	−26	−32	−39	−45	−51
20	30	24	17	11	4	−2	−9	−15	−22	−29	−35	−42	−48	−55
25	29	23	16	9	3	−4	−11	−17	−24	−31	−37	−44	−51	−58
30	28	22	15	8	1	−5	−12	−19	−26	−33	−39	−46	−53	−60
35	28	21	14	7	0	−7	−14	−21	−27	−34	−41	−48	−55	−62
40	27	20	13	6	−1	−8	−15	−22	−29	−36	−43	−50	−57	−64
45	26	19	12	5	−2	−9	−16	−23	−30	−37	−44	−51	−58	−65
50	26	19	12	4	−3	−10	−17	−24	−31	−38	−45	−52	−60	−67

At minus 18 degrees (wind chill), frostbite can occur in 30 minutes. At minus 32 degrees (wind chill), frostbite can occur in 10 minutes. At minus 48 degrees (wind chill), frostbite can occur in 5 minutes.

●●●●●

Reporting Sports

Some people view sports reporting just like any other reporting, except about sports. Perhaps it should be, but it doesn't work that way. Inevitably, for a variety of reasons well outside the scope of this book, sports reporting is a blend of good reporting and local boosterism. Finding that middle ground can be difficult. Local sportscasters or sports reporters perceived as indifferent to the home team can wind up in the (job) loss column themselves. Going too far in rooting for the home team results in boorishness and whining that eventually irritate the audience.

Another common problem in sports reporting is that access to the players may be restricted if the team, school or coach is unhappy with the reporting on the team. Some sports reporters, concerned about the potential difficulties in covering people who are unhappy with the reporter, tend to shy away from controversy or criticism. Some stations wind up sending news reporters to cover controversial local sports stories because the sports reporters either aren't capable of covering the "news" side of sports or are unwilling to ask tough questions and risk alienating the people they cover.

Reporting Scores

The seemingly straightforward delivery of sports scores poses one of the biggest challenges. There is no magic formula. The first thing you need to determine is *which* sports are *how* popular. Radio sports tends to concentrate on play-by-play and scores. Generally, don't give just the winners. The audience may not want a lot of detail, but they want to know who won, who lost and the score. It's also easier to follow sports scores when the announcer consistently gives the winning team first:

```
Boston beat Baltimore 5-to-2 ... Cleveland
over Toronto 7-to-4 ... New York edged Oakland
2-to-1 ... and Detroit shut out Minnesota
3-to-nothing.
```

The repetition of winner-first, loser-second makes it easier to follow, especially when scores are just heard. But notice the variety of expression used to say the same thing. In each case the first team won and the second lost, but vary the way you say it. If possible, no two scores (especially in a row) should use exactly the same words to describe the score. Among the possibilities are *beat, defeated, pummeled, walloped, nailed, drubbed, edged, shut out, blanked, got by, won by, humiliated, squeaked by, trounced, got past* and so on. But make sure you use the right term for the score. Hardly anything sounds as silly as an announcer saying something like

```
Dallas trounced Green Bay 13-to-10.
```

Varying the way you refer to teams is fine, but keep in mind that everyone understands cities, but considerably fewer people know the names of teams. Watch out for *New York, Los Angeles, Chicago* and *Sox.* All have two or more teams.

Television has the advantage of graphics. If you're also going to show the audience the score, you have a lot more leeway on how you say it. On particularly heavy sports days—or for certain sports—it may be best just to run the scores in a crawl, either full screen or at the bottom of the screen.

Common Mistakes

Some general sports reporting cautions. First, the audience assumes that scores are final unless otherwise noted. Make clear if you're dealing with games in progress. Second, don't confuse men's and women's sports. It's incredibly irritating when an announcer gives a series of scores and then notes that those scores were for the women rather than the men (or vice versa). Make clear up front exactly what scores you're giving. Third, college sports involve men's and women's teams; high school sports involve boys' and girls' teams.

● ● ● ● ●

Sports and Teams

Auto Racing

Internationally, the leading types:

FIA (Federation Internationale de l'Automobile)
Formula 1

In the United States, the leading types:

AMA (American Motorcyclist Association)—motorcycle racing
IMSA (International Motor Sports Association)—racing prototypes
IndyCar (Indy Racing League)—"Indy" car racing
NASCAR (National Association of Stock Car Auto Racing)—stock car racing
NHRA (National Hot Rod Association)—drag racing
SCCA (Sports Car Club of America)—Trans-Am racing
SCORE International (High Desert Racing Association)—off-road racing
WeatherTech SportsCar Championship

Baseball—Major Leagues

American League

East	Central	West
Baltimore Orioles	Chicago White Sox	Houston Astros
Boston Red Sox	Cleveland Indians	Los Angeles Angels
New York Yankees	Detroit Tigers	Oakland Athletics (As)
Tampa Bay Rays	Kansas City Royals	Seattle Mariners
Toronto Blue Jays	Minnesota Twins	Texas Rangers

National League

East	Central	West
Atlanta Braves	Chicago Cubs	Arizona Diamondbacks
Miami Marlins	Cincinnati Reds	Colorado Rockies
New York Mets	Milwaukee Brewers	Los Angeles Dodgers
Philadelphia Phillies	Pittsburgh Pirates	San Diego Padres
Washington Nationals	St. Louis Cardinals	San Francisco Giants

Basketball—National Basketball Association

Eastern Conference

Atlantic Division	Central Division	Southeast Division
Boston Celtics	Chicago Bulls	Atlanta Hawks
Brooklyn Nets	Cleveland Cavaliers	Charlotte Hornets
New York Knicks	Detroit Pistons	Miami Heat
Philadelphia 76ers	Indiana Pacers	Orlando Magic
Toronto Raptors	Milwaukee Bucks	Washington (DC) Wizards

Western Conference

Northwest Division	Pacific Division	Southwest Division
Denver Nuggets	Golden State Warriors	Dallas Mavericks
Minnesota Timberwolves	Los Angeles Clippers	Houston Rockets
Oklahoma City Thunder	Los Angeles Lakers	Memphis Grizzlies
Portland Trail Blazers	Phoenix Suns	New Orleans Pelicans
Utah Jazz	Sacramento Kings	San Antonio Spurs

Basketball—Women's National Basketball Association

Eastern Conference	Western Conference
Atlanta Dream	Dallas Wings
Chicago Sky	Los Angeles Sparks
Connecticut Sun	Minnesota Lynx
Indiana Fever	Phoenix Mercury
New York Liberty	San Antonio Stars
Washington Mystics	Seattle Storm

Boxing

Major sanctioning groups are the World Boxing Association (WBA), World Boxing Council (WBC), World Boxing Organization (WBO) and International Boxing Federation (IBF)

Football—National Football League

American Football Conference

East	North	South	West
Buffalo Bills	Baltimore Ravens	Houston Texans	Denver Broncos
Miami Dolphins	Cincinnati Bengals	Indianapolis Colts	Kansas City Chiefs
New England Patriots	Cleveland Browns	Jacksonville Jaguars	Oakland Raiders
New York Jets	Pittsburgh Steelers	Tennessee Titans	San Diego Chargers

National Football Conference

East	North	South	West
Dallas Cowboys	Chicago Bears	Atlanta Falcons	Arizona Cardinals
New York Giants	Detroit Lions	Carolina Panthers	Los Angeles Rams
Philadelphia Eagles	Green Bay Packers	New Orleans Saints	San Francisco 49ers
Washington Redskins	Minnesota Vikings	Tampa Bay Buccaneers	Seattle Seahawks

Football—Arena Football League

American Conference	National Conference
Philadelphia Soul	Arizona Rattlers
Orlando Predators	Cleveland Gladiators
Jacksonville Sharks	LA KISS
Tampa Bay Storm	Portland Steel

Football—Canadian Football League

East Division	West Division
Hamilton Tiger-Cats	British Columbia (B.C.) Lions
Montreal Alouettes	Calgary Stampeders
Ottawa Redblacks	Edmonton Eskimos
Toronto Argonauts	Saskatchewan Roughriders
	Winnipeg Blue Bombers

Golf

Major events sanctioned by the Professional Golfers Association (PGA), the Senior Professional Golfers Association (Senior PGA) and the Ladies Professional Golfers Association (LPGA).

Hockey—National Hockey League

Eastern Conference

Metropolitan	Atlantic
Carolina Hurricanes	Boston Bruins
Columbus Blue Jackets	Buffalo Sabres
New Jersey Devils	Detroit Red Wings
New York Islanders	Florida Panthers
New York Rangers	Montreal Canadiens
Philadelphia Flyers	Ottawa Senators
Pittsburgh Penguins	Tampa Bay Lightning
Washington (DC) Capitals	Toronto Maple Leafs

Western Conference

Central	Pacific
Chicago Blackhawks	Anaheim Ducks
Colorado Avalanche	Arizona Coyotes
Dallas Stars	Calgary Flames
Minnesota Wild	Edmonton Oilers
Nashville Predators	Los Angeles Kings
St. Louis Blues	San Jose Sharks
Winnipeg Jets	Vancouver Canucks
	Vegas Golden Knights

Soccer—Major League Soccer

Eastern Conference	Western Conference
Chicago Fire	Colorado Rapids
Columbus Crew SC	FC Dallas
D.C. United	Houston Dynamo
Montreal Impact	LA Galaxy
New England Revolution	Portland Timbers

(Continued)

Eastern Conference	Western Conference
New York City FC	Real Salt Lake
New York Red Bulls	San Jose Earthquakes
Orlando City SC	Seattle Sounders
Philadelphia Union	Sporting Kansas City
Toronto FC	Vancouver Whitecaps FC

Ultimate Fighting Championship—UFC

Mixed Martial Arts (MMA), fighting in various weight classes

18

Reporting: Seasonal Coverage and the Calendar

Seasonal Reporting

There is a cyclical nature to our lives, and much of that cycle is based on the calendar. Some of it's based on religion; some based on historical events; and some on the seasonal nature of weather. People who live in cold climates spend more time outside in the summer; our major shopping of the year comes in late November and December because of Christmas and Chanukah.

Our non-breaking news coverage tends to mirror those cycles. Every year, we do stories on New Year's resolutions, major holidays, Groundhog Day, Daylight Saving Time, the busiest travel and shopping days, and so on.

The listings in this chapter will help remind you to plan for seasonal, holiday and religious coverage. 'LEGAL HOLIDAY' refers just to the U.S.

Solar and Lunar and the World's Major Religions

The calendar in this section lists the major holidays celebrated in the United States, Canada and Mexico. In addition to the important Christian holidays, the major Jewish, Muslim, Buddhist and Hindu holidays are included.

Unlike the Roman, solar-based calendar, Jewish, Muslim, Buddhist and Hindu calendars are all lunar-based, and all have 354 days in a year (rather than 365). However, the Jewish, Buddhist and Hindu calendars add a month periodically (about every three years) which keeps the calendar generally in line with the seasons. That's why Jewish, Buddhist and Hindu holidays will always occur at the same general time of the (solar) year but on varying days. The Muslim calendar, however, stays at 354 days. That means that, over time, Muslim holidays will cycle through the entire solar calendar. That's why they're listed separately at the end.

• • • • •

Calendar Holidays

JANUARY

1 New Year's Day: LEGAL HOLIDAY. If it falls on a Saturday, it's observed on Friday. If it falls on a Sunday, it's observed on Monday.

6 Epiphany: Observed by many Christians worldwide, although not necessarily on the same date as in the United States.

Dr. Martin Luther King Jr. Day: LEGAL HOLIDAY. Observed on the third Monday in January.

Chinese New Year: January 21–February 19 depending on the moon.

Sarasvati Puja: (sehr AH swah tee POO jah). Hindu festival honoring Goddess Sarasvati, who represents wisdom, intellect and knowledge as well as inspiration, arts and music.

FEBRUARY

2 Groundhog Day

5 Constitution Day: Observed in Mexico.

12 Lincoln's Birthday

14 Valentine's Day

Presidents Day: LEGAL HOLIDAY. Observed on the third Monday in February.

22 Washington's Birthday

Ash Wednesday: Seventh Wednesday before Easter.

Lent: Forty days from Ash Wednesday to Holy Saturday (the day before Easter). Lent starts 42 days before Easter in Orthodox Eastern Church.

29 Leap Day: Almost every four years (2004, 2008, etc.). Technically every 4 years as long as the year can be divided evenly by 4 . . . unless it can be divided evenly by 100, in which case it's not a leap year unless the year can be divided evenly by 400. So 1900 wasn't, 2000 was, 2100 won't be.

Maha Shiv Ratri: (MAH hah shihv rah TREE). Hindu fast, night vigil and feast for God-Goddess Shiva-Shakti (union of will and power), who dances to create, destroy and re-create the universe. Observed in February or March, depending on the lunar year.

MARCH

Daylight saving time starts: In the United States, except Arizona and Hawaii, clocks are set forward one hour at 2 a.m. on the second

Sunday in March. (DST used to start on the first Sunday in April, but the law was changed in 2005, effective in 2007.) Worldwide observance is variable. Note *saving* is singular.

17 St. Patrick's Day

21 (usually) the first day of spring: Some years the first day of spring will be March 20. The vernal equinox.

21 Benito Juarez's Birthday: Observed in Mexico.

Palm Sunday: The Sunday before Easter.

Good Friday: The Friday before Easter.

Easter Sunday: The first Sunday after the first full moon occurring on or after March 21 (March 22–April 25).

Passover: One week occurring in March or April after the first full moon occurring on or after March 21 (14–21 in the Hebrew month of Nisan).

Magha Puja Day: (mahg POO jah). Fourfold Assembly or Sangha Day. Observed to commemorate a special honor in the life of Buddha. On the full moon day of the third lunar month.

Hindu New Year: This doesn't actually mark the beginning of a new calendar year but usually marks the beginning of spring, although it is different in different parts of the country.

Holi: (HOE lee). Hindu festival celebrating the courting of God Shiva by Goddess Parvati and the efforts on her behalf by Kama (God of Love) and Fati (Goddess of Passion).

APRIL

1 April Fools' Day

8 Buddha's Birthday: Observed in Korea and Japan.

14 Pan American Day

15 Income Tax Due: Because of Emancipation Day in Washington, DC, if April 15 falls on a Friday, then taxes are due the following Monday, April 18. If April 15 falls on a Saturday or Sunday, taxes are due the following Tuesday, either April 17 or 18.

Ram Navmi: (rahm NOE mee). Birthday of Hindu God Rama (avatar of Vishnu).

MAY

1 May Day/Labor Day: Observed in Latin America, most of Europe, Russia and the countries of western Asia.

Mother's Day: The second Sunday in May.

Victoria Day: The first Monday before May 25. Observed in Canada.

Memorial Day: LEGAL HOLIDAY. The last Monday in May (May 30 was the original Memorial Day).

Vesak or Visakah Puja: (WEH sock POO jah; note that Vesak and Visakah are pronounced the same). Buddha Day. This major Buddhist festival of the year celebrates Buddha's birth, enlightenment, and death on one day. Observed on the day of the first full moon in May.

JUNE

14 Flag Day

Father's Day: The third Sunday in June.

21 (usually) the first day of summer: Some years the first day of summer is June 22. The longest day of the year with the most sunlight. Summer solstice.

JULY

1 Canada Day: Canadian national holiday.

4 Independence Day: LEGAL HOLIDAY. If it falls on a Saturday, it's observed on Friday. If it falls on a Sunday, it's observed on Monday.

Asalha Puja Day: (AHS lah POO jah). Dharma Day. Commemorates Buddha's first teaching. Observed on the full moon day of the eighth lunar month.

AUGUST

15 Assumption Day: Observed in Catholic countries.

Janmastami: (juhn muhst MEE). In Hinduism, this holiday celebrates the birth of Krishna, believed to be an incarnation of Vishnu and the author of the Bhagavad Gita, the most important book of the Mahabarata. Observed in August or September, depending on the lunar calendar.

Ganesh Chaturthi: (guhn EHSH cha toor THEE). Hindu festival honoring God Ganesha (son of Goddess Parvati and God Shiva) as the challenger/creator and remover of obstacles. Observed in August or September, depending on the lunar calendar.

Saradhas: (shrahd). Hindu festival in which offerings are made for departed ancestors. Observed in August or September, depending on the lunar calendar.

SEPTEMBER

Labor Day: LEGAL HOLIDAY. The first Monday in September.

Grandparents Day: The first Sunday in September.

23 (usually) the first day of fall: Some years the first day of fall is September 22. Autumnal equinox.

Rosh Hashanah: (rah shih SHAH nah). Jewish New Year. In September or October (1, 2 in Hebrew month of Tishri).

Yom Kippur: (YOHM kih PUUR). Jewish Day of Atonement. In September or October (10 in Hebrew month of Tishri).

NavRatri/Durga Puja: (NAHV rah tree/DUHR gah POO jah). Hindu festival of Great Goddess Maha Devi as Durga, protector of the powerless, celebrating her destruction of evil and the restoration of cosmic order. Observed in September or October, depending on the lunar calendar.

Dashera: (dahsh heh RAH). Recounts the rescue of Hindu Goddess Sita (avatar of Lakshmi) by God Rama (avatar of Vishnu) from an evil demon. Observed in September or October, depending on the lunar calendar.

OCTOBER

Columbus Day: LEGAL HOLIDAY. The second Monday in October (October 12 was the original Columbus Day).

Canadian Thanksgiving: The second Monday in October.

31 Halloween

Pavarana Day: (pah WEHR nah). In Buddhism, marks the conclusion of the rains retreat (Vassa) during the rainy season, which corresponds to the monsoon season in Asia; usually the end of October.

NOVEMBER

1 All Saints' Day: Observed primarily by Catholics in most countries.

2 All Souls' Day: Observed primarily by Catholics in most countries. Observed as the Day of the Dead in Mexico.

Daylight saving time ends: In the United States, except Arizona and Hawaii, clocks are set back one hour at 2 a.m. on the first Sunday in November. (Until 2007, DST used to end on the last Sunday in October.) Worldwide observance is variable. Note *saving* is singular.

Election Day: The first Tuesday after the first Monday in November.

11 Veterans Day

20 Anniversary of the Revolution: Observed in Mexico.

Thanksgiving Day: LEGAL HOLIDAY. The fourth Thursday in November.

Advent: The Sunday nearest November 30 marks the start of the Christmas season.

Chanukah: (KHAH nu kah). Jewish Feast of Dedication. Eight days in November or December (starting on 25 in the Hebrew month of Kislev). Various spellings.

Kathina Ceremony: (kah THEE nah). Robe offering ceremony. In Buddhism, the laity gather to make formal offerings of robe cloth.

Observed on a convenient date within one month of the conclusion of the Vassa Retreat.

Anapanasati Day: (UHN puhn uhs TEE). At the end of a retreat (Vassa) for the rainy season, the Buddha presents his instructions on mindfulness of breathing (Anapanasati). This marks the end of the fourth month of retreat.

DECEMBER

8 Feast of the Immaculate Conception: Observed in most Catholic countries.

Nine Days of Posada: Observed in Mexico during the third week in December.

22 (usually) the first day of winter: Some years the first day of winter is December 21. Day of the year with the least daylight. Winter solstice.

25 Christmas: LEGAL HOLIDAY. If it falls on a Saturday, it's observed on Friday. If it falls on a Sunday, it's observed on Monday.

26 Boxing Day: Observed in Canada.

26 Kwanzaa: Observed through January 1.

Buddhist Holidays

Some Buddhist holidays are celebrated at differing times of the year depending on the country. Take the Buddhist New Year, for example. In Thailand, Burma, Sri Lanka, Cambodia and Laos, the new year is celebrated for three days starting with the first full moon day in April. In China, Korea, Vietnam, Mongolia, Nepal, Indonesia, and parts of rural Japan, the new year starts on the first full moon day in January, but the celebration can be in late January or even later, depending on the country. Most of Japan celebrates the new year for at least three days, most often starting on January 1.

Uposatha: (uu poh SAH thah). Observance Day. Four monthly holy days, every month: the new moon, full moon and quarter moon days.

Hindu Holidays

Hindus celebrate many religious holidays, but the diversity of the religion leads different parts of the country and different sects to celebrate different holidays. The dates (above) represent the major Hindu holidays and approximate month in which they occur.

Muslim Holidays

Muharram 1: (moo hah RAHM). Muslim New Year.

Mawlid an-Nabi: (MOU lid). Celebrates the birth of Mohammed (the 12th day of the 4th month).

Ramadan: (RAH mah dahn). Holy month of fasting for Muslims (9th month of the Islamic year).

'Id al-Fitr: (EED ahl fah tr). Shawwal 1. The Muslim celebration at the end of Ramadan (the 1st day of the 10th month).

'Id al-Adha: (EED ahl AHD hah). Dhul-Hijjah 10. Biggest day of celebration in Islam. Pilgrimage day for Muslims (the 12th and last month of the Muslim calendar).

●●●●●

State Holidays

Along with the U.S. national holidays of New Year's Day, Martin Luther King Day, Presidents Day/Washington's Birthday, Memorial Day, Independence Day, Labor Day, Columbus Day, Veterans Day, Thanksgiving and Christmas, listed below are any additional holidays when state offices close.

In most states, a holiday that falls on Saturday is observed the previous Friday, and a holiday that falls on Sunday is observed the following Monday. There are also discretionary holidays for state workers, frequently including the day after Thanksgiving and the day before or after Christmas.

ALABAMA
Robert E. Lee Day: Observed with Martin Luther King Day in January.
Confederate Memorial Day: Fourth Monday in April.
Jefferson Davis's Birthday: Observed on the first Monday in June.

ALASKA
Seward's Day: Observed on the last Monday in March.
Alaska Day: Observed October 18.

ARKANSAS
Robert E. Lee Day: Observed on the third Monday in January with Martin Luther King Day.

CALIFORNIA
Cesar Chavez Day: Observed on March 31.

CONNECTICUT
Good Friday: Observed on the Friday before Easter.

DELAWARE
Good Friday: Observed on the Friday before Easter.
Election Day.

GEORGIA
Robert E. Lee Day: Observed on the day after Thanksgiving.
Confederate Memorial Day: April 26 but observed on a Friday or Monday.
Washington's Birthday: Observed the day after Christmas.

HAWAII
Good Friday: Observed on the Friday before Easter.
Kuhio Day: Regatta Day. Observed March 26.
Kamehameha Day: Hawaiin hero who unified the islands under a monarchy. Observed on June 11.
Statehood Day: Observed on the third Friday in August.
General Election Day.

ILLINOIS
Lincoln's Birthday: Observed February 12.
General Election Day.

INDIANA
Good Friday: Observed on the Friday before Easter.
Election Day.
Lincoln's Birthday: Observed the day after Thanksgiving.
Washington's Birthday: Observed the day after Christmas.

IOWA
Thanksgiving Friday: The day after Thanksgiving.

KENTUCKY
Spring Holiday: Observed on the Friday before Easter (half day).
General Election Day.

LOUISIANA
Mardi Gras Day: Tuesday before Ash Wednesday.
Good Friday: Observed on the Friday before Easter.

MAINE
Patriots Day: Observed on the third Monday in April.
Thanksgiving Friday: The day after Thanksgiving.

MARYLAND
Election Day.
American Indian Heritage Day: The day after Thanksgiving.

MASSACHUSETTS
Patriots Day: Observed on the third Monday in April.

MICHIGAN
Election Day.
Thanksgiving Friday: The day after Thanksgiving.

MISSISSIPPI
Robert E. Lee Day: Observed on the third Monday in January with Martin Luther King Day.
Confederate Memorial Day: April 26 but observed on the last Monday in April.
Jefferson Davis' Birthday: Observed the last Monday in May with Memorial Day.

MISSOURI
Lincoln's Birthday: Observed on February 12.
Truman Day: Observed on May 8 (or nearest weekday).

MONTANA
Election Day.

NEBRASKA
Arbor Day: Observed on the last Friday in April.
Thanksgiving Friday: The day after Thanksgiving.

NEVADA
Nevada Day: Observed on the last Friday in October.
Family Day: Observed on the Friday after Thanksgiving in November.

NEW HAMPSHIRE
Thanksgiving Friday: The day after Thanksgiving.

NEW JERSEY
Lincoln's Birthday: Observed on February 12.
Good Friday: Observed on the Friday before Easter.
Election Day.

NEW MEXICO
President's Day: Observed the day after Thanksgiving.

NEW YORK
Lincoln's Birthday: Observed on February 12.
Election Day.

NORTH CAROLINA
Good Friday: Observed on the Friday before Easter.
Confederate Memorial Day: May 10 but observed on Friday or Monday.

NORTH DAKOTA
Good Friday: Observed on the Friday before Easter.

OKLAHOMA
Thanksgiving Friday: The day after Thanksgiving.

OREGON
Thanksgiving Friday: The day after Thanksgiving.

PENNSYLVANIA
Thanksgiving Friday: The day after Thanksgiving.

RHODE ISLAND
Victory Day: Observed on the second Monday in August.
Election Day.

SOUTH CAROLINA
Confederate Memorial Day: May 10 but observed on a Friday or Monday.
Thanksgiving Friday: The day after Thanksgiving.

SOUTH DAKOTA
Native American Day: Observed on the second Monday in October.

TENNESSEE
Good Friday: Observed on the Friday before Easter.

TEXAS
Confederate Heroes Day: Observed January 19.
Texas Independence Day: March 2.
San Jacinto Day: Observed April 21.
Emancipation Day in Texas: June 19.
Lyndon Baines Johnson Day: August 27.
Thanksgiving Friday: The day after Thanksgiving.

UTAH
Pioneer Day: Observed on July 24 (or nearest weekday).

VERMONT
Town Meeting Day: The first Tuesday in March.
Bennington Battle Day: Revolutionary War battle: August 15 (or nearest weekday).

VIRGINIA
Lee-Jackson Day: Confederate Generals Robert E. Lee and "Stonewall" Jackson: January 16 but observed on Friday or Monday.
Thanksgiving Friday: The day after Thanksgiving.

WASHINGTON
Thanksgiving Friday: The day after Thanksgiving.

WEST VIRGINIA
West Virginia Day: June 20.
Thanksgiving Friday: The day after Thanksgiving.

WISCONSIN
Good Friday: Observed on the Friday before Easter.
Election Day.

19

Reporting: Specialized Coverage

The General Assignment Reporter

Most reporters in radio and television are general assignment reporters. That just means that there's no telling what a reporter might be covering from one day to the next. Today, it's a house fire and traffic tie-ups; tomorrow, it's a city council meeting and pollution control.

Some larger stations still have at least some specialized reporters. The most likely by subject area are education, politics, crime and consumer. Some stations that cover a large territory might also have reporters who specialize in a specific geographic area of the market. They're still general assignment reporters; they just do that reporting in a defined geographic area.

This chapter is designed to help the general assignment reporter cope with the wide variety of topics that he or she might face on any random day.

Business, Economy and Taxes

So many of the stories we deal with on a day-to-day basis—and should deal with more in investigative, enterprise and process reporting—concern money. Some estimates say that as many as a quarter of all the stories we do concern money. Yet business and economic subjects remain perhaps the most underreported and misunderstood of any that we cover.

Part of the problem may be that so many of the people who are involved in reporting and producing the news are young enough that they have too little experience with the financial side of day-to-day survival. Frequently, *young* translates to unmarried, no children, renter and transient, with few ties to the community. Audience members, in contrast, are older, have lived in the community for years, are married, have children, frequently own their own homes and so on. Studies tell us that there's a direct correlation between how long people have lived in a community and how likely they are to watch broadcast news . . . and how often they do so. In other words, the audience is frequently not "just like us." Among other things, they're a lot more involved in the economic life of the community and care a lot more about it. We need to recognize that and respond.

This section will make no one an expert in the field. It's designed as a quick reference guide to demystify some of the most important business and economic terms we encounter every day—keeping in mind the concept that our audience cannot understand what we do not.

Top Money Terms

assessed valuation: Most commonly used in reference to real estate taxes. A house and lot might be *worth* $100,000, but the local government where the house is located may not tax at full value. It may tax at *assessed valuation,* a government-set figure that is a government-determined percentage of the total value. For instance, a community may levy property taxes on an assessed valuation that's set at half the real value of the property. That means you cannot compare the tax *rate* in one community with the tax *rate* in another unless they either tax at the same assessed value (50 percent in this example above) or you adjust for the difference. A mill rate (see *mill rate*) is then set as a tax on assessed valuation. Without knowing local assessed valuation, you cannot calculate the actual effect of a property tax hike. Generally, the best way to deal with property tax stories is to calculate how much the property taxes are on a home of typical value in the community, then talk about how much the taxes on that property will go up or down.

bankruptcy: BE CAREFUL. The term has more than one meaning because there are varying stages of bankruptcy proceedings. Without any other modifiers, this is a legal term meaning that a company's or individual's assets must be sold with the proceeds going to creditors. *Do not use this term incorrectly. You must differentiate between companies or individuals involved in bankruptcy proceedings and those actually bankrupt.* Most often, companies and individuals file for protection under the federal bankruptcy laws, temporarily halting lawsuits and actions by creditors while an attempt is made to reorganize. The three individual bankruptcy proceedings involve filings under Chapters 7, 11 and 13 of the federal bankruptcy law. Chapter 7 is final liquidation. In Chapter 11 (reorganization bankruptcy) an individual or company seeks protection from creditors but remains technically out of bankruptcy as a payment schedule is worked out to avoid bankruptcy. In Chapter 13 an individual's wages are garnished. You need to find out under which chapter or section of the law a person or business is filing. Commonly, you should say that an individual or company is filing for *bankruptcy protection* rather than saying that they're filing for *bankruptcy.*

bonds: Interest-bearing obligations issued (sold) by businesses and governments to raise money. *General obligation bonds* are issued (money is borrowed) by governmental units (with voter or governmental approval) and are secured or guaranteed by the governmental unit's ability to tax. *Municipal bonds* are general obligation bonds issued by a city, county, possession, state, territory, town or village. *Industrial revenue bonds* (IRBs) are actually private bonds that are issued through a governmental unit on behalf of private business. Note that the security (what backs the bonds) may be the government, an agency of the government, the project itself or the private business(es) involved. *Revenue bonds* are bonds backed only by the revenue of the project built with the money raised by the bond issue. What backs the payback of the bonds determines how secure the bonds are.

company, corporation, firm, partnership, professional association, sole proprietorship: The terms *business, firm* and *company* are all synonymous in that they all mean an entity that conducts business. Those terms convey no legal status to the firm or business. Anything that does business may be called a company, business, or firm. Corporations, partnerships, sole proprietorships and professional associations (PAs) are all viewed as legal entities; most are legally created with documents filed with one or more states and one or more federal agencies—the IRS at the very least. A *sole proprietorship* is owned by one person. *Partnerships* involve two or more people. Although usually small, many enormous real estate companies are really partnerships because of some tax advantages. *Corporations* are formed, among other reasons, to limit liability. The corporate "shell" provides an ability to raise substantial funds while shielding the owners of the stock from personal liability (in most cases except fraud). Most corporations and all large ones are regular corporations. Many smaller ones and new ones are Subchapter S corporations. Sub S corporations operate the same as regular corporations except that the profits or losses of a Sub S corporation are passed directly to the limited number of shareholders. *Professional associations (PAs)* are the same as corporations. The name is used mostly by groups of professionals (e.g., doctors, lawyers) because they believe the name sounds better and less impersonal than "corporation" and because state laws do not allow individuals to be shielded from malpractice.

cost of living: The total money needed to pay for goods and services based on varying standards of living normally released with the figures. The difference between cost of living and CPI (consumer price index) is that cost of living includes how people spend their money rather than the fixed marketbasket comparison of the CPI and includes the effect of income taxes and Social Security.

Dow Jones Industrial Average: This is the total cumulative value of one share of stock in each of 30 specific major industrial companies, most of which are listed on the New York Stock Exchange. This is used as a general guide for what's taking place in the stock market because the 30 companies represent a cross-section of U.S. industry and because they're so big. If the Dow Jones Industrial Average is up 11.02, that means the total dollar value of the industrial shares of stock in the companies followed (weighted for stock splits and changes in the stocks sampled) rose 11 dollars and 2 cents from the closing prices the day before. Stock market reports should state whether the Dow was up or down, by how much and the closing (or latest) figure. The next most important information is the volume of trading, with an indication of whether the trading volume was light, moderate or heavy.

Index of Leading Economic Indicators: A Commerce Department measure (index, not dollars) of where the economy is heading based on 12 economic guideposts. The items measured are 1) average work week, 2) average weekly initial unemployment claims, 3) new orders for plant and equipment, 4) vendor performance (companies receiving slower delivery from vendors), 5) net business formation, 6) contracts and orders for plant and equipment, 7) building permits, 8) change in inventories on hand and on order, 9) change in sensitive materials' prices, 10) stock prices (500 common stocks), 11) money supply (M-2), and 12) change in credit (business and consumer borrowing). Note that the eighth item (change in inventories on hand and on order) is late every month, which leads to preliminary figures being released and then adjusted later.

mill rate: A unit of measure by which real estate or property taxes are levied. A mill is a tenth of a cent (one-thousandth of a dollar). The mill rate is the amount of taxes due per thousand dollars of assessed valuation. See *assessed valuation.*

mutual funds: Refers to companies that invest money in businesses, the money market, bonds or other defined investments. Mutual funds get their money from the shareholders or investors in the mutual fund. In addition to being divided by types of investments, mutual funds are also divided into load and no-load. A load fund means that a commission (percentage) is taken with each purchase of shares (typically 2 to 8 percent of the investment) by the fund itself for operation, profit and so forth. No-load means that all invested money goes to the purchase of shares with no commission.

prime rate: A critically important term of dubious meaning. Theoretically, it's the interest rate at which banks lend money to their best, most secure customers. It's important because so many other rates are pegged to it. Most business loans float (go up and down) above prime—commonly 1 to 3 percent higher—adjusted monthly. More and more consumer loans and even some home mortgages and credit card rates are pegged to the prime rate. What makes the figure dubious is that the best, most secure companies frequently borrow money below the prime rate, making the figure arbitrary. The federal discount rate, set by the Federal Reserve Board, is one of the major determinants of the prime rate.

real estate taxes: Always a plural unless used as an adjective. This is actually a combination of taxes levied on all taxable real estate. Normally collected by a local jurisdiction, commonly counties, it's a combination of county tax, school or education tax, plus a variety of taxes for other services. Real estate taxes are assessed in mills based on *assessed valuation* and *mill* rate (see both).

unemployment: Figures are released monthly by the Labor Department. The figures include people the government says are actively seeking employment but who are still unemployed, with seasonal adjustments figured in. Unemployed figures do not include those the government says are no longer looking for work, which is why critics charge that the figures understate actual unemployment. Members of the military are not included in the figures since there's no such thing as unemployed military.

●●●●●

Crime and Legal

Great care must be taken when writing about crime to avoid violating the spirit of our system: People are innocent until proven guilty. That same care also avoids potentially costly libel actions.

Journalistically, we'd probably be better off if we applied the same standards to crime stories that we apply to just about everything else. There's no question that the audience is interested in and concerned about crime, but there's no evidence that the audience cares about meaningless, petty crime that has no implications beyond the one or two people involved. Yet that's exactly what so many stations seem to cover night after night.

Years before her death from cancer, Carole Kneeland, then news director of KVUE-TV in Austin, Texas, determined that the notion "if it bleeds, it leads" really shouldn't be the credo of local TV news. With help from others, she developed five criteria that crime stories had to meet to go on the air:

1. Is there an immediate threat to public safety?
2. Is there a threat to children?
3. Do people in the audience need to take some action?
4. Is there a meaningful impact the story has on the community?
5. Is the story about crime prevention?

A crime story that didn't meet at least one of those criteria didn't go on the air. The effect was to decrease the amount of crime coverage the station did, but Kneeland and others at the station argued that all they really did was apply the same standards for crime coverage that they already applied to other things.

Attribution

Always use qualifiers and attribution when dealing with someone accused of a crime until and unless that person is found guilty in a court of law. Sometimes that attribution can seem cumbersome, but there's no shortcut. Every time you link an identifiable person as a possible perpetrator in an illegal, immoral or questionable activity, you must have some form of attribution. And remember that a person may be identified not only by name, but also by picture or even a description that sufficiently allows that person to be singled out.

Alleged

Alleged is a legal term that generally means *charged.* Alleged will serve as a form of attribution but should not be first choice because it's not a word commonly used in spoken English, and the way it's commonly used will frequently *not* protect a station in a legal action.

LEGALLY
OKAY: Police allege that John Smith committed the
robbery....

Although the attribution in the sentence above is fine, the writing isn't. No one speaks like that.

POOR
USAGE: John Smith allegedly robbed....

This is not the way people speak, nor does this sentence make clear who's alleging that John Smith robbed anyone.

BETTER: `Police arrested John Smith for the robbery....`

ALSO
BETTER: `Police say John Smith robbed ...`

ALSO
BETTER: `Police have charged John Smith with robbing ...`

Note that the first example, "`Police arrested John Smith for the robbery ...`" requires no further attribution for that part of the sentence. Someone was either arrested or not—that's a fact, not a defamatory statement. In our system people are innocent until proven guilty, so there's no problem with *correctly* stating that someone was arrested.

A story that includes details of a crime along with an identifiable suspect is usually best handled by citing police:

PROPER
ATTRIBUTION: `Police say Smith entered the office holding a shotgun and left with a bag stuffed with 20-dollar bills.`

The above contains proper attribution that's both conversational and makes clear the source of the charges.

Misplaced Attribution

Watch out for misplaced attribution:

PROBLEM: `Police arrested John Smith for the alleged robbery ...`

The attribution for *John Smith* is fine, but the *alleged* before *robbery* means you're questioning whether the robbery itself took place. If that's really what you mean to do, make that issue clear. Hardly anyone is *allegedly murdered*. Usually, we know whether the person was killed; at issue is who did it. *Alleged* or any other qualifier is normally both unnecessary and inappropriate in front of the crime. Qualifiers are needed only in reference to the accused.

Cautions

Using a phrase like *the alleged murderer* provides a writing shortcut that may be technically correct but potentially unfair because of the ease with which the audience may either miss *alleged* or not fully understand the critical qualifier. Note also that only someone actually charged with a crime can be considered *alleged* to have done it. Again, if a prosecutor or police say that someone is a murderer, make that clear—and skip *alleged*.

Suspected technically applies to the process of investigation before any charge is made.

ACCEPTABLE: `Police say James Smith is a suspect in the`
`case ...`

The bigger question is whether you should be identifying people who are merely suspects but have not been charged with a crime. Generally, don't identify suspects unless there's a compelling reason to do so. And remember that *suspected* applies only when authorities suspect someone of a crime—not when you do.

Increasingly, law enforcement agencies are identifying *people of interest*. That's just another way of saying that someone is a *suspect*. Be careful. Remember that if police had enough evidence, they'd have charged the person with a crime. Identifying suspects or *people of interest* appears to be a way to have the news media help police gather evidence. Quite a few high profile *people of interest* have never been charged with crimes but have had their reputations damaged by overzealous law enforcement and complicit news media.

Get the Terms Right

Burglary, holdup, larceny, robbery, stealing, theft. *These terms are not interchangeable. Theft* is the general term meaning the unlawful appropriation of someone else's property. *Stealing* and *theft* may be used as alternative descriptions for *larceny* and *burglary. Larceny* is the legal term for *theft,* broken down between petty larceny and grand larceny. Each state determines where the line is drawn, but it's usually pretty low (e.g., $25 to $150). *Burglary* and *robbery* are the terms to describe *how* an unlawful appropriation took place. *Burglary* is frequently regarded as a crime against property involving the unlawful entry into a house or building for the purpose of theft; *robbery* is a crime against people involving the forcible taking of valuables or possessions from a person through the use of weapons or intimidation. *Holdup* may be used for a robbery committed with a weapon, officially called *armed robbery.*

Homicide, manslaughter, murder. These terms are similar in meaning *but cannot be used interchangeably. Homicide* is the unlawful death or killing of someone, as opposed to lawful state or military action. *Manslaughter* is also killing someone but normally without malice, sometimes unintentionally. This is a formal legal charge and generally carries a considerably lighter potential penalty than murder. *Murder* is the premeditated killing of someone or, frequently, killing someone during the commission of another crime (such as robbery).

Top Crime and Legal Terms

acquitted, innocent, not guilty: All these terms mean the same thing, although neither judges nor juries actually declare someone accused of a crime *innocent*. However, because of potential confusion either because the audience missed the word *not* or the announcer dropped it, some consider it better to use *acquitted* or *innocent* rather than *not guilty*.

arraignment: A court proceeding in which a person charged with a crime is informed of the charges against him or her. At this proceeding, bail may be set, a defense attorney may be appointed, and a plea may be entered.

civil, criminal: *Civil* actions concern violations of private (individual, business or governmental agency) rights. Civil suits seek monetary damages and/or relief by a court order. *Criminal* actions are brought by a governmental unit charging the commission of a crime. Criminal charges may result in a fine or imprisonment or both.

concurrent sentence: Sentences for more than one crime in which the guilty party serves the sentences at one time (concurrently) rather than successively. See also *cumulative sentence*.

cumulative sentence: Sentences for more than one crime in which the guilty party serves the sentences one after the other. The same as accumulative—although *cumulative* is a better word—and the opposite of concurrent. See also *concurrent sentence*.

deposition: Sworn testimony of a witness that is taken outside of court.

felony, misdemeanor: Both terms relate to the commission of a crime but differ in the severity of the charges and potential punishment. A *felony* is normally a serious charge carrying a potential punishment of a lengthy (one year or more) prison term or death. A *misdemeanor* is a less serious charge usually carrying a potential punishment of a fine and/or a shorter term in jail or a workhouse.

grand jury: Typically, a group of 12 to 23 individuals who are empaneled to hear evidence about potential wrongdoing and empowered to decide whether formal charges (an indictment) should be issued against someone.

indict, indictment: Use these words only in the legal context of bringing charges. *Indictment* involves the formal charges placed by a grand jury against one or more people, organizations or businesses alleging the commission of a crime. Charges brought without a grand jury are called an *information*.

jail, prison: Both *prisons* and *jails* do the same things: confine people convicted of crimes and some people awaiting trial. Normally, a *jail* serves to confine people convicted of lesser charges and serving shorter sentences. All penitentiaries are *prisons*.

pardon, parole, probation: *Pardon* means forgiveness. It is the release from sentence for someone accused and convicted of wrongdoing. Note that the person pardoned is not absolved from the wrongdoing but is simply released from confinement or the prospect of confinement. *Parole* is the release from confinement (usually for good behavior) before a full sentence is served. *Probation* is the release from the *prospect* of confinement (suspension of sentence) for someone who has been found guilty of a crime. Normally, the person must remain on good behavior and is under supervision.

plea bargain: Negotiation between the prosecution and defense in a criminal proceeding that results in a reduced charge and reduced sentence or other arrangement in exchange for a guilty plea.

●●●●●

Education

When stations look over a list of what their audience is most concerned about—either a list they've constructed by surveying their audience or a list supplied by a consultant—education is always near the top.

Despite all the national, political discussion, education is fundamentally a local issue. There are some national mandates, but most of what happens in education is determined by a local board and administration within the guidelines established by a state board of education or the equivalent.

For the K (kindergarten) through 12 grades, states commonly have a commissioner or superintendent of education. That person is most often appointed by the governor, but it's an elected position in some cases. States frequently determine educational minimums like the number of school days per year and the number of credits required for graduation and so on. A state office or a board may also prescribe minimum statewide testing results.

From a public school standpoint, most states offer half- or full-day kindergarten, and kids continue in elementary school through fifth grade. Middle school commonly includes grades 6, 7 and 8, with high school 9 through 12. For a variety of reasons—most often economic—an increasing number of communities are trying alternative combinations.

On a local basis, it's common to have an elected school board. It's frequently a nonpartisan election, which means candidates are not identified by party affiliation. The school board is responsible for hiring and overseeing a superintendent for the school district. The superintendent then oversees a central administration staff and is typically responsible for hiring and managing principals for the various schools in the district. There are a number of variations on this theme, so check on how your local system operates.

Private schools typically are required to follow certain key state guidelines, but since they normally do not receive local or state tax dollars, they are largely free to administer themselves as they see fit. There is also an increasing trend toward home schooling, where one or both parents take on the responsibilities for schooling kids at home. Sometimes those students can also get involved with public school after-school activities. Sometimes a student may be home schooled because the parents want nothing to do with the public school system.

While private schools do not normally receive public tax dollars, there are a variety of plans with school vouchers taking place. Under that system, parents may be eligible for a voucher (a predetermined amount of tax dollars) that can go to either the local public school or another public school or even a private school—wherever the child goes. In a 5–4 decision, the U.S. Supreme Court upheld the constitutionality of school vouchers, but some state courts have held that a given state constitution does not permit vouchers.

In most places in this country, the biggest source of school funding comes from local property taxes. But because courts found that poorer school districts offered fewer educational opportunities, a varying amount of state money commonly supplements local tax dollars to help toward evening out the per pupil support system. At the same time, there appears to be a growing trend in having state government pick up more of the tab for public education. Again, check on how things work in your state.

Higher education commonly operates differently. Some states have a board or commission that oversees public higher education; some do not. As higher education expenses have risen and states have cut budgets, more and more state schools argue that they have moved from "state-supported" to "state-assisted." Some not too jokingly worry that they're moving rapidly toward simply being "state-located."

As expenses have increased and relative state support has dropped, student tuition and fees have picked up more and more of the operating costs. Depending on the size of the state, there are commonly different tiers of state institutions. The top rung includes the large research institutions; the second rung might include smaller or more specialized research institutions or even non-research institutions; a third rung might be two-year (freshman and sophomore) or community colleges. As state money has become tighter, there has been a tendency to limit duplication among state schools, and more schools now have subject areas of defined strength where extra resources are put. Other than requirements needed for accreditation, private universities are largely free to operate as they choose.

Top Education Terms

accreditation: A process by which an outside organization certifies the minimum qualifications of the staff, facilities and operation of an educational organization. For instance, the National Council for the Accreditation of Teacher Education sanctions most teacher-education programs, and there are six regional accreditation associations for colleges and universities.

alternative schools: Generally, public schools set up by states or school districts for students not succeeding in traditional public schools.

at risk: Describes students with socioeconomic challenges, such as poverty or teen pregnancy, which may place them at a disadvantage in achieving academic, social or career goals.

Brown v. Board of Education (of Topeka, Kansas): The 1954 Supreme Court decision that banned racially segregated schools.

busing: Usually refers to the racial integration of schools by busing students to achieve racial balance. Note that most students are bused simply for transportation and not to achieve any form of integration.

charter schools: Schools that receive public funding but are independent of traditional public schools.

Common Core: Developed by a group of government and business leaders (and promoted by the Obama Administration), it's a set of grade-by-grade standards for what should be learned in English and math. Most states have adopted some or all of the standards, which was a requirement to receive special federal school funding dollars.

corporal punishment: Generally refers to spanking or paddling students for disciplinary reasons. At this writing, 19 U.S. states permit corporal punishment. Most are in the South, Southwest and Midwest.

Individuals with Disabilities Education Act (IDEA): A 1975 federal law, originally known as the Education for All Handicapped Children Act, where federal money goes to schools that must then guarantee that all children with disabilities receive a free public education.

magnet school: A school that specializes in a particular field, such as science or the arts, to attract students from elsewhere in a school district.

No Child Left Behind Act of 2001: Signed into law in 2002, the bill was structured on four principles: accountability, choices for parents, more local control and using research to determine what works. At this writing, the law has become less popular because, many have charged, it emphasizes testing more than actual learning.

tenure: Most commonly refers to the controversial practice of near-guaranteed employment for teachers and professors who have successfully taught at one place for a certain period of time and met other job requirements.

Title I, VII and IX: Title I is the nation's largest federal education program. Created in 1965 during the War on Poverty, Title I of the Elementary and Secondary Education Act addresses remedial education programs for poor and disadvantaged children. Title VII refers to a federal program to make non-native students proficient in English. Title IX is commonly noted in regard to sports programs; it bars gender discrimination in schools that receive federal funds.

● ● ● ● ●

The Environment

Historically, the environment has shown up as a major local issue only when there's been a major local environmental problem: a particularly polluted river, a toxic waste site or spill, controversial battles over land use and endangered animals. When the local problem has been addressed, the environment has tended to fade as a pressing issue.

Global warming/climate change has changed that. While individuals and groups may disagree over how severe or immediate the threat of global warming, few now deny its existence. That's raised the consciousness on the issue and led to increased news coverage, including new coverage on how the people and businesses in each area contribute to making the environment better—or worse.

Top Environment Terms

altered weather patterns: The theory that global warming will, among other consequences, lead to unnatural changes in the weather. Note that natural occurrences, like El Niño, can also alter weather patterns.

carbon footprint: The measure, in units of carbon dioxide, of greenhouse gases added to the environment by individuals, groups or organizations. Calculations can be made of the direct or primary contribution based on fossil fuels consumed and the indirect or secondary contribution made by others (individuals or organizations) whose services we use.

Clean Air Act: Air quality regulation started in 1955, with The Clean Air Act coming in 1963 and with significant changes in 1967, 1970, 1977 and 1990. The act defined air pollution and provided for federal authority to regulate it.

Clean Water Act: First passed in 1972 with significant amendments in 1977 and 1987, the CWA defined water pollution and provided for federal authority to regulate it.

endangered species: A species that is in danger of extinction through either natural (e.g. overpopulation of predators) or unnatural (e.g. use of pesticides) conditions.

fossil fuels: Non-regenerative sources of fuel found within the earth's crust as a result of millions of years of pressure on the remains of animals and plants, where energy is given off as a result of burning. Examples include coal, oil and gas. Non-fossil fuels include nuclear, hydroelectric, geothermal, solar and wind power as well as wood and some other materials.

global warming: The increase in the average temperature of the earth's air and water. Generally attributed primarily to the burning of fossil fuels, which has resulted in the accumulation of greenhouse gases, which trap the heat produced on earth and prevent that heat from escaping into space. There is concern that as heat builds up, there will be significant changes in the climate and melting of glaciers, which could increase the water level of the oceans, resulting in coastal flooding.

greenhouse gases: Gases in the earth's atmosphere that prevent heat from escaping into space, thus forming a "greenhouse" effect, trapping the heat in the earth's atmosphere and raising the temperature of the earth's air and water.

nuclear power: The generation of energy through nuclear technology—most often nuclear fission, the splitting of the nucleus of an atom. In 2016, Watts Bar 2 in Tennessee became the first nuclear power plant to go on line in the U.S. since 1996. Nuclear power supplies almost 20 percent of U.S. electricity, and another four nuclear power plants remain under construction in the U.S.

ozone: At the earth's surface, ozone is a pollutant. In the atmosphere, a part of the stratosphere called the ozone layer, ozone helps to filter harmful ultraviolet rays from the sun.

renewable energy: The generation of energy by using natural resources that regenerate themselves naturally. Most commonly, hydroelectric (water), windmills (wind), solar (sun), geothermal and some others.

risk assessment: The term frequently applies to public health or the environment and involves the determination of the amount of risk involved in any enterprise or activity along with the potential size of the loss.

●●●●●

Geography

As with many things in life, the geographic lines identifying where we are and where we're near are not as clear-cut as we might like. Even terms like *here* and *there* can get us in trouble, depending on where we are and where the audience is. *Local* usually works well, although from one end to the other within a market may not seem very local. It gets worse beyond that.

We frequently refer to stories as being *regional,* and the government and private business frequently release data by regions, but there is no universal agreement about where one region starts and the next one begins. To an Easterner, Texas may be in the Southwest, but to a Texan or a New Mexican it all depends. And some terms we think of as *geographic* are really more *political.*

Major U.S. Geographic Terms

Appalachia: Geographically, the term applies to all of the area through which the Appalachian Mountains pass. However, we commonly mean the poorer areas of eastern Tennessee, eastern Kentucky, southeastern Ohio and western West Virginia.

Bible Belt: A subjective phrase that is variously applied to parts of the South, Midwest and Southwest. Limit the use of this phrase to quotes.

Corn Belt: North central Midwest (where corn is a major product), including parts of Ohio, Indiana, Illinois, Iowa, Nebraska and Kansas.

Cotton Belt: Parts of the South and Southeast where cotton is (or was) grown.

Deep South: Generally viewed as Alabama, Georgia, Louisiana, South Carolina and Mississippi.

Down East: The southeastern part of Maine.

Eastern Shore: Parts of Maryland and Virginia east of the Chesapeake Bay.

Great Lakes: Forming part of the border between the United States and Canada. From west to east, they are Lake Superior (bordering Minnesota, Wisconsin and Michigan), Lake Michigan (bordering Wisconsin, Illinois, Indiana and Michigan), Lake Huron (bordering Michigan), Lake Erie (bordering Michigan, Ohio, Pennsylvania and New York) and Lake Ontario (bordering New York).

Great Plains: The grasslands of the United States, running from North Dakota, South Dakota, Nebraska, Kansas and Oklahoma to Texas and including portions of Colorado, Wyoming and Montana.

Gulf Coast: Running along the Gulf of Mexico, it includes the western shore of Florida and the shores of Alabama, Mississippi, Louisiana and Texas.

Nevada: Pronounced neh VA dah (as in Canada), not neh VAH dah (as in ah ha).

New England: Connecticut, Maine, Massachusetts, New Hampshire, Rhode Island and Vermont.

New York City: Includes the five boroughs of Manhattan, Queens, Brooklyn, the Bronx and Staten Island.

North Slope: The area of Alaska north of the Continental Divide and draining into the Arctic Ocean, running across northern Alaska.

Outer Banks: The islands along the coast of North Carolina.

Sea Islands: The islands along the coasts of South Carolina, Georgia and Florida.

Sun Belt: Generally viewed as those states in the South and Southwest from Florida all the way west into California.

Voice of America Pronunciation Guide

One of the best places to locate pronunciations of names in the news— both geographic and people—is the Voice of America Pronunciation Guide (pronounce.voanews.com). You can look up pronunciations from a long list of names (mostly international) in the news or type in exact or approximate names in order to find the pronunciation. Along with a phonetic spelling, VOA also provides an audio file to hear how the name should be pronounced.

Major World Geographic Terms

Asian Subcontinent: Bangladesh, Bhutan, India, Nepal, Pakistan and Sri Lanka.

Baltic states: Formerly part of the Soviet Union, the independent states of Latvia, Lithuania and Estonia.

British Isles: The group of islands including Great Britain, Ireland and the adjacent islands.

Caribbean: The Bahamas, Cuba, Hispaniola (Dominican Republic, Haiti), Jamaica, Puerto Rico and the West Indies.

Central America: The southernmost part of North America: Belize, Costa Rica, El Salvador, Guatemala, Honduras, Nicaragua and Panama.

China: Use for mainland China (People's Republic of China). Note that the Chinese capital is Beijing (bay JING), formerly known in the West as Peking. Use *Taiwan* (tye-WAHN), formerly known as Formosa, for the island country off China. Note that China considers Taiwan to be a renegade province.

down under: Marginal reference for Australia, New Zealand and some of the other countries in the area, which are better referred to as being in the South Pacific.

Far East: The easternmost part of Asia: China, Japan, North and South Korea, Taiwan and Hong Kong. Technically also refers to Siberia, but don't use the term that way.

Germany: East (German Democratic Republic) and West (Federal Republic of Germany) Germany reunified in October 1990. The capital is Berlin.

Great Britain: Includes England, Scotland and Wales. The United Kingdom includes Great Britain and Northern Ireland. Ireland itself is separate.

Indochina: Part of Southeast Asia including Cambodia, Laos and Vietnam.

Latin America: Countries south of the United States, where Romance languages (Spanish, Portuguese, French) predominate.

Maritime Provinces: Nova Scotia, New Brunswick and Prince Edward Island in Canada.

Middle East: Afghanistan, Cyprus, Egypt, Iran, Iraq, Israel, Kuwait, Jordan, Lebanon, Oman, Qatar, Saudi Arabia, South Yemen, Sudan, Syria, Turkey, the United Arab Emirates and Yemen. Note that *Middle East* refers to a general region that crosses continents.

Nordic countries: A general reference to the Scandinavian countries, including Denmark, Norway, Sweden, Iceland and Finland.

Persian Gulf: The major oil shipping waterway to the Gulf of Oman and the Arabian Sea, bordered by Bahrain, Iran, Iraq, Kuwait, Saudi Arabia, Qatar and the United Arab Emirates.

Scandinavia: Denmark, Iceland, Norway, Sweden and, arguably, Finland.

West Indies, the: Barbados, Grenada, Trinidad, Tobago, all Virgin Islands (British and U.S. islands of St. Croix, St. John and St. Thomas), Anguilla, Antigua, Dominica, St. Lucia, St. Vincent, St. Christopher-Nevis, Guadeloupe, Martinique and the Netherlands Antilles (Aruba, Bonaire, Curaçao, Saba, St. Eustatius and St. Martin). Common usage places the West Indies as part of the Caribbean, and that description is acceptable.

● ● ● ● ●

Government

The federal government is divided into three branches: executive (White House, federal agencies); legislative (Congress) and judicial (the federal court system, including the U.S. Supreme Court). All must operate within the current interpretations of the Constitution by the federal courts and, ultimately, the U.S. Supreme Court.

The give and take of those three branches shape the contours of the system. The executive branch proposes policies, makes appointments and administers the law. The legislative branch passes laws (which the president signs or vetoes). Financial matters generally originate in the House of Representatives, commonly in response to presidential initiatives. High-level presidential appointments and international treaties must be approved by the Senate. Exceptions are those who work for the president in a personal, staff capacity, such as the national security adviser and press secretary.

Although Congress enacts legislation, the laws themselves are administered by the various federal agencies under the control of the executive branch. Those agencies—and the courts—promulgate rules and regulations based on their interpretation of congressional law and the legislation itself. Any rule or regulation may be changed by the implementing agency or by congressional law, assuming presidential approval or congressional ability to override a presidential veto. Legislation passed by Congress may be vetoed by the president but can only be changed by Congress. The process is commonly called a system of checks and balances or the separation of powers.

State governments frequently operate in a similar manner to the federal system. States have either a legislature or a general assembly. Massachusetts and New Hampshire call it a General Court, and North Dakota and Oregon call it a Legislative Assembly. All states have a senate; Nebraska has a unicameral legislature, so the senate is the only game in town. All other states also have a house of representatives except California, Nevada, New Jersey, New Mexico, New York and Wisconsin, which have assembly members, and Maryland, Virginia, and West Virginia, which have delegates.

All states have counties except Alaska, which has boroughs, and Louisiana, which has parishes.

Top Government Terms

adopt, approve, enact, pass: Amendments, ordinances, resolutions, and rules are *adopted* or *approved*. Legislative bills are *passed*. Laws are *enacted*. Committees *approve* legislation or plans of action.

bill, legislation: A *bill* is proposed legislation. *Legislation* is what a bill becomes after enactment.

conservative, left, liberal, moderate, right: We use these terms all the time; unfortunately, their meanings are, at best, subjective and may say more about the political views of the writer than about the person being labeled. Generally, it is best to avoid the terms unless someone so described agrees with the label or the term is used in a bite.

departments: Federal departments: Department of Agriculture, Department of Commerce, Department of Defense, Department of Education, Department of Energy, Department of Health and Human Services, Department of Homeland Security, Department of Housing and Urban Development, Department of the Interior, Department of Justice, Department of Labor, Department of State, Department of Transportation, Department of the Treasury, Department of Veterans Affairs. All are headed by secretaries (except Justice, which is overseen by the attorney general); all are appointed by the president and confirmed by the Senate.

European Union: The idea behind the EU is the promotion of economic and social progress of the member nations—along with enabling the combined strength of the countries to form a strong economic world unit. Predecessor organizations include the European Economic Community and the Common Market. The 28 current members include Austria, Belgium, Bulgaria, Croatia, Cyprus, Czech Republic, Denmark, Estonia, Finland, France, Germany, Greece, Hungary, Ireland, Italy, Latvia, Lithuania, Luxembourg, Malta, Netherlands, Poland, Portugal, Romania, Slovakia, Slovenia, Spain, Sweden, and the United Kingdom. Candidates for admission at this writing: Albania, Macedonia, Montenegro, Serbia and Turkey. Use *European Union* on first reference, E-U second reference. At this writing, the "Brexit" vote in England will result in that country pulling out of the EU . . . although the timetable is not yet clear.

filibuster: The process of using legislative rules to make (or threaten to make) long speeches to prevent proposed legislation from coming to a vote.

legislative bodies and titles: Some local governing units have city councilors, some have aldermen; some state legislative bodies are legislatures, some are assemblies; Louisiana has no counties; they're parishes. In Alaska, they're boroughs. Make sure you know the correct local terms before writing.

Medicaid: A joint federal-state program for the poor, disabled and elderly that helps to pay for health care.

Medicare: A federal insurance program for the elderly and disabled that helps to pay for health care.

NATO (North Atlantic Treaty Organization): Western defense and mutual interest organization. The 28 members are Albania, Belgium, Bulgaria, Canada, Croatia, Czech Republic, Denmark, Estonia, France, Germany, Greece, Hungary, Iceland, Italy, Latvia, Lithuania, Luxembourg, Netherlands, Norway, Poland, Portugal, Romania, Slovakia, Slovenia, Spain, Turkey, United Kingdom and the United States. Headquarters is in Brussels, Belgium. Use *NATO* first reference.

OPEC: Organization of the Petroleum Exporting Countries. The 13 members are Algeria, Angola, Ecuador, Indonesia, Iran, Iraq, Kuwait, Libya, Nigeria, Qatar, Saudi Arabia, the United Arab Emirates and Venezuela. Use *OPEC* first reference.

Supreme Court: The nine justices appointed by the president and confirmed by the Senate make ultimate decisions in court cases in the United States through final interpretations of the Constitution. The Chief Justice is *of the United States* (not *of the Supreme Court*). Others are Associate Justices of the Supreme Court.

● ● ● ● ●

Health and Medicine

Reporting health and medical stories can be especially tricky. First, they can be technical, and few reporters are trained in the technical aspects or the jargon involved. Second, those most likely to pay the closest attention are those most in need of new developments and discoveries. If anything, stories about possible breakthroughs should be underplayed to avoid arousing misplaced hope.

The Patient Protection and Affordable Care Act and the Health Care and Education Reconciliation Act of 2010

Both bills were signed into law by President Barack Obama in March 2010, and they have resulted in significant changes in health care in the United States. Among the earliest provisions to go into effect: ending lifetime limits on health care coverage, the elimination of non-coverage for pre-existing conditions, more access to preventive care and allowing young people to stay on parents' insurance policies until age 26. Mandatory health care coverage went into effect in 2014. "Obamacare," as the law has become known, was upheld in major rulings by the U.S. Supreme Court in 2012 and again in 2015. At this writing, President Donald Trump and the Republican Congress plan to repeal the ACA.

HIPAA

Reporting on health matters has become more difficult because of a provision of HIPAA, the Health Insurance Portability and Accountability Act of 1996. The Department of Health and Human Services regulations implementing HIPAA went into effect in April 2003. Basically, the regulations make it a crime to release any health-related information about anyone unless the person has specifically authorized disclosure. The privacy provisions of the federal law apply to health information created or maintained by health care providers who engage in certain electronic transactions, health plans and health care clearinghouses. That includes hospitals, physicians, emergency medical personnel, health plans and people who work with the above groups. Police, fire-fighters and law enforcement agencies are not covered, meaning you can, for example, ask police about someone's health condition. Police don't normally have anyone's health records. However, a combined ambulance and fire department may make it impossible to get information from both of those areas. Family members aren't covered, nor are journalists, although journalists could be liable for invasion of privacy depending on how they got the information. A family member can choose to release health information, even if that family member had to ask another family member's permission to see the information. There are serious civil and criminal penalties for violations of HIPAA, enforced by the HHS Office of Civil Rights.

Hospital Conditions

Most often, the medical conditions of hospital patients are issued after medical care has been administered. Someone is injured or becomes sick; the person is taken to a hospital. Keep in mind that the extent of injuries at a traffic accident, for instance, bears no relationship to the condition given out by the hospital. Someone police describe as "seriously" injured at the scene could easily be in "fair" or even "good" condition according to the hospital. Police may well describe what the injuries look like at first glance; the hospital will give out a condition after doctors have worked on the patient.

When information is released at all, hospitals provide condition information within a broad framework of how the patient is doing. While there's no absolute uniformity here, these are the conditions and what they generally mean:

undetermined: Means just what it says. Patient is in E-R (emergency room) and not yet diagnosed.

treated and released: Patient received treatment but was not admitted to the hospital.

good: Patient is usually conscious, comfortable and alert. Vital signs are within normal range and stable. Prognosis is good.

fair or satisfactory: These mean the same thing. The patient is usually conscious but may be uncomfortable and may not be fully alert. Vital signs are within normal range and stable. Prognosis is fair.

poor: This term is seldom used today but means somewhere between fair and serious.

serious: The patient is seriously ill or injured. Vital signs are not within normal range and are not stable. Prognosis is uncertain.

critical: The patient is in life-threatening condition. Vital signs are not within normal range and not stable. Prognosis is unfavorable.

stable: Used in conjunction with some of the terms above (e.g., the patient is in serious but stable condition). This means the patient's condition is not changing and is not expected to change in the immediate future. If someone tells you the patient is in *critical but stable condition,* get more information. That really doesn't make much sense.

Make sure you use whatever condition the hospital has given you. Never invent your own—not even based on what someone at the scene may have said.

Top Health and Medical Terms

abortion: The deliberate termination of pregnancy. Given the controversial nature of the subject, make sure stories are done even-handedly, including the references to the two sides. It's probably best to use *pro-life* and *pro-choice* rather than *pro-life* and *pro-abortion* or *anti-abortion* and *pro-choice.* The procedure known by opponents as partial birth abortion or PBA is referred to by the medical community as dilation and extraction, commonly called D & X, intact D & X, D & E or intrauterine cranial decompression. There are probably about 3,000–4,000 cases a year, nationwide, but there are no reliable numbers. The procedure involves dilating the cervix and partially removing the fetus, feet first. A cut is then made in the back of the fetus' head and a vacuum tube extracts the fetus' brain. That contracts the head and allows the rest of the fetus to be removed more easily. The procedure is usually performed in the fifth month or later. Opponents argue that the procedure is never required; proponents argue that there are cases when it's the safest medical procedure to save the life of the mother.

AIDS (acquired immune deficiency syndrome): A virus that destroys the body's immune system, leaving it subject to a variety of other ailments. AIDS is transmitted by body fluids, usually sexually. Use *AIDS* first reference. Note that there's a big difference between someone testing positive for the HIV virus and someone with AIDS. Someone who has tested positive for HIV has been exposed to the virus. That person may or may not contract AIDS at some unknown time in the future. Write stories carefully.

Alzheimer's disease: A degenerative disease, characterized by a loss of mental function, most commonly in elderly people.

cancer: A series of different and only marginally related diseases characterized by a rapid and destructive growth of cells.

Centers for Disease Control (CDC): Located in Atlanta, the CDC monitors illnesses across the country and especially the spread of illnesses. Use *C-D-C* second reference, and note that *Centers* is plural.

Down syndrome: A congenital disease, characterized by some level of mental retardation and facial characteristics. Used to be known as *Down's syndrome* but the *'s* has disappeared over the years.

drugs: The term *drugs* has come to mean illegal drugs. Generally, use the word only in that context. If you mean medicine, use that term to refer to legal drugs used for treatment of illness or injury. Avoid *medication;* it's just a longer way of saying medicine.

epidemic: A widespread outbreak of a disease. May be declared only by a medical authority.

Food and Drug Administration (FDA): Oversees most food, drugs and cosmetics. Use full name first reference.

flu: Short for *influenza.* Don't confuse the flu with a cold; the flu can be serious stuff. Primarily involves the lungs and not the intestines. *Flu* okay first reference.

Medicaid/Medicare: Medicaid is a joint federal-state program for the poor, disabled and elderly that helps to pay for health care. Medicare is a federal insurance program for the elderly and disabled that helps to pay for health care.

National Institutes of Health (NIH): The center of federal, government-run health and medical research, located near Washington, DC. Use *N-I-H* second reference, and note that *Institutes* is plural, and it's *of* health.

20

●●●●●

The Business of News

At a time when the news landscape is changing as rapidly as it is, it's increasingly critical for prospective news people to understand the business context within which news happens.

The point is that news doesn't just rain down from the sky, and its continued existence—to say nothing of continued employment—depends heavily on companies making money by supplying news and information.

As employment in the newspaper industry plunged, starting in 2007, with 40 percent of newspaper newsroom jobs lost over the next eight years, plenty of people wrote off broadcast news as well. But the TV news job losses of 2008 and 2009 were temporary drops based on a weak economy rather than a fundamental shift in the news marketplace that we've seen in newspaper.

This chart below makes clear what the trend has been in newspaper and television employment since 2000. Daily newspaper employment

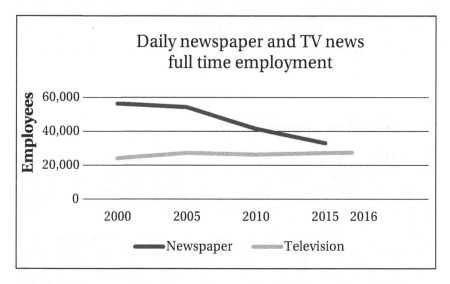

Figure 20.1 Newspaper data from ASNE. TV data from RTDNA/Hofstra University Survey. There is no 2016 data for newspapers because ASNE decided to stop calculating and releasing it.

actually peaked in 1990 at 56,900; TV news employment peaked in 2001 at 29,700—a temporary surge fed by the dot-com bubble, but current TV news employment is not far below that all-time high.

Over this time period, there's been a small but steady shrinkage in the number of daily newspapers, and a larger shrinkage in the number of TV stations producing local news. But the size of those newspapers and the staff producing those newspapers have dropped dramatically. In TV, station consolidation has meant that there are fewer TV news-rooms, but they're producing more and more news and running that news on more and more stations. Consequently, even as the number of TV newsrooms originating local news has been shrinking, the size of those newsrooms has grown enough to keep employment high. As this is written, TV news employment is now at its second highest level ever.

Why? Simple. TV news continues to make money, and stations (and the companies that own them) continue to invest in news. The average TV station is running a record amount of news—5 hours and 30 minutes per weekday at last count.

What about public radio and public television? First of all, public television really isn't much of a player in local news. Yes, national and international news exists Monday through Friday on PBS, but you can find daily local newscasts on only a handful (literally, a handful) of public stations. I've always thought that that should be a national scandal, but clearly most people don't seem to care.

Probably the best broadcast news in this country, day in and day out, is on National Public Radio. But NPR is a business, too, and if it doesn't take in the millions of dollars it consumes to cover news, then it, too, will be endangered. And money is tight at NPR right now.

The business of news, then, isn't always about profit as such, although it clearly figures in the equation, but it is very definitely about revenue and expenses.

● ● ● ● ●

The Predicted Demise of TV

When TV was first publicly introduced at the RCA pavilion at the 1939 World's Fair in New York, a New York *Times* article dismissed it with this now-famous critique: "The problem with television is that people must sit and keep their eyes glued on a screen; the average American family hasn't time for it."

I'm old enough to remember when pundits predicted the demise of each of the three major networks: ABC, CBS and NBC. I remember in 1986 when media observers noted that the new Fox TV network couldn't possibly succeed because there just wasn't room for another network.

In 1983, ABC and Westinghouse sold their Satellite News Channel to CNN, in essence declaring that there just wasn't room for a cable news competitor to CNN. So when Fox announced the start of Fox News Channel in 1996, experts again predicted that it couldn't possibly succeed.

I remember reading in the 1990s the rather widespread expectation that the number three and, certainly, the number four news stations in TV markets would either go out of business or at least get out of the local news business. Today, 87 percent of the 150 biggest TV markets have three or more separate, English language newsrooms producing local news. Only two markets in the top 100 don't make that cut.

For more than 15 years, I have read about the impending demise of the TV "upfronts." The upfronts involve the summer sale of a portion of the advertising for the networks' upcoming TV season starting in the fall. They predicted it again for the 2016–2017 TV season . . . and they were wrong again.

I once worked for a dean who decimated the centerpiece of the broadcast news program at the school because he blindly accepted some "expert's" prediction that the half hour TV newscast was all but dead. That was more than a dozen years ago—well before local TV stations added hundreds of additional half hour newscasts.

Certainly, not every venture in television has been successful, but I've assembled this list of inaccurate predictions of the demise of TV as a warning. The disappearance of TV has been predicted since before the medium even got started. Its continued expansion and even existence have always been met by skeptics whose regular pronouncements and expectations of imminent failure have gone unrealized. The lesson to take away is to be careful about predicting the future—especially the future demise of television.

● ● ● ● ●

A New Model for News?

Back in 2000, quite a few of us traveled to Tampa, Florida, to examine the "next big thing" in news. It was called convergence, and, in this case, it involved a new building housing the Media General co-owned Tampa *Tribune*, WFLA-TV and combined website TBO.com. Many hailed this convergence and cooperation of media as the future of news. I was fascinated by the concept, and I was firmly convinced that this was the best model for journalism education. But as I wrote after visiting, I didn't see much real convergence actually taking place in Tampa, and it wasn't clear that it was ever going to happen on a widespread, commercial basis. It didn't, and in 2012 Media General sold off all its newspapers and became just a local TV and digital company.

In 2017, Nexstar Media took over Media General. TBO.com is part of the Tampa Bay *Times*, which bought the competing *Tribune* and shut it down.

There are at least some "converged" news operations, perhaps most notably the *Deseret News* and co-owned KSL-TV and radio in Salt Lake City. But convergence did not become the new model in news, and there are actually fewer cooperative ventures between TV stations and newspapers today than a few years ago—and the trend is down rather than up.

There are a variety of reasons why convergence didn't develop the way many expected. Probably the two most important are the internet and the FCC.

Although newspapers and TV stations competed against each other in newsgathering, they never really competed for audiences. The decisions to read the paper or watch the news on TV were largely independent of each other; most newspaper consumption took place in the morning, and prime TV news time was in the evening. Convergence seemed to make sense. Until the internet. Everyone competes head to head online, so while the convergence of jointly–owned stations and papers might grow, convergence among stations and newspapers without common ownership is not likely, and the newspaper push for online paywalls makes this form of convergence less and less likely in the future.

There was also an expectation that the FCC would loosen its rules against new co-located newspapers and TV stations. At least some in the business thought that the combination of newspaper and TV would lead to a more profitable combination. The subtext actually involved the far more profitable TV station propping up a declining newspaper. But the FCC didn't change its policies, and reaffirmed that decision in 2016, although there is some discussion about allowing a waiver for failing newspapers. Today, most combined newspaper and TV groups have split the two media apart.

● ● ● ● ●

The New TV Newsroom

The latest RTDNA/Hofstra University Survey shows again that the TV news business isn't limited to TV anymore. Three-quarters of stations provide local news content to one or more other media—beyond their own station or website. Almost half of TV news departments are involved in some sort of cooperative arrangement with another medium. The bigger the news staff and the bigger the market, the more likely the involvement, although the trend on this is definitely down. Just a few years ago, about two-thirds of TV stations participated in some sort of convergence or cooperative venture.

Percentage of TV News Departments Providing Content to Other Media—2016

	Another local TV station	TV in another market	Cable TV channel	Local radio	Website not your own	Mobile device	Other
All TV	15%	19%	5%	45%	11%	26%	6%
Big four affiliates	15	18	5	46	10	26	6
Other commercial	21	21	5	26	16	32	5
Market size:							
1–25	29	19	5	29	19	29	2
26–50	12	20	2	49	15	24	12
51–100	13	14	10	47	8	30	4
101–150	14	16	1	48	9	27	7
151+	9	31	2	44	11	18	9

Just under 30 percent of TV stations are involved in some sort of shared services (or similar) arrangement with another station. In these arrangements, one station oversees or even conducts most or all of another station's operation. It's all about saving costs and making more money.

In the table above, "other" was most often an affiliated TV station or a newspaper.

● ● ● ● ●

Where the Money Comes From

The business model itself has changed. TV still generates most of its income from advertising, and for stations that run local news, half of total station revenue comes from news. Station websites have become increasingly profitable (over three-quarters of news directors who know whether their website makes a profit say the answer is yes), but the biggest growth area for station revenue is a steady jump in cable and satellite carriage fees. Labeled "retransmission," it's the money cable, satellite and telco companies pay to broadcasters to include those local channels on the cable or satellite system. Of course, the networks want a share of that money as well—commonly one-third to one-half. Local station revenue from retransmission is now estimated to be 12 to 15 percent of total station revenue.

SNL Kagan, a financial research firm, estimates that broadcast retransmission fees from cable, satellite and telco companies will hit nearly $8 billion in 2016 and close to $12 billion by 2022. For comparison, it was $2.4 billion in 2012. Statista estimates total TV ad revenue for 2017 will be $76.5 billion. eMarketer estimates that 2017 is when total digital advertising surpasses TV. Digital is estimated at 38.4 percent of all advertising dollars versus 35.8 percent for TV. By contrast, newspaper is projected to be 6.6 percent of the total, falling below radio at 7 percent.

Stations are also expecting to make money on mobile, although the business model there still isn't clear.

There may also be some changes in station programming that could significantly affect both revenue and employment. TV stations get their programming from three sources: 1) Network, assuming they're affiliated with a network, like ABC, CBS, Fox, NBC, CW, and so on; 2) Syndicated programming, like the daytime talk shows, some game shows and some off-net, older network shows and older episodes of current network shows; 3) Local programming, almost all of which is news.

The network programming includes the prime time lineup in the evening as well as most sports and some daytime shows. There was a time when the networks paid the stations to run network programming (really, to run the commercials in the programs), but that time is long gone. Today, almost all stations pay the networks for the programming the networks produce. It's called "reverse compensation," and that compensation comes primarily in the form of stations paying the network a portion of their retransmission revenue. That relationship is not likely to change anytime soon, but more and more stations are re-evaluating their syndicated programs.

Most stations pay for syndicated shows through a mixture of barter and cash. That means they give up some of their commercial time to the companies supplying the syndicated programs (barter) in addition to paying cash to the syndicator for the programming itself. As that programming has become more and more expensive, in both time and cash, stations are starting to look at creating more local shows to replace costly syndicated ones. That's part of what's behind the steady increase in the amount of local news that stations produce, but stations are also starting to look into other local information/entertainment programs.

● ● ● ● ●

Ratings

There are some who argue that *ratings* is a dirty word, synonymous with the worst pandering to the lowest common denominator. But ratings are just numbers, and people in the business who say that they don't pay attention to ratings—or care how many people watch or listen to the news—are fools or liars. The business is about informing, perhaps enlightening, and definitely engaging the audience. But if no one is out there listening or watching, then newscasters are just talking to themselves.

There are two critical terms to define in order to understand ratings: rating and share. Both are percentages. In television, rating is the percentage of homes watching a TV program of all the homes that have a television set (that's estimated at just over 95 percent of all homes). In radio, it's the percentage of people listening to a particular station of all the people who have radios. In essence, it's a competitive measure of how a TV program or radio station is doing against all the choices in life: eating, sleeping, working, watching another station, and so on.

For example, in TV, a rating of 15.4 means that 15.4 percent of all the homes that could watch that program had that program on. If we're looking at a local station, it's 15.4 percent of the station's local market. If we're talking about a network program, then it's 15.4 percent of the country. What's going on with people in the rest of the 84.6 percent of the homes? Some are watching other channels; some are listening to radio instead; some are reading; some are sleeping; some aren't home and so on.

The other term is share. It's also a percentage, but it's a competitive measure against competitive media. A TV program that has a 15.4 rating, for example, might well have a 26.1 share, for example. That would mean that—of the homes that have TV on—26.1 percent are watching that particular program.

In radio, it's the percentage of people listening to a particular station as opposed to the percentage listening to other stations.

So if you know exactly what people are watching or listening to, then share will always add up to 100 percent. Ratings, in contrast, will never add up to 100 percent simply because there will never be a time when everyone (or every home) is watching TV or listening to radio at the same time.

● ● ● ● ●

The Scope of Media Use

Part of the difficulty of peering into the future of news is that there's a lot we don't really know even though we frequently pretend that we do. But let's start with what we do know. Media use is the number one life activity for the average American adult. Even more than sleeping. Way more than work. After all, we don't work seven days a week, but we do consume media every day. Over two-thirds of the waking day (69 percent), we use one—or more—media. Amazingly, over 40 percent of the time that we spend with media, we're doing nothing else. Not working. Not eating. Not traveling somewhere. Just consuming media.

Television remains the 800 pound media gorilla. TV use towers over any other medium. Yes, TV viewing is down slightly, but it still towers over all other media. That's not just what we found in our extensive Middletown Media Studies' observational research; it's what Nielsen continues to find in its studies of TV and online usage. Nielsen numbers released in the first quarter of 2016 put total average TV viewing at 5 hours and 4 minutes per day. Per person . . . per day. Here's the comparative list of time spent with media for U.S. adults 18+:

TV	5+ hours per day
Radio	1.8
Phone	1.7
Internet on PC	0.9
Tablet	0.5
Game console	0.2
Multimedia device	0.2
DVD/Blu-Ray	0.1
Video on smartphone	0.04

Television also dominated video viewing: 95 percent of video watching was on a TV; 4 percent was on the internet; 1 percent was on a smartphone. And four and a half hours of the 5+ hours per day involved watching TV live. TV dropped 3 minutes a day from the year before; smartphone use was up 37 minutes from the previous year, a huge jump.

Generally, the older the viewer, the more they watch TV. Young adults, 18 to 24, were the lowest in TV viewing at 2.2 hours per day.

Pew Research Center's study on news, from the first quarter of 2016, found that Americans "show a clear preference for getting news on a screen, and the TV screen still leads the way." But, the research also found that while the dominance of TV was clear among Americans 50+, 18 to 29 year olds reported they "often" got news online.

●●●●●

Media Use Is More Complex Than It Used to Be

A few decades ago, media use was a lot simpler. There were morning and afternoon papers, four television stations, a bunch of radio stations and magazines, and that was about it. Today, we have fewer newspapers but more of everything else. And more choices beyond that, most notably the internet. Same number of hours in the day, but a staggering fragmentation of options, most shouting, "watch me," "listen to me," "read me."

And we do. And since we still only have 24 hours in a day, we seem to cope by piling on. The assumption had generally been that as new media came along, it displaced older media. Not today. Perhaps led by the computer, which really taught us how to multitask, we are more and more using two or more media at the same time. Not just young people, but almost everyone. In our last study, over 30 percent of media use involved two or more media at the same time. Much of that involved two or more different uses of a computer (e.g. email and software), but much of it either involved the computer and another medium (most often TV) or two or more other media.

● ● ● ● ●

It's Hard to Measure Media Use

There are a lot of reasons why it's so hard today to measure media use. The use of two or more media at the same time is part of the problem. You can observe that complexity (as we did in our research), but it's nearly impossible to ask someone about it. We looked at 17 media in our research. If we asked people about each possible pair, it would take 136 questions. And that wouldn't get at three or more media at the same time, and, yes, people do that, too.

Part of the problem relates to the staggering number of media choices. It's hard enough to keep all the choices straight much less remember which ones you used and for how long. How accurately could you reconstruct your media life, even from yesterday, much less a broader question like whether you're using a given medium more or less than you used to or more or less than another? Unfortunately, much of what we hear about media use we get from questions like that via phone surveys. It's interesting data, and it may help us see developing trends, but, as we proved in our observational studies, it's strikingly inaccurate.

The biggest problem in these self-reported surveys is that we're simply not very good at estimating how we use our time. Another part of the problem relates to media bias. The fact is, we've been conditioned to understand that some media use is generally "good" and some media use is generally "bad." We know the answers, and it undoubtedly biases our responses.

In the first Middletown Media Studies, when we compared phone survey, diary and observation, we observed that people used 130 percent more media than they said they did, but the discrepancies weren't consistent from one medium to the next. People weren't far off on their estimation of how much time they spent with print media, but they underestimated their TV use by 160 percent.

In Middletown Media Studies II, we called people after we observed them and asked whether, on the day they were observed, (which, in most cases, had been the day before), they read the newspaper, listened to the radio, used the computer, went online, watched TV . . . and, if so, how much? We had just observed them, which means they should have been extremely conscious of their media use. Even so, they substantially overestimated their use of newspapers and the computer, but underestimated their TV use by almost 50 percent. It's not that survey research doesn't work, it's that there are serious limitations to asking people about behavior, especially when some of that behavior is considered "good" and some is considered "bad." That's why a lot of phone surveys have people saying they watch less and less TV, even while Nielsen's far better set-top boxes are still recording high viewership.

The situation is further complicated by a lack of standards for judging internet use. Internet use was initially measured by "hits" until advertisers (who are the real reason audience is measured at all) understood that the numbers were largely meaningless and easy to manipulate. We moved to page views, which is still in use. Some argue that time spent online is a better measure, although, from an advertising standpoint, it tends to undervalue the brief but frequent time spent with search.

Cross-checks on internet usage have found major discrepancies between the numbers reported by the websites themselves and the numbers that outside, independent companies were able to measure. Not surprisingly, the websites themselves always reported far higher usage than that reported by outside, independent companies.

When I looked at this issue for the last edition (2013), I found that estimates for daily internet usage varied from a low of 40.8 minutes per day to a high of 2.5 hours per day. That inconsistency struck me as part of the reason that the internet doesn't get the level of business it feels it deserves. Let's see how that's changed with the latest (2015) estimates of time spent online:

Nielsen (18+)	1.75 hours per day
Ofcom (age 16+)	2.9 hours per day
comScore	"about 3 hours per day"
Flurry Insights	3.3 hours per day (mobile apps alone)
GlobalWebIndex	6.2 hours per day (ages 16–64)

Why are there such differences in some of the estimates? There are a variety of reasons, but one of the biggest problems is that many of the surveys are conducted online. That's a huge problem if you want accurate numbers. The latest Pew Research Center studies found that at least 15 percent of Americans do not use the internet. At all. Some of that's economic; some a fear or distaste for technology or a concern for privacy; some people simply aren't interested. A 2015 Pew study found that a third of all Americans do not have broadband at home. That's not much changed from a few years earlier. What that means is that 15 to 33 percent of Americans aren't included in an online survey. That's not a problem if you want to learn about typical online behavior, but it's not all right if you want to learn about typical American behavior. For example, an online only survey that found that the average user spent 2 hours per day online would actually mean that the average American spent between 80 and 102 minutes per day online when you take into account all the people who aren't online at all or don't have broadband at home (where people are most likely to participate in a survey). The lesson here is to read the fine print about research methodology before you simply buy into the numbers. Any numbers.

● ● ● ● ●

What We Think We Know About Media Use

Media use is a lot like real estate—it's all about location. TV is the dominant medium at home, radio is the dominant medium in the car, the computer is the dominant medium at work. Anywhere else, and it's all about mobile. That's pretty much what you'd expect . . . if you thought of it in those terms. And you should. We have a tendency to look at media consumption based on overall minutes or hours of use, but media consumption is heavily based on where the consumer is located.

Of course, you can consume news anywhere and via any medium. The most critical variable in whether and how much news someone consumes is age. The older the people, the more likely they are to consume news and the more of it they consume. Education has a role as well, but it's very much secondary. Gender and ethnicity play almost no role.

In a couple of national surveys, when I asked people where they got most of their news, local TV came out on top, by more than a two to one margin over the second choice. We found the same thing in the Middletown observational studies. But that's overall. For 18–34 year olds, the internet beats out TV.

● ● ● ● ●

What We Don't Know About Media Use

We know that newspaper circulation is down, and it has plummeted as a percentage of the total U.S. population, but the picture in TV is less clear.

We know that the typical local television station has most often seen its audience drop over the last few years, especially at night. That's certainly important to those stations, but it doesn't answer the bigger, societal question: Is that audience slipping in the midst of a general decline in TV news viewing? Or is it a decline because the audience has more and more choices for TV news, and so a stagnant audience is spreading out? Or is the audience for TV news growing, but the choices for viewing are growing even faster? We don't know for sure because it's so hard to look at it that way. While Pew's "State of the Media" reports a decline in TV viewing, its methodology hasn't kept up with changes in the TV news business, and more and more TV news goes uncounted.

As this is written, 714 TV newsrooms are producing news for those 714 stations and running news on an additional 328 stations. A total of 1,053 stations.

In Pew's State of the Media 2016, the audience for network news was stable, but local TV news went down after a couple years of increases. Cable TV news went up; newspaper went down. But Pew's methodology doesn't measure all TV news, just some. Most, to be sure, but Pew doesn't include the news on 271 TV stations in the U.S.—more than 25 percent of all local stations that run local news. That's about 85 more unmeasured TV stations than were unmeasured by Pew just five years ago. Logic suggests that whatever decline there has been in local news may well have gone not to other media but to the many and increasing number of local TV stations that Pew doesn't include in its measurement.

None of that means that it won't all turn around for TV, and that the audience won't fall off precipitously. But it hasn't yet, and it doesn't appear that things will change in the near future.

It's also unclear exactly how the internet figures into the news mix. We know that news and information websites are used primarily between 8:30 a.m. and 5 p.m. In other words, they're used at work. Does that make them secondary news outlets? But if people are getting the news online at work, will that mean they cut back on news at home? If so, for all newscasts or just some?

How much news people get from online sources is harder to calculate. While news and information websites are capable of amazing depth and breadth, there's a difference between capability and actual usage. Most people do not spend much time at a given news website. Chartbeat found that most people (55 percent) spent 15 seconds or less at a given website. Pew and comScore found that at the top news website, the average visit lasted under 4 minutes. Overall, the average time spent per visit to a newspaper website is just over 1 minute. comScore reports that total time spent on news websites is under 4 minutes per day. That's more than it used to be, but, at least in time spent, it's not rivaling any traditional media.

• • • • •

So Where Are We Going?

First, let's focus on the parameters for the debate. It's really not whether there's a future for news. Every reasonable measure of how people spend their time—as well as what they say they're interested in—makes clear that people have a huge and, if anything, growing appetite for news and information.

The debate is about which media will supply that news and what form that news consumption will take.

The bottom line on the future is that we really don't know who the winners and losers in the news field will be. No one knows. Not for sure. Some of that is because we really can't see into the future, and some of that is because we're much too early in another media evolution to know with certainty how it will come out. Besides, news consumption is permanently evolving, so we're talking about predicting the future that now appears possible, not the future we cannot yet imagine.

As we try to figure out where we're heading, let's start with a few more things we know based on what people do and what people say they want.

■ There's a surprisingly consistent view of what news is, and that's true across all different demographics. Most adults (18+) draw clear distinctions between the local TV newscast and the cable talk shows (like Bill O'Reilly and Rachel Maddow) and the entertainment-oriented TV programs (like *Entertainment Tonight* and *Inside Edition*). They watch what they want, but they know the difference. Interestingly, young people, 18 to 24 years old, didn't view Jon Stewart and his *Daily Show* as news any more than people aged 55 to 64 did. A lot more young people knew what it was and watched it, but they also knew it wasn't a news show.

■ People want their news right up to the minute. Over 90 percent said it was somewhat or very important. That's probably at least part of why people respond favorably to live ("breaking") news reports.

■ Almost three-quarters of American adults say it's very or somewhat important to be able to watch TV news when they want. Undoubtedly, this is at least partly the influence of the internet and the whole notion of people being able to get what they want when they want it.

■ People want anchors to deliver TV news. Interestingly, two-thirds of younger adults, 18 to 34, wanted anchors to deliver the news, considerably higher than older adults (35+). That's relevant because it's a lot harder to have anchors guide people through the news if it's all on demand or an assemble-your-own online approach.

■ Just over 40 percent of adults said they'd like to assemble their own newscasts, but 46 percent said they wouldn't. The answer divided by education; the more educated, the more interested in assembling their own. In line with this, in the earlier days of the internet, more and more stations were offering users an opportunity to assemble their own newscasts online. Today, so few stations are offering that option that I stopped asking the question in the RTDNA Surveys in 2015. It appears that people really don't want to work that hard at receiving what is basically a passive news product.

■ Just over 60 percent of adults said they'd like to interact with TV news. Here the divide was age, with over 70 percent of the 18 to 34 year olds saying yes. A holdover, perhaps, from video games.

So what does all this mean? You can decide that for yourself, but here are some of my expectations:

■ The internet has clearly led to a greater demand for user control and convenience, but it's not clear who's going to supply that or how. I expect TV to remain the medium of choice for both news and entertainment. People love TV, and they want to watch it on the biggest screen available. Take a look at the sales figures for new television sets and you'll see what I mean.

■ Look for an increasing number of niche markets developing in news and information, like small screen—a rapidly growing number of people get at least some of their daily news from their mobile device (mostly smartphones). Much of that comes via Facebook, but Facebook doesn't produce the news. Most of the actual news suppliers are the same media that we've been getting news from. In other words, so far, we have seen few new, major players in the news business for mobile; it's just an extension of existing, established brands, including newspapers, networks, stations and aggregators like Google.

■ There's a lot of loyalty to established, traditional media. That will likely translate into the present established brands dominating the news and information fields in the future, regardless of platform. This will be particularly important as TV and the computer and, perhaps, mobile merge. In the future, we may distinguish between them—if at all—by how many diagonal inches or whether they're portable.

■ Newspaper's triple problems of aging consumers, rising production costs and a shrinking advertising base (especially classified) will lead to radical changes in newspapers in the next 10 years. Some will cut back on the days of publication (Saturday will probably be the first to go), some papers may become boutique subsets of their websites, some won't make it at all.

■ As this is written, more and more newspapers are moving to paywalls for their online information. Some are doing this primarily to try to slow or reverse erosion of paid subscriptions, and some are simply designed to bring in more revenue. Whether these changes will work for newspapers may depend on how we define success. Paywalls should slow subscription erosion but won't eliminate it. Most people won't pay, but, for at least some papers, enough will pay to make it a viable (if scaled-back) business model. But that scaled-back survival will also make newspapers more and more niche players, reaching fewer and fewer better-off consumers. Almost no television station is even considering a paywall. Most are hoping more newspapers establish them because TV stations know that those newspaper pay-walls increase readership at free TV websites. Newspaper paywalls may buy newspapers some time to change their business models; paywalls will not be the new business model.

■ The move to digital will probably slowly lead to dozens, maybe eventually hundreds of all-news or nearly all-news local TV channels as well as more all-weather and mixed specialty channels. This is taking place because the TV switch from analog to digital allows stations to broadcast multiple channels within each station's allotted digital spectrum. In smaller markets, some of those additional digital channels are showing up as new stations, affiliated with CW or MyNet or others. In larger markets, we're seeing more and more specialty programming on those extra digital channels.

■ What will really lead to change in media won't be declines in readership or fragmented viewership as much as advertising opportunities and media business models. Right now, traditional media are as threatened by their own business ineptitude as by media competition. They're being saved—especially TV—by the inability of media companies to make meaningful money from the web and by the web's disorganization, lack of user measurement standards and viable advertising alternatives to traditional media. So far, the real money online and in mobile is being made not by the media companies that produce content but by Facebook and Google, which simply make content available to users. So far, neither Facebook nor Google (Alphabet) has shown an interest in getting into the news origination business.

■ Just because it's new doesn't mean people will care. People will adopt new technology to the extent that it allows them to do what they now do better, easier or more cheaply. Plenty of new efforts and ideas won't measure up.

■ Progress and change always happen faster when looking back on it than when you're living it. Wholesale media changes have not happened yet and will not happen overnight. Partly that's because change doesn't happen that way. Partly it's because we're not dealing with a vast dissatisfied group of consumers desperately searching for wholesale changes. When asked what their choices are for news delivery, people give answers that largely mirror their present use. In other words, they're generally fairly happy with what they have, and that will affect how quickly change happens—or doesn't.

In the end, this we know for certain: For the foreseeable future, people will want to see and hear and read news and information, and those who want to provide it must learn how to tell stories in pictures and words. The rest is detail.

●●●●●

Summary

News is a business, and its survival depends on a business model that enables it to take in more money than it costs to produce news. TV still dominates the media jungle—both in time spent overall and in where people get most of their news. And the amount of TV news being produced keeps growing, year after year. Measuring media use is difficult, and that difficulty, coupled with problems in methodology and media bias, sometimes leads us to misleading or inaccurate media use numbers. Still, it's clear that we're in a period of significant change.

Young adults get more news from the internet than TV; more and more people generally are getting news online; and mobile devices are becoming increasingly important delivery systems for both news and information. Although there are a variety of new efforts in news delivery, so far the traditional players are the leading suppliers of news, and it's clear that news consumption is not shrinking, even though it is fragmenting.

The latest RTDNA/Hofstra University Survey shows again that the TV news business isn't limited to TV anymore—or just news. More than three-quarters of stations provide local news content to one or more other media beyond their own station or website: another TV station, a cable channel, radio, another website, mobile and more.

More and more people are getting news and information on mobile devices, but it's too early to know how that will affect the industry.

●●●●●

Key Words & Phrases

profit . . . revenue . . . expenses . . . advertising . . . cable and satellite carriage . . . retransmission fees . . . market area . . . network, syndicated and local programming . . . rating . . . share . . . media use and location . . . smartphones . . . paywalls . . . news aggregators

● ● ● ● ●

Exercises

A. Make a list of the TV stations, radio stations and newspapers in your market area. Which stations run news, and how much do they run? Do they produce their own news or get it from somewhere else? If somewhere else, where? Make a list of all the online media in your market area that produce *local* news. Characterize the kind, detail and amount of local news that they run.

B. How have the news media in your market area changed over the last five or 10 years? Who's running more, and who's running less? Check on length of newspapers and number (and size) of pages, TV newscasts added or dropped, TV stations that have started news departments or terminated them, radio stations that used to run news and now don't, and ones that now run news but didn't before. Compare broadcast-based and print-based news websites. Are there new online news and information websites in your area? If so, who's doing them and how do they compare with websites from traditional media companies? Which local news websites have paywalls and how do those paywalls work?

C. Make a list of the TV stations in your market area that run news on another medium (list all the media that each is on).

D. Make a list of all the cooperative ventures that the TV, radio stations and newspapers in your market area are involved with.

E. What are the local stations doing on mobile? Are they using apps? How do those work, and do they charge for them?

TV Script Form and Supers ... Glossary

There is no universal script marking system for television. Every station seems to do things a bit differently. Newsroom computer systems dictate some designations, but most systems allow stations to customize the look and approach to suit themselves. Most newsroom computer systems are integrated with control room equipment to make the appropriate supers virtually automatic—assuming they've been entered into the system correctly. This chapter lays out a reasonably typical system which can be used as a base suitable for alteration.

Abbreviations

CG: Character generator. Designate what it's to look like by using separate lines and uppercase and lowercase to correspond to use on air. Sometimes abbreviated CH, CI or CY (after Chyron, the company that once dominated the field).

CU: Close-up, standard bust shot for a single anchor.

Gfx: Graphics. Note what it is.

IN: In cue of SOT in VO/SOT.

MATTE: To indicate more than one live video source on the screen at the same time.

OUT: Out cue of SOT in VO/SOT.

PKG: Reporter package that ends with standard signature (sig) close unless otherwise noted (e.g., *Jane Smith, XXXX-TV, Cityville*). Sometimes abbreviated PK.

SOT: Full screen sound on tape.

SS: Still store (electronic). Sometimes designated as *BSS* (box still store) or *FSS* (full [screen] still store). Make clear what it's to be.

3-shot: Three-shot on camera. Since most stations have more than three anchors, designate which three. Also note the order, for example, Jean/Jan/George where Jean and Jan are the usual co-anchors and George either is normally on the right doing, for example, sports, or is a reporter who is to be sitting on the right.

2-shot: Two-shot on camera. Because most stations have more than two anchors, designate which two (although it may be understood that it means the two news anchors unless otherwise noted).

VO: Voiceover; presumes natural sound under unless designated as silent (VO/sil).

● ● ● ● ●

Script Form

Standard Anchor Read

To indicate standard medium/close-up shot of the anchor who's reading the copy:

VIDEO	AUDIO
CU: Jean	((Jean)) Three more arrests in the latest drug roundup on the west side today.

Standard 2-Shot

To indicate a standard 2-shot:

VIDEO	AUDIO

2-shot: Jean & Jan	((Jean))
	    Three more arrests in the latest drug roundup on the west side today.
	    ((Jan))
	    It's a follow-up to the two dozen arrested . . .

Standard Anchor Read with Gfx

To indicate a medium/close-up shot of anchor with box graphics:

VIDEO	AUDIO
CU: Jean BSS: drugs	((Jean)) Three more arrests in the latest drug roundup on the west side today.

Anchor with Voiceover

To indicate anchor read to voiceover copy with super:

VIDEO	AUDIO
CU: Jean BSS: drugs	((Jean)) Three more arrests in the latest drug roundup on the west side today.
VO———— CG: West Cityville IN: **:02** OUT: **:06**	It's a follow-up to the two dozen arrested yesterday at the Village Apartment Complex.

Note the *IN:* and *OUT:* after the super, giving the time during which a super can be run.

Anchor with VO/SOT

To indicate a VO/SOT:

VIDEO	AUDIO
CU: Jean BSS: drugs	((Jean)) Three more arrests in the latest drug roundup on the west side today.
VO———— CG: West Cityville IN: **:01** OUT: **:05**	It's a follow-up to the two dozen arrested yesterday at the Village Apartment Complex. Police Chief George Smith says it's all part of a new "get-tough" approach.
SOT———— CG: Chief George Smith Cityville Police IN: **:08** OUT: **:13**	((————SOT————)) "We're going to go in there and clean things up. The people of the city have a right to live in peace, and we're going to keep up the pressure until we've gotten rid of every one of them."
VO————	((Jean)) Officers confiscated cocaine, marijuana, and L-S-D.

Remember after SOT to note who is reading and whether it's VO or on camera.

Anchor VO/SOT with Package Intro

To go into a reporter package:

VIDEO	AUDIO
CU: Jean BSS: drugs	((Jean)) Three more arrests in the latest drug roundup on the west side today.
VO———— CG: West Cityville IN: **:02** OUT: **:06**	It's a follow-up to the two dozen arrested yesterday at the Village Apartment Complex. Police Chief George Smith says it's all part of a new "get-tough" approach.
SOT———— CG: Chief George Smith 　　　Cityville Police IN: **:08** OUT: **:13**	((————SOT————)) "We're going to go in there and clean things up. The people of the city have a right to live in peace, and we're going to keep up the pressure until we've gotten rid of every one of them."
VO————	((Jean)) Officers confiscated cocaine, marijuana, and L-S-D. Reporter Sam Jones says the county prosecutor plans to file hundreds of charges.
SOT/PKG————	((————SOT/PKG————))

● ● ● ● ●

Supers

Names

STANDARD NAME SUPER. Notice that in the previous examples, name supers took up two lines while place supers occupied one. With a few exceptions that's the way supers should appear on the air. For most people supers, the first line gives the name, the second line the reason why that person is on the air:

CG: Molly McPherson
　　　Airline Spokesperson
CG: Ann Bishop
　　　Witness

Note that even if you use all caps for the script, you'll have to use uppercase and lowercase for supers. Otherwise, whoever types in the supers won't know how to spell a name like *McPherson.* Make sure to use gender neutral terminology. People who fight fires are called fire-fighters, those who fight criminals are police officers.

NAMES WITH COMPANY IDENTIFIERS. Generally, specific company names are not used in supers unless the story is about that company or about several specific companies. In the latter case the super might read like this:

CG: John Smith
State Savings Bank Manager

But if John Smith has been sought out simply because he's in banking, use this:

CG: John Smith
Bank Manager

PEOPLE IN AUTHORITY. People who are in some position of authority require some different handling of supers. There should be no need to super the president or vice president of the United States. The governor of your own state may be supered on one line:

CG: Gov. Pat Smith

Everyone else runs two lines. In most cases the name goes on the first line and the title on the second:

CG: Dana Greene
Cityville Police Chief
CG: Dana Greene
Village County Sheriff
CG: Dana Greene
Ohio Lt. Governor
CG: Dana Greene
Alaska Governor

TITLE AND RANK. Titles or ranks are used in the first line with the names in the case of clergy, the military, and police and fire officers who are *not* the people in charge:

CG: Rev. Ralph Taylor
United Methodist Church

CG: Sgt. Ralph Taylor
U.S. Army

CG: Capt. Ralph Taylor
Cityville Police Dept.

POLITICIANS. Politicians—U.S. and state—should be supered with federal/state and House/Senate designation along with name on line one and party affiliation and place represented (excluding district number) on line two:

CG: U.S. Sen. Jane Doe
        (R) Kansas
CG: U.S. Rep. John Doe
        (D) Detroit
CG: Indiana Rep. Betty Smith
        (R) Indianapolis

Remember that *congressman/congresswoman* has no real meaning (all senators and representatives are members of Congress); don't use the term.

CANDIDATES FOR OFFICE. Super all candidates for public office, even those who currently occupy elective or appointive office, by party affiliation and the office they're seeking. You can make clear in the story itself if any of the candidates now hold some office:

CG: Betty Smith
        (R) Governor Candidate
CG: John Smith
        (I) Legislature Candidate

DOCTORS. There are too many doctors of too many different things to use *Dr.* in a super preceding a name anymore. Medical practitioners should have the appropriate letters follow a comma after the name:

CG: Jane White, M.D.
        Family Medicine
CG: Stephen Glenn, D.D.S.
        General Dentistry
CG: Elizabeth Flint, D.O.
        General Osteopathy

Do not use either *Dr.* or *Ph.D.* in a super:

CG: Henry Appleman
        Cityville School Supt.
CG: Louise Appleman
        OSU Economist

INITIALS AND ACRONYMS. Minimize both initials and acronyms in supers. The same guidelines apply for supers that apply to copy. If the organization is well enough known to use initials or an acronym first reference, then it's okay for a super. Acceptable initials: AFL/CIO, CIA, FBI, NAACP, NFL and a few others. Otherwise, write it out:

CG: Ken Jones
       United Auto Workers

CELEBRITIES. Celebrities are best identified with either their last major work or, if that's not appropriate, a general identifier:

CG: Mark Harmon
       "NCIS"
CG: Jim Gaffigan
       Comedian

NAME ALIAS. If someone is on the air who does not wish to be identified, have the person pick an alias, and put it in quotes:

CG: "Patrice"
       Rape Victim

SOMEONE NOT ON CAMERA. An exception to the two-line super is the use of a voice of someone who will not be seen, either for more than five seconds of a first bite or not at all. In that case, identify as follows:

CG: Voice of:
       Sam Jones
       Gay Homeowner

MULTIPLE NAMES. If more than one person is on the screen, it may be necessary to call for a super screen right or screen left. But be careful about the timing on this:

CG: John Smith (screen rt.)
       Auto Mechanic

UNUSUAL SPELLING. And if the spelling is unusual, make clear that the way you've spelled it is correct:

CG: John Smythe (sp ok)
       Charged with murder

In the last two examples those directions on screen location and spelling apply only to stations that manually enter the supers into the system. Newsrooms that are completely computerized simply need to enter the correct codes to make it happen properly.

MOS. *MOS* is short for *man-on-the-street* (although including both men and women). There's normally no reason to super MOSs. That's assuming that you've just gone out on the street to collect *short* comments from people about some issue in the news that you're using in a montage of bites.

CREDITING OUTSIDE HELP. When crediting outside help, like a courtroom sketch artist or a freelance photographer, use the same form as a *voice of* super:

CG: Artist:
Sam Smith
CG: Photojournalist:
Janet Jones

Location, Date and Miscellaneous

LOCATORS. The first rule is to think about whether you need a locator at all. If the story is about disposable diapers and you *happened* to shoot it in North Cityville, don't bother with a super. If it could have been anywhere, let it be.

If the story is outside the core city of coverage, super the name of the town, county, area—however the place is known:

CG: Marysville
CG: Delaware County

If the story is within the core city of coverage, use whatever broad terminology local residents use:

CG: Downtown Cityville
CG: East Cityville

If a specific address is necessary (especially on a crime story), use it all (including street, road, city, etc.):

CG: 2201 Velvet Place
Cityville

The second rule for using locator supers is to make sure that they're going to run over location video—not a tight shot of some document or a medium shot of a person who's been interviewed. Locators are inevitably a balancing act between being as broad as possible and as meaningful as possible.

DAY AND DATE. The viewer understands that video on the news was shot that day for that story. If that's not the case or there might be any question, then make sure the video is properly identified. A story on farm produce prices using last week's general farm video probably doesn't need a super. It probably really doesn't matter when that video was shot. But a story about John Smith being charged with a crime shouldn't run over any unidentified video of John Smith unless it's from that day. Crime video must always be specifically dated.

Be as general in dating as you can, given accuracy and context. If you're doing month-by-month comparisons, exact dates are not relevant:

CG: February
CG: Last Month

If you're using video from last Tuesday:

CG: Last Tuesday

That's almost always preferable to the exact date. If the event you're showing happened during the current calendar year, leave off the year; if it happened in a previous year, use the whole date:

CG: January 15
CG: January 15, 2016
CG: January 2016

If all else fails and you absolutely must use a particular piece of previously shot video, and it can't go on unidentified but an exact date isn't known or doesn't make sense, use:

CG: File Tape
CG: File Video

This is an absolute last resort.

The only time a super saying *this morning* would be used on the air would be on a morning or noon show to indicate how timely the video is (or to show a comparison with later video, which would be so marked). The same concept would apply for *tonight*.

LOCATOR AND DATE. Locators may be used with dates:

CG: January 15
       Nassau County
CG: Tonight
       North Cityville

IDENTIFYING OUTSIDE VIDEO. Video must also be identified if the station (or the station's network) didn't shoot it. That includes movie video, video from other networks, public service announcements and commercials, with clarifying "courtesy" in parenthesis:

CG: (courtesy) Columbia Pictures
CG: (courtesy) Public Service Announcement
CG: (courtesy) Commercial

On movies or music videos, just courtesy the distributor or producer, not the title. Spell out *public service announcement.* Most people don't know what *PSAs* are.

●●●●●

Glossary of Broadcast and Online Terms

actuality The "actual" sound of someone in the news on audio tape. This applies only to a newsmaker, not a reporter. *Bite* is the television equivalent.

affiliates Stations with an agreement with one of the networks in which the stations have first call on programs carried by the network. Today, most TV affiliates pay the networks for the programs (and the commercials within them). It's called reverse compensation because it used to be the networks paying the stations. In radio, larger stations are paid, but smaller stations are not, depending on the size of the audience the station delivers.

anchor The *talent* on the set who delivers the news. Also used to refer to on-the-set talent who present sports and weather.

app Short for *application,* it's software designed for a particular purpose, most commonly, software downloaded for mobile use.

assignment desk, editor Common in TV, rare in radio except the largest stations, this is the nerve center of the newsroom. Assignment editors, working at the assignment desk, schedule stories for reporters to cover and photographers to shoot. The desk may also perform research for reporters and other news people.

ax Common abbreviation for *accident.*

B-roll An old film term: Pictures shot to accompany reporter or anchor script. See the second definition of *cover shot.*

background/bg Usually in TV, the natural sound on video that is run at lower volume, under the voice of a reporter or anchor. Same as *wild sound under* or *natural sound under.*

backtiming Timing a story or, more commonly, a newscast from the back forward to help ensure that the newscast ends on time.

beat An area of coverage that a reporter deals with on an ongoing basis, e.g., health, consumer, police.

bg See *background/bg.*

billboard Used variously, but most commonly as an announcement on the air—sometimes by a commercial announcer, sometimes by a newscaster—that a particular advertiser is sponsoring a news program or segment.

bite The selected section of sound on tape (SOT) of a news maker or news event on TV to be run at full volume as SOT (see *SOT*). The TV equivalent of a radio *actuality*.

blog Short for *web log*. Individual or group commentary or observations online.

bridge Used variously but usually refers to an internal stand-up (see *stand-up*) within a reporter package (see *package*).

BSS *Box still store. See SS.*

character generator Electronic equipment that produces supers (titles, also called lower thirds) used to identify people, places and things on TV. Abbreviated *CG:* (sometimes *CH:* or *CI:* or *CY:*, short for common brand name of Chyron) on script paper.

chromakey The electronic merging of two video sources. Often the generation of pictures behind news, sports and weather anchors.

close-up/CU A picture in which the subject is framed fairly tightly on the screen, generally no wider than head and shoulders.

cold open Starting a TV newscast with video or a bite from the lead story rather than starting with the anchor or a standard show open.

copy Scripts written for a newscast.

cover shot (1) A scene of video used to cover or bridge what would otherwise be a jump cut (see *jump cut*) or simply to bridge scenes for time transitions; (2) in some shops, *cover shots* or *cover video* refers to video that accompanies narration. Also called *B-chain* or *B-roll*.

crawl Text running across (usually) the bottom of the screen.

crowdsourcing In media, generally asking people in the audience (online or mobile devices) to determine or verify information.

CU See *close-up*.

cut A direct, abrupt change from one video scene to another. The most common form of editing in TV news.

cutaway Same as first definition of *cover shot*.

dayside The newsroom staff who work generally between 8 a.m. and 7 p.m., culminating in the early evening news. See *nightside*.

dissolve A video cross-fade in which one image is slowly (typically one-half to three seconds) replaced with another image. This softer form of editing (than cuts) is used most often in features to denote scene changes or passing of time.

domain The end of the basic web address, after the period but before any slashes.

drive times The time periods when radio station audiences are generally highest, because so many people are in cars. Morning drive usually runs from 6 a.m. to 10 a.m. weekdays (peak radio listening overall). Afternoon drive usually runs from 3 p.m. to 7 p.m. weekdays.

dub   As a noun, a copy of audio or video material. As a verb, the act of copying audio or video material.

ENG   *Electronic news gathering.* The term applies to videotape or digital video (rather than film) material from the field.

ESS   *Electronic still store.* See *SS.*

establishing shot   Typically, the first shot in a video story, which shows the general context of the location rather than a tighter shot of some of the details.

evergreen   A story, typically a feature, that can be held for later airing because it's not timely.

feed   Video or audio from an outside source, e.g., a network or a station's live truck.

Flash   Animation program for web pages from Adobe.

font   Set of typeface styles in a character generator. See *character generator.*

FSS   *Full (screen) still store.* See *SS.*

future file   Filing system (physical file or on computer) to keep track of events coming up in the future, usually involving days of the month and months of the year. Sometimes called *futures file.*

gfx   Common abbreviation for *graphics.*

gif   *Graphics Interchange Format,* mostly used for illustrations and graphics on the web.

green screen   In TV, most commonly used in weather, it's a green screen or board which allows the chromakey or superimposition of video or maps behind a weathercaster or other talent. Technically, any color could be used, but green is chosen because whoever is in front of the green screen can't wear that color (and not wearing bright green is easy to do).

handout   A press release given or sent to the news media.

heavy   In a newscast, means that the show is running long and something will have to be cut back or eliminated. See *light.*

html   *Hypertext markup language* for coding instructions on the web.

hyperlocal   News about a much smaller community than we commonly see covered, most often a geographic area.

ifb   *Interrupt feed* or *fold back.* Usually refers to both the anchor's and reporter's earpieces and the audio that goes through it on live shots. Designed for the reporter to hear the station audio without his or her own voice and enables the producer or director to talk directly to the anchor or reporter to provide cues or information.

IN Script notation to mark in cue of SOT in VO/SOT. See also *OUT.*

interactivity Generally, the ability of the audience to respond and participate in an activity, either online or through television.

jpeg Joint Photographic Experts Group, compression format for photos.

jump cut An unnatural movement between edits caused by the internal editing of material such that two similar but not identical or flowing video shots are placed next to each other. The result is a discernible *jump* in the picture.

kicker An unusual, light or humorous story, usually short, run at the end of a newscast.

lav Short for *lavaliere,* a small mic that clips on to clothing.

light In a newscast, means that the show is running short and something will have to be expanded or added. See *heavy.*

livechat In media, generally software that allows a live connection between an audience and a live person.

localizing Finding a local news aspect to a story that is not otherwise directly related to your community.

long shot/LS Similar to an establishing shot, this is a picture showing a wide view of the story the camera is capturing. Same as *wide shot/WS.*

MATTE Split screen, indicating more than one live video source on the screen at the same time.

medium shot/MS Between a close-up and a long shot, the medium shot shows some detail of the picture without getting too close.

message board A web page where comments can be posted.

mix minus An engineering term referring to the elimination of the reporter's or anchor's audio through an ifb, thus preventing feedback or disconcerting delayed audio.

MP3 *Motion Picture Experts Group, Audio Layer 3,* an audio compression format used for downloading.

MPEG *Motion Picture Experts Group,* a system for digitizing and compressing video for downloading. Pronounced m-peg.

multimedia Online, generally refers to the mixed use of text, audio, video, graphics, animation, and so on.

natural sound The actual sound of whatever is being recorded (audio or video), generally intended to be run under a reporter's or anchor's voice. Same as *wild, ambient, nat or background sound.*

nightside The newsroom staff who work generally between 2 p.m. and 11:30 p.m., culminating in the late evening news. See *dayside.*

O & O　Abbreviation for *owned and operated,* stations that are actually owned and run by the networks rather than just affiliated with the networks.

OUT　Script notation to mark out cue of SOT in VO/SOT. See also *IN.*

outtakes　Audio or video material recorded for a story but not used on the air.

package　A report, usually put together by a reporter, usually including the reporter, reporter voiceover, natural sound, and one or more interview segments (bites). Usually abbreviated *PKG,* sometimes called *pack.* Normally ends with standard signature (sig) close (or out) unless otherwise noted.

paywall　Requiring payment in order to access an online site.

pixels　Short for *picture elements,* the tiny circles of color that make up a video screen. The more pixels, the more detail and sharper the image.

podcast　Material available for download to be played on a computer or portable electronic device.

pool　Generally refers to the use of shared (or pooled) resources, most commonly a single photographer or group of photographers at an event where all media can receive and use the material.

pre-pro　Short for pre-production, the advance production of material done prior to the newscast.

producer　A *field producer* works with a reporter to determine the audio and video aspects of a story. A *segment producer* typically oversees the writing and production of various segments within a newscast (e.g., health, consumer). A *show producer* or *line producer* typically oversees the writing, graphics, sequence and, to varying degrees, content of a newscast. An *executive producer* typically oversees one or more newscasts and the producer or producers who handle those newscasts. Depending on the station, the *executive producer* is likely to be the number 2 or number 3 management person in the newsroom (after the news director and assistant news director, if the station has one).

PSA　Most commonly used as an abbreviation for *public service announcement,* spots run for free by radio and TV stations for non-profit events or organizations. Also refers to *pre-sunrise authority,* by which certain AM radio stations operate at reduced power between 6 a.m. and average monthly sunrise.

Quicktime　Video format developed by Apple.

rating　The percentage of people or households listening (radio) or watching (TV) of all the people or households who could listen or watch (in the defined area and have a radio or TV). See *share.*

reader　In TV, a story to be read by an anchor on camera.

SEO *Search engine optimization,* the process of choosing words, especially in headlines or key words, to maximize the ability of search engines to locate material.

share The percentage of people or households listening (radio) or watching (TV) of all the people or households who are listening or watching at that time. See *rating.*

sig out, sig close The standard line used by reporters to end all packages. Typically something like *Sue Smith, WXXX-TV, Cityville.*

sil Abbreviation for *silent,* indicating there is no usable audio on a piece of video. See also *VO.*

slug The word or phrase identifying a given story on assignment listings and show rundowns. Also refers to the slug line plus the initials or last name of the writer, the date and the newscast the story is being written for, all of which generally appear in the upper left or across the top of the page.

SNG *Satellite news gathering* as opposed to in the studio or via microwave.

SOT *Sound on tape,* usually used to indicate that a segment of video should be run at regular, full audio level (with accompanying picture).

spots Radio and TV term for commercial announcements.

SS *Still store* (electronic), frequently designated as *BSS, box still store* (the box accompanying an anchor shot), or *FSS, full (screen) still store* (where the video fills the screen).

stand-up A story or segment of a story during which a reporter at the scene talks on camera.

stick mic Handheld microphone. See *lav.*

streaming For computers and mobile devices, a system of sending and receiving a continuous flow of audio and/or video. That flow could be live streaming (as it's being sent) or material available for streaming on demand.

super The superimposition of lettering over video, most commonly names and titles. Sometimes called *lower-thirds* because many (but not all) supers are placed there.

sx Common abbreviation for sports. Also sometimes *Spx.*

tag Scripted close to a radio or TV package, story or commercial, usually at least one full sentence.

talent People who perform on the air, including newscasters, weather and sports but not usually reporters.

tease, teaser Usually a short bit of information on an upcoming story that is used to *tease* the audience so they will continue to listen or watch the newscast, especially used just before commercials.

toss The introduction of another person or video by an anchor or reporter.

url *Uniform resource locator,* the address of a web site.

visuals   Pictures or graphics accompanying a story. See *B-roll.*

VO   *Voiceover,* used to indicate anchor or reporter reading during a video segment. Presumes voiceover natural sound unless indicated otherwise (VO/sil).

voiceover   See *VO.*

voicer   In radio, a story read by a reporter, with the reporter's voice (and perhaps natural sound under) the only audio on the tape (no actualities).

VTR   *Videotape recording.*

webcast   Audio or video feed on the web, usually streamed live.

wide shot, WS   See *long shot/LS.*

wild sound   See *background/bg* and *natural sound.*

wrap   In radio, a voicer that includes one or more actualities. Also a time cue directing talent or reporter to conclude presentation or interview.

wx   Common abbreviation for *weather.*

Index •••••

Italicized entries reference words that appear in defining terms sections of Chapters 7, 17, 18, 19 and 21.